BREAKING CHAINS

Comparative Urban and Community Research

Series Editor, Michael Peter Smith

BREAKING CHAINS
Social Movements and Collective Action

Comparative Urban and Community Research

Edited by

Michael Peter Smith

Volume 3

Transaction Publishers
New Brunswick (U.S.A.) and London (U.K.)

ISSN: 0892-5569
ISBN: 0-88738-860-4
Printed in the United States of America

Volume 3 comprises volume 14 of *Comparative Urban Research*

Contents

Comparative Urban and Community Research is an annual review devoted to theoretical, empirical and applied research on the processes of urbanization and community change throughout the world. The format of *Comparative Urban and Community Research* enables the publication of manuscripts that are longer and more richly textured than the articles a quarterly journal can feature.

Submission requirements: 1) papers should be double-spaced; and 2) author's name, affiliation, address and telephone number should appear on a separate sheet.

This volume was prepared with support from the Department of Applied Behavioral Sciences of the University of California, Davis. Editorial correspondence and manuscript submissions should be addressed to *Comparative Urban and Community Research*, Department of Applied Behavioral Sciences, University of California, Davis, CA 95616.

BREAKING CHAINS: AN INTRODUCTION

Michael Peter Smith
Editor

The role of new social movements in producing urban, societal and political change has been a significant theme in urban research and theoretical debate since the 1960s. The 1990 volume of *Comparative Urban and Community Research* brings together three theoretical essays, four historical and contemporary case studies and a policy study, representing the latest thinking on this theme. A major thread connecting the contributions to *Breaking Chains* is their shared interest in the central causes and consequences of emergent modes of collective action that are related to, yet transcend, conflicts between organized labor and industrial capital in the productive sphere. The articles in this issue call to our attention the activities of the diverse players engaged in major political struggles over community, place and culture; urban services; racial, ethnic and gender inequalities; environmental degradation; and state violence.

The first three articles enrich the theoretical debate on the interplay of structure, agency, class, community and social transformation. While acknowledging the importance of the local bases of grass-roots urban movements, Sidney Plotkin warns of certain dangers inherent in the defensive enclave consciousness of place-based movements. Joseph Kling and Prudence Posner try to preserve class analysis as the most appropriate context within which to interpret such alternative bases of collective action as city, constituency and community mobilization. In sharp contrast, Carl Boggs welcomes the localism and variety of new social movements in the urban, environmental and feminist domains, seeing them as signs of grass-roots democratization which defy the elitist tendency to reduce these different forms of cultural politics to epiphenomena of the global class struggle.

Michael Harloe's finely detailed, comparative-historical study assesses the relationship between reformist housing movements, the labor movement, the state and the rest of civil society in Western Europe and the U.S. during the late nineteenth and early twentieth centuries. His comprehensive review of the social construction of alternative ideologies and state policies toward housing in response to the "social question" underlines the importance of the historical antecedents of contemporary urban developments.

In a comparative case study, Susan and Norman Fainstein show how various community mobilizations in New York City based on territory, ethnicity and client status differ from similarly based forms of collective action in other large U.S. cities that have more responsive political regimes. Their analysis rests on a comparison of the different ways that grass-roots movements are linked to partisan electoral politics in different cities.

A theoretically important case study of urban social movements in Mexico

City by Diane Davis treats urban politics as a contested terrain, in which new social movements seek to overcome political constraints embedded in the corporatist state structure of Mexico, whose ruling party has resolved class conflict in the productive sphere by appeasing the specific concerns of industrial capital and organized labor. The state policies resulting from this accommodation have exacerbated urban problems and fanned the discontent of Mexico City's urban popular and middle classes. Davis views the urban social movements of Mexico City as a sign of political democratization linking community mobilization over urban policies to new electoral coalitions at the national level.

Similarly, David Smith and Su-Hoon Lee's study of the movement for political democratization of the South Korean state carefully details the political relations among business elites, organized labor, technocrats, the military, the intelligentsia, the student movement and the urban semiproletariat in South Korea's ongoing struggle to democratize state and society. This article places the agency of these social actors within the structural constraints that the global economy and domestic institutions are placing on the democratization process.

The final contribution to Volume 3, by Gregory Squires, also sheds light on the structure-agency question, by focusing on the relationship between global economic restructuring and growing racial inequality in U.S. cities. Based on his assessment of this relationship, Squires argues that urban politics and state-policy responses to deteriorating race relations must encompass major economic reforms in the social organization of work. His policy analysis implicitly cautions both the civil rights movement and those who would entirely abandon the politics of production in a presumably postmodern world that politics cannot be separated from economics and that the domains of production, culture and collective action are radically interconnected.

A special note of thanks is due to Ira Katznelson of our editorial board for his willingness to kibitz on the ironies of "breaking chains" and for his important editorial contributions to this volume of the review.

COMMUNITY AND ALIENATION: ENCLAVE CONSCIOUSNESS AND URBAN MOVEMENTS

Sidney Plotkin
Vassar College

The ideal of "community" has understandably become a unifying theme for activists in and scholars of urban movements. Real communities, though, all too often draw their militancy and strength from feelings of encirclement, entrapment, and estrangement, attitudes that are captured here in the idea of "enclave consciousness." Enclave consciousness is an important example of how archaic, premodern habits have tended to persist in spite of the pressures and requirements of modernity. More specifically, for the U.S. case, the essay suggests three historic patterns of law, ideology and economic practice that favor enclave consciousness in many community movements today. Although movements inspired by enclave consciousness have distinct organizational advantages, the stress here is on the moral and political dangers associated with strategies built around enclave defense.

In the rhetoric of the old workers' movement, no value stood higher than "solidarity." This single, powerful term fused an image of the workers' appreciation of their common interests as a class with their strategic commitment to organization and unity against capital. Solidarity emphasized the bond of labor as the common experience of humanity, independent of national or local context. That the Polish workers' movement in the 1980s took "Solidarity" as its name suggested its self-conscious association with the historical cause of labor. For many radical activists and scholars in the West, this invocation of "solidarity" may have seemed quaint and out of tune with progressive action in the advanced states of capitalism, where the labor movement has faded and given way to a variety of urban-based community movements.

Indeed, in the polemics and analysis of contemporary Western radicalism, "community" seems for many to have taken the place once held by "solidarity." Analysis and support for neighborhood resistance is thought by some urban scholars to represent the maturing of a genuinely popular radicalism, one that comes out of the direct experience and aspirations of people and that honors their traditions (Boyte, 1980; Sale, 1980). Community movements, it is argued, inject new life, new spirit and cohesion into the fragile bonds of working-class communities, especially at a time when the traditional vehicle of organized labor is on the wane (Kotler, 1969; Morris and Hess, 1975). Grass-roots urban action is thought to reveal the potential for democratic self-rule by the people as against domination by centralized corporate and bureaucratic elites (Williams, 1981; Bowles, Gordon, Weisskopf, 1983; Bowles and Gintis, 1986). By emphasizing direct self-government at the local level, community movements can experiment with new de-centralist technological and organizational forms, and thus lay a basis for a different kind of society (Illich, 1978). By no means are all students of urban movements so optimistic. There is in the literature uncertainty and skepticism, though typically such doubts focus more on the limited strategic power of urban movements than on possible tensions in the value of urban community itself (Saunders, 1981; Castells, 1984).

The point of this essay is not to add to the debate over class and community as alternative bases of radicalism. I have no illusions about the current health of the labor movement or about the rise of working-class consciousness. Instead I argue that the shift from "solidarity" to "community," whatever its strategic wisdom for radicals, is fraught with political and moral difficulties. Whatever the failures of the workers' movement, the symbolic appeal to labor solidarity is aimed at overcoming divisions of ethnicity, nation, religion and race in the name of the common interests of workers as a class. Community offers, in its place, the desirable ideal of local solidarity and democracy.

Community, however, is not an unambiguous value; its connotations of inner connection can often be accompanied by related feelings of separateness from the larger society, fears of encirclement by aggressive outside forces and anxieties about connections with an external world that is seen as dangerous, hostile and best kept at bay. When such attitudes are present, community and alienation can fuse together in an embittered and partisan solidarity. Community thus can become a euphemism for racial and ethnic hatred, loathing of the poor, or contempt of the "other." This is certainly not an unfamiliar point. Instead of treating such tendencies as exceptions to the rule of community, though, they should be seen as close to the center of the value itself. In light of the class, race and status differences of contemporary society, the idea of community entails social alienation as well as consensus, militant partisanship as well as mutual aid. This thesis is furthered by the suggestion that the term "enclave consciousness" is a clue to what must be confronted as the darker side of community.

To help explain the idea of enclave consciousness, the paper will look briefly at reappraisals of localism by radicals, suggest some of the roots of localism in the U.S. context, examine how such localist tendencies affect the content of enclave consciousness and, finally, weigh the political significance of enclave consciousness for urban movements.

Radicalism and Localism

Captivated by the progressive spirit of the Enlightenment, Marx and Weber were at least as skeptical of local community as they were of the benefits of modernity. Localism, as it evolved out of European feudalism, was a political outlook serviceable mainly to the reactionary interests of landed nobility.

Because Marx and Weber believed that the forces of capital accumulation and bureaucratic rationalization were enormously more powerful than the local resistance, both were sure that capitalism would undermine localism; whatever remained of enclave consciousness would give way to more modern, rationalist outlooks (Marx and Engles, 1948; Weber, 1946: 230-1).

In the mid-twentieth century, modern critical theorists rejected the probability of proletarian revolution, explaining the absence of revolution, in part, by calling attention to the breakup of local communities and their replacement by mass, consumer society. The centralized controls of advanced industrial capitalism would block working-class consciousness by promoting the private appetites of the consumer mentality. An antipolitical sense of alienation would grow out of mass consumerism and civic privatism; technological domination would flourish; genuinely radical change was unlikely (Mills, 1956; Marcuse, 1964; Habermas, 1973).

When the New Left burst on the scene in the 1960s, its activists and writers were inspired much more by this critical theory of mass society than by the Old Left faith in modernization as the necessary step toward socialism. For the New Left, centralized bureaucratic powers and large-scale institutions of any type or ideology were inherently destructive of human interests. Such institutions were everywhere the sources of militarism, imperialism, racism and environmental destruction. The New Left contributed to radical thought a much needed re-evaluation of the relationship between scale, rationality and human needs. It also supported, and in some important respects inspired, a variety of urban-based social movements that arose to challenge the policies of centralized institutions. In the advanced states of capitalism, struggles for human-scale communities became the new outlet for radicalism. "Our knowledge has been misguided in the direction of globalism," wrote one communitarian. "We must come to recognize 'neighborhood as the source of revolutionary power and local liberty as its modest cause'" (Kotler, 1969: xii; cf. Williams, 1981).

There is more to the story of community than this, however. Some urban movements struggled to preserve the "we-feeling" of community by asserting the alien character of the "other." In the 1960s, separatist themes first played crucial roles in the Black-Power and "community-control" movements in minority neighborhoods. Whites then gladly used the rhetoric of "community control" to justify their own reactionary battles to keep blacks away from "their" schools and neighborhoods. More recently, similar attitudes have empowered community activists of all colors to fight the erection of neighborhood shelters for the homeless, drug users and AIDS victims.

The motivations of local activism have been all too often mixed up with motives of race and class prejudice and with deep-seated fears of the stranger. In fact, if we look candidly not only at the communal aspirations of urban protest, but at the kinds of things rejected by community activism, the moral ambiguity of New Left decentralism becomes inescapable. Especially in the crucial area of land-use protests, community activists rarely make political or moral distinctions between the kinds of projects they find offensive. As often as not, neighborhood protestors are as quick to reject projects aimed at fulfilling social needs–especially those of the poor, the nonwhite and the sick–as they are the profit-oriented projects of corporate elites. Unless theorists and strategists of urban movements take such distinctions seriously, they will not have adequately thought through the complexities of community as goal or strategy.

Certainly, one meaning of community is the strong bond of human connection and identity that people experience with respect to neighborhood and place. This "we-feeling" prompts that important and valuable sense of group solidarity that allows us to feel at one with others and the earth. Community, in this sense, is the antidote for alienation. But community does not, as we sometimes seem to think, logically preclude alienation, for communities may feel separate or estranged from other communities. As this sense of communal alienation deepens, it can feed on its own suspicions, becoming hostile, even brutal, in its "foreign" relations with neighboring communities. The feelings and relationships of community can thus give rise to a solidarity that is militantly partisan. These are the tendencies captured in the term "enclave consciousness."

At least two kinds of questions are suggested by an attempt to come to terms with enclave consciousness. One is strategic: How can community movements overcome their inward-looking tendencies to mount an effective opposition to centralized corporate and political power? The other is more analytical, though it embodies crucial normative interests, too: How has enclave consciousness managed to survive rationalization, retaining a foothold in a world ruled by global forces of political, economic and technical power?

The latter issue, which is closer to the focus of this paper, is a question of the persistence of traditional institutions and habits of thought in the face of modernity. As Veblen (1967), among others, has argued, the power of past institutions to inhibit reason in the present must never be underestimated. Old cultural patterns often long survive the conditions and exigencies which originally brought them into being. Continuing in force, old ways can influence the outlooks of new generations and mold patterns of behavior, finding a cultural niche even amid the seemingly antagonistic and overwhelming conditions of a new order. Indeed, the very slowness of cultural adaptation may well help people survive the impulsions of change, though long-ingrained habits can also retard the capacity of people to respond rationally to change, that is, with all the tools potentially at their disposal. Unless we are willing to stick to a quasi-religious faith in the automatic workings of "the dialectic," we have to be prepared to face up to the heavy hand of anachronism as it weighs on the present order, shaping and slowing the possibilities of rational adaptation to change. One example of such anachronism is the continued grip of localism, even in the most advanced industrial cultures such as the U.S. In at least three distinct (though interrelated) forms–law, ideology and economic practice–an enduring localism underpins and reinforces the persistence of enclave consciousness, giving it a kind of traditional reaffirmation and legitimacy that allows enclave consciousness to live on, even thrive, as a form of partisan solidarity, or alienated community, in the midst of such giant institutions as the nation-state and global capitalism.

Streams of Localism

Legal Localism

Among the more important factors favoring the ideological, especially the class, character of European labor politics has been the existence of strong centralized states. Centralized states give political power and politics a national focus; they help to concentrate political struggle on broad ideological themes (Body-Gendrot, 1987). Decentralized governments, meanwhile, are more free to arrange their own particular patterns of politics, patterns that can run the gamut from effective pluralist competition to "carte blanche for vested interests" (Lowi, 1979: 259; Elkin, 1987: Chapter 3). The U.S. never developed a centralized state along European lines. While the powers of local governments in this country are tightly hemmed in by the authority of state constitutions, the confinements of the Dillon Rule and enormous fiscal pressures to attract and hold private capital, they are nonetheless relatively free, in comparison with European cities, to manage their internal policies and organize their political relationships, especially in the key area of land use (Peterson, 1981; Swanstrom, 1985; Elkin, 1987; Plotkin, 1987).

In addition, the federal structure of political power (including especially the local basis of representation in Congress), coupled with the decentralized nature of the national electoral and party systems, has always insured that national policies permitted a large measure of discretionary control to remain in the hands of state and local officials (Lowi, 1979). Most important, though, legal localism in the U.S. has never been simply a matter of the formal power of the larger cities. It has also involved ideological aspirations toward home rule, grass-roots democracy and self-government that, especially when combined with the political and economic power of local ruling groups, has encouraged a proliferation of powerful little governments and quasi-governments (e.g., special districts, public authorities, suburban governments, etc.) both within and beyond the formal boundaries of cities. These have had a huge influence on the administration of urban growth as well as the distribution of its benefits and costs (Plotkin, 1987).

The U.S., for all the nationalization of its corporate and military power, nonetheless has a political system highly attuned to the pressures of local and regional groups, especially the more localized interests of capital and the middle class. Such pressures have found their way into the political system in part because the government was itself originally designed to favor the representation of just such narrow, territorial voices.

Local jurisdictions and interests have played an unusually important role in the U.S. political tradition since its beginnings. The creation of American political institutions was strongly influenced by the fact that the nation's first colonists carried over from England local political traditions that reflected her feudal past. England, after all, was governed into the late sixteenth and early seventeenth centuries by a "Tudor Polity" that answered first to the local landed aristocracy (Huntington, 1968). Although England gradually abandoned the localist representative tradition after her Civil War, there was no need for the U.S. to do so. Here, the early merchant towns were already equipped with the legal power to administer their affairs along commercial lines; the local bourgeoisie had no feudal aristocracy with whom to settle accounts and no need to demand centralized power as a means of breaking up the rule of local notables. American colonial towns were in many ways akin to medieval enclaves, inasmuch as "they were established by people who broke away from existing social restraints and who formed relatively closed societies with new social structures" (Frug, 1980: 1097). Early American politics were defined as much, or even more, by the animosities and antagonisms within the property-owning classes, especially divisions between landed and commercial capital, as well as between larger and smaller farmers. All of these interests were heavily reflected in the geo-political terms of competing urban and rural enclaves, what today's urban political economists call "growth politics" (Swanstrom, 1985; Feagin, 1988). Not for nothing did James Madison define "factions" by their tendency to form not only in favor of their own interests, but against "the rights of others and the permanent and aggregate interests of the community" (Madison, 1961).

At the same time, land-based property differences, fueled by varying social and religious traditions and already-strong regionalist sympathies, encouraged great distrust of centralized political power. After the American Revolution, when the new national government was organized, the leading interests settled on a federal compromise that allowed the scattered ruling elites to dominate their own local and state bailiwicks pretty much on their own terms (Dahl, 1961). Meanwhile, the key national institutions of Congress and the Presidency were left to express loose pluralistic coalitions of local powers. Consider, for example, that in American national government there remains no provision for a national, or at-large, political constituency to elect the president or either part of the Federal Legislature (Schwartz, 1988). In crucial ways, the American Founders achieved the nationalization of political power only at the price of preserving a good deal of the old Tudor system of fragmented political power, which was rooted in the specific economic interests of regional and local constituencies. As Madison reminded those who feared an overly strong national government, there was little in the proposed government to modify the tendency for politicians "to sacrifice the comprehensive and permanent interests of the State (much less the national government) to the particular and separate views of the counties or districts in which they reside" (Madison, 1961: 296, parentheses added). In American politics, local factions, driven by a notable sense of their interests as enclaves, had a strong legal position from which to make their fight.

Ideological Localism

If the legal framework encouraged localism, so did the populist tone of the nation's democratic and antiauthoritarian ideals. There are firm roots for such ideological localism–what Veblen called "a quasi-anarchistic scheme of social control" (1915: 46)–in the agrarian protests of the early American farmers, the political philosophies of Thomas Jefferson and Thomas Paine and not least in the spiritual rebelliousness of the American Protestant tradition. Americans have long believed that society should foster grass-roots political action as the natural field of egalitarian democracy (Seidelman and Harpham, 1985: 6; Tocqueville, 1945). This tradition, which inspired Saul Alinsky and much of the contemporary populist left, celebrates local association and direct forms of political action as the most appropriate and representative vehicles of democracy. Alinksy may well have stated the key principle of ideological localism when he insisted that "if the people have the power...in the long-run they will, most of the time, reach the right decisions" (1946: xiv).

Essential to the populist celebration of direct action is a related set of beliefs holding that "small units of social and political organization" are "the citadels of all the values associated with democracy" (McConnell, 1966: 91). Small-scale democracy enjoys this virtue because the majority it seeks to embrace is supposedly more homogenous than the mixed and conflicting populations of larger units. Small jurisdictions are more likely to encompass neighborhood people who think, feel, live and own more or less alike. Thus, small communities tend to an outlook–an enclave consciousness–that sees its primary political conflicts with the society outside, not within. In fact, as critics of small jurisdictions have noted, this way of thinking can end up justifying the authoritarian repression of minorities as well as majorities, while supporting the social power of leading economic interests (Madison, 1961: 81; McConnell, 1966). As far as the ideology of small-scale, populist democracy is concerned, however, such criticisms are beside the point. For the populist democrat, the important thing about grass-roots democracy is that it projects the voice of seemingly united and organic communities against an alien and demanding outside world.

The homogeneity of small grass-roots constituencies has other important consequences for the content of the political demands made by populist enclaves. Because people who identify with little constituencies regard the interests and values of their neighbors as essentially like their own, members of the enclave will probably feel impatient with ideological discussions that reexamine or challenge dominant values. Taken as given expressions of homogeneous community preferences, the enclave will seek to transmit its "common" interests outward in very concrete ways. These will typically take the form of demands for specific economic benefits, or for privileged exemptions from responsibilities to the larger society–the typical pork of American congressional politics–or, as is typical of urban land-use fights, the exclusion of unwanted industrial or social projects. In other words, small constituencies are more likely than large ones to reject appeals designed to overcome partisan solidarity; that is, to build linkages and coalitions among different segments of the society or to fuse the common interests of the enclave and wider society. Such ideas are "less recognizably in the interest of [the] readily definable groups" (McConnell, 1966: 115). The populist pragmatism of small constituencies is thus unlikely to represent serious ideological threats to the established order. In sum, for all the enthusiasm and seeming radicalism of direct-action politics, the political implications of ideological localism tend to be conservative (McConnell, 1966: 115; Lowi, 1971: Chapter 3).

Economic Localism

Legal and ideological localism favor diffusion of ethnic, racial and political identities, but there is an economic root to American localism, too. The idea of economic localism, with its ring of protectionism and unfree trade, may seem odd at first, especially in the context of the U.S., which has always celebrated the virtues of open markets. Still, it is not hard to understand the logic of economic localism once the economic and social pressures of urban capitalism are examined.

In capitalist cities, where business investment is the main force behind change, urbanites have a tough time just maintaining their neighborhoods. The dynamics of business-led change are extremely powerful, and they regularly threaten household and neighborhood stability. "Each neighborhood experiences constant inflows and outflows of residents, materials and money" and, as noted above, there is not much that individual neighborhoods can do to control such changes (Downs, 1981: 1; Harvey, 1973; Molotch and Logan, 1987). This dynamism, moreover, is strongly encouraged by the boosters of local-growth politics, who themselves manifest enclave consciousness as they actively compete with rival towns to pull in the greatest possible flows of external investment at the other's expense (Veblen, 1967: 142-65; Peterson, 1981; Swanstrom, 1985; Feagin, 1988).

Naturally, local residents struggle against the bad consequences of expansion and change; no one wants to see his or her life shaken (Elkin, 1987: 43). But struggles to contain urban land-use changes usually end up as efforts to confine the neighborhood to existing members, curbing competition for whatever locational advantages the residents may possess. As Weber argues, when local groups try to close their socio-economic relations in this way they usually take "some externally identifiable characteristic of another group of (actual or potential) competitors–race, language, religion, local or social origin, descent, residence, etc.–as a pretext for attempting their exclusion." For this reason, among others, Weber sees neighborhood as "an unsentimental economic brotherhood" for which socio-economic separatism is anything but an alien policy (Weber, 1978 (vol. 1): 342, 360ff).

Economic tendencies toward exclusion are heavily encouraged in modern capitalist cities. There, the exclusionary rights of private property not only determine the social and spatial organization of the city, but also form the first legal defense against environmental change (Plotkin, 1987). One expression of this economic exclusionism is the Neighborhood Improvement Association tradition of community organizing, which developed primarily "to protect property values and community homogeneity," usually by "excluding members of lower classes and racial minorities" (Fisher, 1984: 73).

Economic localism reflects a proprietary aspect of communalism, a kind of possessive communalism. Very much part of the enclave consciousness, possessive communalism suggests the belief that private interests are best nurtured and guarded by their setting in a socially restrictive enclave of kindred interests. The enclave–"our neighborhood"–thus comes to be seen not so much as a warm, affective "community" as a collective property for the safekeeping of private possessions.

Possessive communalism, in this sense, represents a blending of the older partisan solidarity with the more private, individual motivations of modern property, what MacPherson (1962) called the liberal ethos of "possessive individualism." Possessive communalism reflects an understanding that the private economic and social interests of neighborhood members are joined inextricably together by the residents' common occupation of an area. These interests, the residents believe, can best be protected if they act as if their locale was a kind of communal private property in need of joint regulation (Nelson, 1980). Justifying the militant antibusing efforts of one working-class Brooklyn neighborhood, a local activist invoked this idea of possessive communalism with a suggestion that his community was a private membership club. "You have do it to keep out the undesirables," he explained. "It's a cooperative effort of neighbors. They have the right to pick their neighbors" (Rieder, 1985: 82).

Legal, ideological and economic localism strengthen the "strong forces working toward cultural heterogeneity and territorial differentiation in the urban system" (Harvey, 1973: 84). They help to explain a cultural and political context that gives rise to parochial, rather than class, activism, to closed, rather than open, social relationships (Weber, 1978 (vol. 1): 43-6). It is necessary to look at the situation in such terms to understand how urban social conflicts are culturally structured (Smith, 1988). These ideas, though, do not get us close enough to the content of enclave consciousness itself. For this we need to move from frame to substance.

Enclave Consciousness

In enclave consciousness, people see their neighborhood as home territory, a familiar environment of people, buildings and space, surrounded by alien threats. Enclave consciousness is first of all a political orientation to the defense of such a place (Cox and McCarthy, 1982: 196). As opposed to a politics of ideological commitment, enclave consciousness reflects the desire "to give politics first a location rather than simply an abstract structure" (Morris and Hess, 1975: 9). Based on a sensibility of firm interconnection between social relations and the urban, built environment of houses, sidewalks, yards, stores, churches, parks, lots and streets, the enclave consciousness has much to do with the spirit, custom and collective self-understanding of a more or less well-defined neighborhood. The result is "a tenacity of neighborhood sentiment" (Molotch and Logan, 1987: 101).

The roles of communal feeling and territorial identity as elements of enclave consciousness should not be exaggerated, however. Especially in the privately oriented culture of the United States, sentiments of possessive communalism are bound to be linked closely to feelings of possessive individualism. We need not wholly reject the idea of community, or even reduce it to a question of rational, self-interested action, to recognize that community can serve as a political mask for what are felt to be primarily individual, family or household interests (Frieden, 1979). Indeed, what lends the enclave consciousness its peculiar social character is the way that possessive individualistic elements are combined and blended in the American context with social and economic ties to neighborhood and place.

Tocqueville caught one aspect of this fusing of private and social identities when he noticed that, in America, democratic individualism rarely meant isolation from others. Individualism, he argued, *did* draw people away from society at large, but it also attracted them to smaller social circles, inclining them toward family and friends, not atomism and blind self-seeking (Tocqueville, 1945 (vol 2): 104). Thus, "many values of popular individualism are really familial...with control, security, comfort and convenience being sought for the family" (Gans, 1988: 3). The concerns and fears of the private household, in this sense, are never far from the center of the enclave's interests.

The neighborhood can lend valuable support to the varieties of family and household in modern American life, of course (Molotch and Logan, 1987: 103-10), but, for modern enclave consciousness, these are primarily gifts to the safekeeping of household interests. Thus, while celebrating community, neighborhood households that embody the enclave consciousness also regularly strive to preserve privacy and social distance between themselves to retain their otherwise individual, apolitical character. The instrumental connection between household and neighborhood is an important factor behind the strongly protective or defensive cast of much community activism. It helps explain why effective political and social action is likely to require the presence of an immediate common threat (Weber, 1978 (vol. 1): 361). As one protester recognized, the possibilities of community organization around more abstract ideals are remote; attacks on children and property form the most reliable reasons for activism. In his words, "There's only one kind of activism you can have in Canarsie: you can organize (people) around protecting their bucks or their kids" (Rieder, 1985: 173).

As an ingredient of enclave consciousness, the importance of threat should not be overemphasized. Given the militant inheritance of partisan solidarity and the instability and change that accompany urban capitalist life, households and communities are genuinely "vulnerable places" (Rieder, 1985: Chapter 3). Residents feel that they must remain alert to external dangers emanating from the wider society and market. Control, security and minimization of risk are constant preoccupations of the enclave consciousness. As Gans writes, "the goal of popular individualism is hardly separation from other people," especially inasmuch as others are needed to watch out for and fight against unwanted changes in the environment (Gans, 1988: 3-4). Somewhat like the plebs of Machiavelli's Florence, today's urban protestors use collective action not so much to gain power for themselves as a group, but to be left alone in their neighborhoods and to avoid domination by the powerful (Machiavelli, 1970: 116).

The collective desire to avoid external control makes neighborhood independence a major theme of enclave consciousness. Like the private household, people feel that the neighborhood should be able to stand on its own two feet. Buttressed by beliefs in its hard-earned independence, members of the enclave feel they owe little to the larger society. Except perhaps for religious commitments to a wider church community, or the call of an emergency, and therefore temporary, coalition with neighboring areas, the enclave consciousness rejects ties to other neighborhoods, much less to wider units of political association such as mass movements, trade unions or political parties.[1] Some even argue, echoing Madison's fears of the predominance of local factions, that the enclave consciousness predominates in America today (Savas, 1987: 304; Gans, 1988: 114).

In place of "national community," the enclave consciousness seeks the distinctively autarkic ideal of communal independence, leading many urbanites to believe they have "a right to avoid entanglement in the affairs of the larger society" (Rieder, 1985: 95). A New Jersey protester, for example, animated by state efforts to move AIDS patients into a nearby nursing home, said as much when he declared, "These AIDS people come from a decadent society...I'm talking about sex and degenerates passing drug needles in Newark...NIMBY (not in my back yard). You said it, NIMBY! That's what we believe" (*New York Times*, 1988; parentheses added). Even where the enclave consciousness takes more humane forms, though, as illustrated by one recent study of community activism in Paris, it seems devoutly to crave communal separateness. When student architects working with the neighborhood sought to give graphic representation to the residents' urban longings, the residents wanted "an island of communal life, with gardens and patios surrounded by medium-rise housing" insulating it from the larger city beyond (Body-Gendrot, 1987: 135).

Like the Paris protester, the anti-AIDS activist in New Jersey apparently believes that his own neighborhood is an "island," that it has the potential to be a stable, internally coherent and decent place, a setting capable of regulating its own healthy affairs. Neighborhood, for the enclave consciousness, thus becomes something close to a complete expression of essential relationships, with a happy integrity of its own that is distinct from metropolitan or national systems. In other words, the modern enclave consciousness has much in common with the world view of pre-industrial, country-and-town life, which Robert Weibe so well captured with his phrase "the island community." Like their rural forbearers, members of today's urban enclaves still manage "to retain the sense of living largely to themselves" (Weibe, 1967: 2).

Given the dynamics and pressures of centralized capitalism, the enclave's yearning for independence is laden with anxiety. Feelings of neighborhood marginalization and exploitation can run rampant when centralized institutions make surprise announcements of new development projects, or suddenly warn of long-simmering environmental threats (Apter and Sawa, 1984: 235). Nor is the primal fear of urban violence just the statistical hyperbole of conservative politicians. Poor, working- and middle-class urbanites understandably feel that their enclaves are squeezed between the economic depredations of the corporate and political elite and the random street attacks of drug users. For the enclave consciousness, the city is manipulated by greedy forces from above and beset by uncontrollable violence from below. It is an arena of predatory interests, a conflict-ridden system aimed at controlling, exploiting and ultimately destroying the enclave.

Enclave struggles thus become a matter of "them" against "us." Enclave consciousness reflects, in this sense, a "subordinate value system" that neither fully supports nor radically rejects the dominant value structure (Parkin, 1971: 88). This subordinate outlook adapts to the outside social structure by maintaining a posture of tense skepticism with respect to external authority, and militant rejectionism when it comes to the lower classes. Nor does such contempt work only in one direction. The enclave consciousness leaves plenty of room for black as well as white racism, as well as color-blind classism; ruling-class neighborhoods and suburbs are hardly exempt from it either. Throughout the ranks of society, externally induced changes in the community are suspect and the wider society is seen to have no justifiable reason for ever changing things. As one progressive city planner explained after meeting with a group of neighborhood opponents of a new industrial park, the protestors seemed to believe that "there are *never* circumstances that justify forcing some residents to move," even to make way for a project beneficial to workers in the city as a whole (Clavel, 1986: 102, italics in original). Clearly, the end result of the enclave consciousness is the classic mercantilist policy of "beggar thy neighbor," as community groups regularly seek to export or exclude the perceived "bads" of urban life while fencing in the goods (Harvey, 1973; Stone, 1987: 9).

Such tendencies, rife in Alinsky's influential theory of community organization, are commonplace in neighborhood self-defense fights (Alinsky, 1946; Fisher, 1984; Castells, 1983: 60-5). At its core, Alinsky's approach can be read as a systematic effort to awaken the enclave consciousness, although rarely to inform it with an explanation of the forces that make the larger social system tick. Cleveland's recent experiment with urban populism, in the form of the Kucinich administration's effort to take on the city's banks and utilities, is a case in point. There was nothing in the Alinsky theory of activism to prevent Kucinich from moving toward racist appeals when his political future was in peril (Swanstrom, 1985). As Feagin suggests in the case of Houston, working-class racism is so endemic to that city's political culture that class-oriented community politics have been virtually stymied altogether (Feagin, 1988).[2]

Spirited by moral outrage against elite manipulation and lower-class depredation, the enclave consciousness channels the political activism and resistance of ordinary people mainly into demands to "leave us alone." With its characteristically defensive, exclusionary and reactive character, the resulting politics is a "geopolitics of local community," in which "deterrence, counterforce, holding ground, securing borders, flanking maneuvers and standing fast" are "central organizing concepts" (Rieder, 1985: 234). Each enclave becomes a mini-fortress, always prepared for the next big fight, though without requisite stores of strategic weapons. As the siege mentality prevails, all efforts are concentrated on restricting the power of elites or the underclass to penetrate the community. As Boyte himself notes (1980: 191), much community organizing in the 1970s reflected a "marked localism, or tendency to concentrate on those problems closest to home and to be suspicious and skeptical about involvement in any broader or larger organizational forms and coalitions addressing 'bigger issues.'"

In sum, the enclave consciousness tends toward a rigid and undifferentiated exclusionism. It is a consciousness reluctant to make social or moral distinctions between environmental dangers arising from the modern physical and technical processes of urbanization and the more primitive fear of strangers. Even where the focus of community action is not racial or social exclusion, though, but rather a suddenly discovered, internal environmental threat, typical enclave demands center on corrective action by external institutions or a buyout of the affected homes, not basic changes in patterns of social-economic planning, decision and investment (Freudenberg, 1984).

To gain such action, enclave consciousness can motivate people to support much-more-than-ritualistic participation in electoral or interest-group politics. Indeed, given the dissipation of local party structures and the wiring of a mass electorate into modern telepolitics, militant forms of direct action have emerged as prime strategy for community activists. The siege mentality, coupled with a penchant for excited urban dramas to attract the camera, encourages activists to shout "no!" to power. Protest meetings, angry denunciations of city and corporate leaders, referendum and petition campaigns, marches to and around the centers of urban power, rent strikes, sit-ins, lie-ins and assorted other forms of bureaucratic sabotage are now familiar features of "street-fighting pluralism" (Yates, 1977). Expanding the intensity, if not always the scope, of conflict has become the name of the game in the geopolitics of enclave defense. It is worth noting, however, that much of the noise of street demonstrations can be a "facade that is more imposing than the substance behind it," (Henig, 1986: 225), for community activist groups are themselves often internally divided by social and political conflicts and only weakly representative of their own community sentiment (Rieder, 1985).

Prolonging Politics

Enclave consciousness does not thrive because the urban working-class has been conspiratorially tricked into mistaking its interest. The enclave consciousness is an historical product of diverse cultural traditions and deep-seated political-economic patterns that have profoundly shaped the experience of labor in America. And while intraclass divisions have not always prevented class alliances in the U.S. (the history of the labor movement, for example, is a mixed story of cooperation as well as conflict among groups within the working class) it remains true that we have to face up to "the deep racial and ethnic differences that molded American politics in practice" (Kazin, 1988: 49). Such differences are one reason the "many signs of ferment and social conflict in American cities remained largely within segments of the working class" (Smith, 1988: 79). It may well be that radicalism in America meets its limit at the enclave. The enclave consciousness is a weak link in the chain of labor history, but for all that, it is still important as a defense against the totalization of power by modern capitalist society (Habermas, 1973). Perhaps it would be worthwhile to count some of the blessings of the enclave consciousness.

First, at a time when "we are witnessing a shrinking of the realm of the possible and a shrinking of the realm of the public" (Henig, 1986: 243), enclave consciousness is one force that actually keeps open public dissent and oppositionism in American culture. For all its limitations, enclave consciousness inspires a kind of functional unruliness in urban politics–functional, that is, to the continuation of politics and the making of popular demands in an increasingly apolitical and privatized society. This consciousness contains more than a little of the legacy of what Veblen called the ancient "quasi-anarchistic scheme of social control resting on insubordination" (Veblen, 1954: 46). This unruly, quasi-anarchistic quality supports the making of what amount to irrationally rational demands to be left alone by, rather than to participate within, institutions of domination. That is why the so-called politics of NIMBY poses uniquely puzzling dilemmas for centralized state and corporate power. The exclusionary demands of NIMBY are simply not as subject to cooptation as were the participatory demands of the 1960s (Katznelson, 1981; Plotkin, 1987). Today, central and urban governments may continue to "engage in regressive social engineering," but now they must expect street fights before they will get their way (Mollenkopf, 1983: 294; Huntington, 1984; Yates, 1977).

More, for all its restrictiveness and negative-mindedness, the enclave consciousness does offer a powerful rationale of empowerment. Community resistance is evidence against the dour image of politics taught by sociologists of "the mass society" (Mills, 1956). Citizens who fight to secure their homes and communities from intervention by high-level controllers manifest alienation, but not apathy. They show a will and capacity to question authority. Their actions belie what Marcuse, following Mills, saw as the repressive quiescence of a "one-dimensional" citizenry, whose powers of reasoned criticism have been wholly incorporated by centralized media empires, including the national state itself (Marcuse, 1964). Political consciousness in the lower ranks of society, even in its unreconstructed, enclave form, is less flat and quiescent than critical theory has suggested.

Neighborhood activism may be an example of what Mills called "the lower common sense" (Mills, 1956: 313), but it *is* reasonable to question the siting of dangerous industrial projects and the destruction of urban neighborhoods. Clearly, community opposition to environmental and industrial dangers does not exemplify what Marcuse called "The Great Refusal." As a more diminutive refusal, though, enclave politics is not without consequence for crucial human interests: the preservation of community and nature, the protection of life and health and the reduction of socially unnecessary human misery and ecological waste. These are not secondary values. The unruliness of the enclave consciousness is functional to their preservation, too, at least in the short run.

Finally, if the enclave consciousness helps spawn a politics of exclusion, exclusion can sometimes give way to more socially responsible perspectives. Under certain conditions, urban enclaves have forged alliances with other groups and pursued more universal goals. To take one example discussed elsewhere: Mexican-Americans from the poor west side of San Antonio, Texas, who used Alinksy-type organizing strategies to defend *barrio* interests, did not let the enclave perspective prevent them from joining with white, middle-class environmentalists to fight a regional shopping mall that threatened the city's sole source of water (Plotkin, 1987: Chapter 5). What is doubly important about this illustration is the way that Mexican-American organizers developed a practical understanding of the interconnections between environmental issues and issues of corporate-led urban development. The defenders of the *barrio* joined the mall fight not only to protect the city's pure water, but also as a means of regulating capital flight from downtown to the suburbs; they saw the mall issue as one way to raise larger questions about the social as well as spatial planning of their city.

Similarly, in the very different context of Laurinberg, North Carolina, poor blacks, whites and Indians recently coalesced to fight the location of a treatment plant for hazardous wastes. According to the town's white mayor, it was not only environmental fears that brought the town together, but also a sense of exploitation by arrogant outside elites. The treatment plant people came here "because they thought we were ignorant," said the mayor. "They thought we would roll over and die a long time ago." Instead, the town's fight expanded the conception of the enclave; the struggle itself "produced a growing sense of unity and strength among blacks, whites and Indians in an area where racial divisions had been the norm" (*New York Times*, 1986: A18). In a number of American cities, neighborhood organizations have taken on economic issues with much more than merely enclave significance, such as tenants rights and rent controls, red-lining by banks and insurance companies, ownership of municipal facilities and corporate disinvestment (Clavel, 1986; Swanstrom, 1985).

Conclusion

Community-based movements clearly are not inherently racist and reactionary. Neither, however, are they inherently democratic and socially responsible. The point is that enclave consciousness is a strong tendency within communitarian politics. It is best understood not as a distortion of an otherwise egalitarian, democratic communalism, but as an institutional pattern that reflects traditions of stratification and alienation that have been handed down from the past only to assume modern, capitalistic and bureaucratic forms. Thus, the main argument in this paper is that community and alienation are not mutually exclusive terms. Enclave consciousness is one way of conceiving their possible relation. There is, of course, nothing new or surprising about noticing the tendency of groups in similar economic and social situations to divide against one another. Leftist activists and scholars know all too well how traditional ethnic and racial animosities are regularly used by elites to "divide and rule" underlying populations. The name Willie Horton resonates as the most recent, potent example. Still, communitarians and Marxists have tended, albeit in different ways, to understate the reactionary power of tradition to shape modern institutions and outlooks.

Communitarians write as if the reactionary elements of community are marginal to its more positive feelings of "we-ness." Presumably, for them, enclave consciousness can be stripped away from the more benign tendencies in group solidarity through democratic discussion of its irrationality. Perhaps this is true, but communitarians will still have to face the issue of whether the ties of community can stand up to the potential loss of "the other" as unifying enemy, or whether they will have to find a new "other." This could be capital, of course, but then communitarians would end up on the even more dangerous turf of class struggle, precisely the discourse they regard as either anachronistic, wrong headed or ill-suited to U.S. conditions.

For Marx himself tradition represented little more than a temporary historical moment of irrationality. In one of his most famous sentences, Marx declared that "The tradition of all the dead generations weighs like a nightmare on the brain of the living" (Marx, 1970: 97, 99). The analogy is telling. Nightmares are imaginary and temporary states of an unhappy and frightened consciousness. Freud aside, they last only as long as sleep. Once awakened, sleepers can shed their feared visions and confront the day. With tradition as mere temporary delusion, it is not hard to understand why Marx could anticipate the proletariat's slow awakening from its nightmare, that morning of revolution when workers finally tear away "all superstition in regard to the past."

Tradition deserves more credit; it is not a temporary delusion. The past inheritance of culture, built on centuries, on millennia of learned belief, on fears, animosities, envies and jealousies, stoutly reinforced by prevailing habits and institutions, persists as a central pattern in the world of consciousness, including the modern consciousness. Cultural history is not part of an illusory "superstructure" of ongoing life. It is a primary shaping factor in the use and organization of social and productive forces; it helps form the core of those everyday attitudes and suspicions that people bring to their encounters with the world. The past gives culture and consciousness the only footing that people can understand and make sense of. For ill as well as good, it channels their responses to the present and shapes the possibilities of the future. If "the revolution of the nineteenth century must let the dead bury their dead," as Marx said, a genuinely democratic communist revolution was unlikely, for the dead are never fully buried. "The dead," as William Kennedy has written, "even more than the living, settled down in neighborhoods." Radicals have to find a way of making their own peace with the dead.

Acknowledgements

The author would like to express his thanks to Joseph Kling, Prudence Posner, Michael P. Smith and the anonymous referees of this journal for their help in clarifying the arguments of this paper.

Notes

1. Logan and Molotch correctly point out that such tendencies were much less true for black protest in the 1960s. Then, "the activist thrust was against the larger system" (1987: 138). However, even the systemic radicalism of black protest was not immune to territorial forms of cooptation (Katznelson, 1981).

2. The tragic findings of such case studies are backed up by broader national samplings of opinion. A National Opinion Research Center study found that for most white ethnic groups in the U.S., 43 percent or more of those questioned believed that "White people have a right to keep blacks out of their neighborhoods if they want to"; for Eastern European Catholics, the percentage agreeing was 58 percent (Harrigan, 1985: 79). It is no surprise, then, that Jimmy Carter could run for the presidency in 1976 by declaring his commitment to protect the "ethnic purity" of American neighborhoods, or that 12 years later George Bush would make a black rapist the unifying symbol of political fear in white, working-class communities.

References

Alinsky, S. (1946) *Reveille for Radicals.* Chicago: University of Chicago Press.

Apter, D.E. and Sawa, N. (1984) *Against the State: Politics and Social Protest in Japan.* Cambridge: Harvard University Press.

Body-Gendrot, S.N. (1987) Grass-roots mobilization in the thirteenth arrondissement of Paris: A cross-national view. In C.N. Stone and H.T. Sanders (Eds.), *The Politics of Urban Development.* Lawrence, KS: University of Kansas Press: 125-43.

Bowles, S. and Gintis, H. (1986) *Democracy and Capitalism, Property, Community and the Contradictions of Modern Social Thought.* New York: Basic.

Bowles, S., Gordon, D. and Weisskopf, T. (1983) *Beyond the Wasteland, a Democratic Alternative to Economic Decline.* New York: Doubleday.

Boyte, H. (1980) *The Backyard Revolution.* Philadelphia: Temple Univ. Press.

Castells, M. (1984) *The City and the Grassroots.* Berkeley: University of California Press.

Clavel, P. (1986) *The Progressive City, Planning and Participation, 1969-1984.* New Brunswick: Rutgers University Press.

Cox, K.R. and McCarthy, J.J. (1982) Neighborhood activism as a politics of turf: A critical analysis. In K.R. Cox and R.J. Johnston (Eds.), *Conflict, Politics and the Urban Scene.* New York: St. Martin's Press: 196-219.

Dahl, R. (1961) *Who Governs?* New Haven: Yale University Press.

Downs, A. (1981) *Neighborhoods and Urban Development.* Washington, D.C.: Brookings.

Elkin, S.L. (1987) *City and Regime in the American Republic.* Chicago: University of Chicago Press.

Feagin, J. (1988) *Free Enterprise City: Houston in Political and Economic Perspective.* New Brunswick: Rutgers University Press.

Fisher, R. (1984) *Let the People Decide, Neighborhood Organizing in America.* Boston: G.K. Hall, Twayne.

Freudenberg, N. (1984) Citizen action for community health: Report on a survey of community organizations, *American Journal of Public Health, 74*, 444-48.

Frieden, B.J. (1979) *The Environmental Protection Hustle.* Cambridge: MIT Press.

Frug, G. (1980) The city as a legal concept, *Harvard Law Review, 93*: 1053-1154.

Gans, H.J. (1988) *Middle American Individualism, the Future of Liberal Democracy.* New York: Free Press.

Habermas, J. (1973) *Legitimation Crisis.* Boston: Beacon Press.

Harrigan, J.J. (1985) *Political Change in the Metropolis*, third edition. Boston: Little, Brown.

Harvey, D. (1973) *Social Justice and the City*. Baltimore: Johns Hopkins University Press.

Henig, J.R. (1986) Collective responses to the urban crisis: Ideology and mobilization. In M. Gottdiener (Ed.), *Cities in Stress*. Beverly Hills: Sage: 221-46.

Huntington, S.P. (1968) *Political Order in Changing Societies*. New Haven: Yale University Press.

Huntington, S.P. (1984) *American Politics, the Promise of Disharmony*. Cambridge: Harvard University Press.

Katznelson, I. (1981) *City Trenches, Urban Politics and the Patterning of Class in the United States*. Chicago: University of Chicago Press.

Kazin, M. (1988) "The historian as populist, a review of Herbert Gutman, power and culture, essays on the American working class," *New York Review of Books* (12 May): 48-50.

Kotler, M. (1969) *Neighborhood Government*. New York: Bobbs-Merrill.

Logan, J.R. and Molotch, H.L. (1987) *Urban Fortunes, the Political Economy of Place*. Berkeley: University of California Press.

Lowi, T.J. (1971) *The Politics of Disorder*. New York: Norton.

Lowi, T.J. (1979) *The End of Liberalism*, second edition. New York: Norton.

Machiavelli, N. (1970) *The Discourses*. Baltimore: Penguin.

MacPherson, C.B. (1962) *The Political Theory of Possessive Individualism*. New York: Oxford University Press.

Madison, J. (1961) Federalist papers, nos. 10 and 46. In A. Hamilton, J. Madison and J. Jay, *The Federalist Papers*. New York: Mentor: 77-84; 294-300.

Marcuse, H. (1964) *One-Dimensional Man*. Boston: Beacon.

Marx, K. and F. Engels (1948) *The Communist Manifesto*. New York: International Publishers.

Marx, K. and F. Engels (1970) *The Eighteenth Brumaire of Louis Bonaparte*. In Selected Works, in one volume. New York: International Publishers.

McConnell, G. (1966) *Private Power and American Democracy*. New York: Random House.

Miliband, R. (1977) *Marxism and Politics*. New York: Oxford.

Mills, C.W. (1956) *The Power Elite*. New York: Oxford University Press.

Mollenkopf, J.H. (1983) The Contested City. Princeton: Princeton Univ. Press.

Molotch, H. and Logan, J. (1987) *Urban Fortunes, the Political Economy of Place*. Berkeley: University of California Press.

Morris, D. and K. Hess (1975) *Neighborhood Power*. Boston: Beacon.
Nelson, R.H. (1980) *Zoning and Private Property Rights: An Analysis of the American System of Land-Use Regulation*. Cambridge: MIT Press.
Parkin, F. (1971) *Class Inequality and Political Order*. New York: Praeger.
Peterson, P. (1981) *City Limits*. Chicago: University of Chicago Press.
Plotkin, S. (1987) *Keep Out: The Struggle for Land-Use Control*. Berkeley: University of California Press.
Rieder, J. (1985) *Canarsie, the Jews and Italians of Brooklyn Against Liberalism*. Cambridge: Harvard University Press.
Saunders, P. (1981) *Social Theory and the Urban Question*. New York: Homes and Meier.
Savas, E.S. (1987) *Privatization, the Key to Better Government*. Chatham, N.J.: Chatham House.
Schwartz, N.L. (1988) *The Blue Guitar: Political Representation and Community*. Chicago: University of Chicago Press.
Seidelman, R. and Harpham, E.J. (1985) *Disenchanted Realists, Political Science and the American Crisis, 1884-1984*. Albany: SUNY Press.
Smith, M.P. (1988) *City, State and Market: The Political Economy of Urban Society*. New York: Blackwell.
Stone, C.N. (1987) The study of the politics of urban development. In C.N. Stone and H.T. Sanders (Eds.), *The Politics of Urban Development*. Lawrence, Kans.: University of Kansas Press.
Swanstrom. T. (1985) *The Crisis of Growth Politics: Cleveland, Kucinich and the Challenge of Urban Populism*. Philadelphia: Temple University Press.
Tocqueville, A. (1945) *Democracy in America*, vol. 2, P. Bradley (Ed.). New York: Random House.
Veblen, T. (1915) *Imperial Germany and the Industrial Revolution*. New York: Viking Press.
Veblen, T. (1953) *The Theory of the Leisure Class*. New York: Mentor.
Veblen, T. (1967) *Absentee Ownership and Business Enterprise in Recent Times*. Boston: Beacon.
Weber, M. (1946) *From Max Weber, Essays in Sociology*, H. Gerth and C.W. Mills (Eds.). New York: Oxford.
Weber, M. (1978) *Economy and Society: An Outline of Interpretive Sociology*, 2 vols., G. Roth and C. Wittich (Eds.). Berkeley: University of California Press.
Weibe, R.H. (1967) The Search for Order. New York: Hill and Wang.
Williams, W.A. (1981) "Radicals and regionalism," *Democracy*: 1.
Yates, D. (1977) *The Ungovernable City*. Cambridge: MIT Press.

CLASS AND COMMUNITY: THEORIES OF ACTIVISM IN AN ERA OF URBAN TRANSFORMATION

Joseph M. Kling
St. Lawrence University

Prudence Posner
Associated Colleges of the St. Lawrence Valley

The populist tradition in the U.S. views "citizenship," "constituency," and "community" as the bases of collective action. This tradition is in conflict with the Marxian notion of class as key to the emergence and form of social movements. While there is much truth in the populist viewpoint, it underestimates the role of class structures in contemporary capitalist society. These structures shape the grievances that working people experience and disguise the larger social and economic interests that they share. This paper begins the process of reconciling the class/community dichotomy by situating "community" itself, as a concept, within a framework premised on the notion of class conflict in capitalist society.

Moving the People: Class or Community?

In recent decades one of the most controversial debates relating to the problem of activism has focused on the nature of the aggregate to be mobilized for change. Is it the working class that one seeks to organize? What of "new" working classes? Or has the fundamental locus of struggle become nonclass groups, such as women and racial and ethnic minorities?

Membership in the working class is usually defined, in these debates, by the fact that surplus value is extracted from a person's particular activity as a producer of goods or services. This broadly follows Marxist-oriented understandings of class. On the other hand, collective grievances exist which cannot be traced directly to an individual's class position. Alain Touraine, for example, argues that with the decline of industrially based capitalism and the rise of a managerial, or "programmed," society, it is the position of groups within the frame of larger bureaucratic and cultural apparatuses that forms the basis for domination, control and, ultimately, resistance. "What is crucial now is no longer the struggle between capital and labor in the factory," he writes,

> but that between the different kind of apparatus and user-consumers or more simply the public–defined less by their specific attributes than their resistance to domination by the apparatus...the defense against such apparatus is no longer carried out in the name of political rights or

> workers' rights but in support of a population's right to choose its kind of life and in support of its political potential, which is often called self-management. Political action is all pervading: it enters into the health service, into sexuality, into education and into energy production (Touraine, 1981b: 6-7).

Movements organized around issues of culture, identity, life-style or place have come to be known, in recent discussions of social change, as new social movements (see Luke, 1989; and Olofsson, 1988 for surveys of this literature).

As Luke suggests, there is neither an agreed-upon definition of new social movements nor a consensus as to the criteria which might qualify groups as such. True, most observers "seem to know a new social movement when they see one" (Luke, 1989: 125). It is not surprising, though, that we have failed to ground a concept which has been used to explain phenomena as disparate as the civil rights movement in the U.S. and the movements for political democracy in Eastern Europe (Omi and Winant, 1986; Touraine, 1981a). New social movements, it turns out, lack a centering theoretical principle, and can only be understood in relation to the particular societies, histories, cultures and political and economic structures within which they take shape. We know that such movements are organized around grievances and identities which are distinct from the workplace and the process of production, that they are made up, among others, of "informational 'new middle-class workers,' anti-industrial resistance groups...and traditional culture defense groups" (Luke, 1989: 149). More than that we do not know, because theory has reached no more precise level of articulation.[1]

In the context of the debates over activism in the U.S., one can perhaps get a handle on this issue by thinking of the new social movements as grounded in *citizen-based* or *constituency-based* identities. Constituency members are tied to social action either through their being socially singled out and subjected to discrimination as persons, or in the fact that they reside in a common area, usually a neighborhood, which generates both communal identity and locally based political interests. Thus, women, in the face of market and workplace discrimination or repressive traditions regarding family roles, have common social interests as women; at the same time, women who live together in a neighborhood may be brought together around specific needs for, say, a local day care center or health clinic. Again, thinking about new social movements in constituency terms is particular to a society which has always had a fragmented, pluralist political structure, combined with strong, yet often conflicting, interest-group and populist traditions.

While the activist debate in the U.S. might be described generally as one between those who look primarily to class as the basis for movement organization and those who look to constituency or aggrieved citizenship, it can also be approached in terms of the distinction between class and community. The locus of class-based organizing is clear: the workplace and the areas where the workers reside, neighborhoods resting somewhere in the vicinity of the plants which dominate the classic industrial city and mill town. Citizens and constituency members, on the other hand, are not necessarily identifiable as workers in the strict sense of direct producers who exchange their labor power for a wage. The locus of constituency-based organizing, therefore, is often thought of as "the community," where these citizens live, and from which they commute to all sorts of work in a variety of settings. Since most constituency interests transcend locality, it is the need to think in terms of a *locus of organizing* that leads to the terminological class/community distinction in contemporary discussions of social movements.

Overview of the Debate: The New Populism or The New Marxism?

There is a long tradition in the U.S. which relies on "citizenship" as the basic category through which to understand collective political action. This tradition challenges the primacy of the Marxian notion of class as the key to both the emergence and direction of social movements.[2] It is associated with middle-class progressivism and the agrarian populism of the decades preceding World War I, and traces its roots back to Jeffersonian ideas of the American commonwealth (Evans and Boyte, 1986, esp. Chapters 1, 4 and 5). It receded between the wars as class issues, in response to the Great Depression, came to the fore. Labor unions, led by the CIO drives, became the primary social-movement formation, and the American Communist Party exercised a significant impact on progressive politics.

After World War II, labor's influence diminished and class concepts of organization lost salience. Community organizer Saul Alinsky put forth a concept of workers as citizens, whose first responsibility was to society as a whole, not to their union and certainly not to their "class."[3] The American labor movement embraced both Cold War ideology and corporate unionism (see, for example, Green, 1980: 208; and Bluestone and Harrison, 1982: Chapter 5). C. Wright Mills wrote *White Collar*, which introduced the notion of an exploited, or new, middle class, and challenged traditional Marxian notions of class struggle and collective organization, during these years (Mills, 1967, originally published, 1951).

In the early 1950s, under the battering of McCarthyism and a general anti-left hysteria, there was no large-scale organizing presence of either populist or class-based orientation. In May 1954, however, Brown vs. The Board of Education was decided. A year and a half later, 1 December 1955, in Birmingham, Alabama, Rosa Parks refused to go to the back of the bus. The Civil Rights movement was under way.[4]

There is no room in this paper to do justice to the history of American social movements since the end of World War II, but it is not an unfamiliar story. In summary, there have been four major social movements in America since the silences of the McCarthy era: civil rights/black power, student/anti-war, women's and community action.[5] It is notable that none of the major post-war American social movements are class-based. All are built around the citizenship notion of the populist tradition, rather than the class identity concept of the Marxist tradition.

The resurgence of citizen-based movements led to a resurgence of populist theory in the realm of social and historical analysis. For example, the agrarian movement of the 1880s and 1890s, once analyzed in terms of the farmers as a kind of peasant class of small landowners caught in the jaws of an expanding industrial capitalism, now came to be seen as a people's movement not subject to categorization in terms of class.[6]

Organizers such as Mike Miller of the Organize Training Center in San Francisco, Wade Rathke of ACORN (Associated Community Organizations for Reform Now), policy theorist Frank Reissman of *Social Policy* magazine and historian and social theorist Harry Boyte took the emerging neopopulist ideas and applied them to the community and public-interest movements that which had begun to appear in the 1970s. Boyte explicitly reintroduced the notion that what was occurring was citizen- or constituency-based political action. "We can distinguish several main traditions of citizen advocacy with roots in the 60s and earlier..." he wrote,

> the geographically based method of community organizing largely developed by the late Saul Alinsky; the kind of public interest advocacy pioneered by Ralph Nader; constituency organizing that brings together and mobilizes those concerned with specific issues and abuses...
>
> Despite the differences, all have themes in common that roughly define the "citizen advocacy" tradition. They represent an old American practice of cooperative group action by ordinary citizens motivated by civic idealism and specific grievances... (Boyte, 1980: 7-8).

There was much force to the populist argument. Beginning, for example, with the publication of E.P. Thompson's *The Making of the English Working Class* (1963) and the development of the new social history, research consistently confirmed that social support networks based on culture, tradition and community were major motivating forces for collective action among working people (Dawley, 1976; Gutmann, 1977; Hobsbawm, 1959; Sewall, Jr., 1980; Wilentz, 1984). Indeed, that political identities based on ethnicity, nationality, race, gender and locality are genuine sources of resistance and organization in their own right, and not examples of some sort of false consciousness to be corrected by activists who see more deeply into political and economic realities, has established itself as a fundamental principle in much of Western Marxist practice.

Still, many observers argued against the simple abandonment of class-based social analysis. Erik Olin Wright and Ira Katznelson worked at reconceptualizing the notion of class. Wright, taken with the breaches made into the armor of the Marxist framework by the rise of a middle class that seemed, in its way, as exploited by the new bureaucratic capitalism as workers were in theirs, tried an ambitious reformulation of class theory. It was built to incorporate what he called "contradictory class positions" (Wright, 1979: Chapter 2; 1985: 26-37).

Katznelson's deconstruction of the notion of class into four levels, in such works as *City Trenches* and the introductory chapter to *Working-Class Formation*, almost precisely parallels Wright's. A major difference, however, is that Katznelson tied his reconceptualization directly to the emergence of nonclass-based social movements, particularly those which emerged in the urban black community. For this reason, his approach proves somewhat more fruitful in attempting to understand the relationship between class structures and constituency-based organizing.

So brief an overview cannot indicate the full complexity of the ways in which class theory, since the 1970s, has been reworked. The point, however, is to suggest that class-based theories that recognize the basic insights of neopopulist thinking do exist. They provide a starting point for the attempt to reconcile, at least partially, the activist dilemma precipitated by the class/community split. It is to this effort at consolidation that we now turn.

Castells: The Capitalist City and Constituency Mobilization

If Marxism is so powerful a tool of analysis, neopopulist theory properly inquires, why has it failed to account for the character of many of the major social movements in the industrialized West? The answer of analysts such as Manuel Castells is simple: Marxism was never a unified theory of change. Its first part dealt comprehensively with the concept of class structure. Its second, however, dealt with the notion of class struggle and, given the historical juncture at which Marx wrote, was unable to elicit an adequate account of the ways in which working people would become mobilized. Since the two parts of Marxist theory are, in many ways, logically distinct, it is possible to reassess its understanding of social movements, while retaining its basic analysis of the role of surplus appropriation in shaping social structure. For those unwilling to abandon the centrality of class when shifting perspective from social structure to social movements, the essential theoretical question becomes, in the formulation of Castells (1983: 298): *how is the connection to be established between the structure and the practices?*[7]

The traditional Marxian answer has always been through the class-based vanguard party. "Leninism became an integral part of Marxism," Castells writes, "not only because of the triumph of the Soviet revolution, but because only the theory of the party can establish a bridge between structures and practices in the Marxist construction" (1983: 299). The problem, of course, is that the class-based party movement has never been the sole form of resistance to political domination. This historical fact becomes especially clear after World War II, with the worldwide unfolding of constituency movements built around such issues as black nationalism, various ethnic nationalisms, community resistance to industrial encroachments, feminism and environmentalism.

In the face of these realities, a number of responses are possible. Marxism can insist that all social movements, at bottom, are reducible to class movements, or it can dismiss these movements as having no independent historical significance. These arguments, however, are variants of a mechanical and logically indefensible reductionism. A third response is to attempt to retain the fundamental impact of class on historical development, while at the same time incorporating the relevance of nonclass-based movements into the theoretical and empirical understanding of social change.

Castells's contribution is to have conceptually and empirically linked constituency movements to class structures through the notion of *urban space as medium*. Space, he reminds us, is as much a material dimension of production as are land, labor and capital, for the ways in which goods are produced are inseparable from the ways in which space itself is appropriated to produce them. The story of how this process of spatial reorganization worked in terms of the development of industrial capitalism is well known and familiar: with the invention of the steam engine and the emergence of the factory system, family producers are uprooted from their cottages in and around the rural village. They are forced by social conditions to locate in concentrated regions that are organized and structured in terms of the interests of the owners and controllers of the newly industrialized means of production. Thus is born the *capitalist city*, whether a manufacturing center such as Manchester, or a market and financial center such as London.

It is how people experience the domination and the control that flows from the spatial form associated with the modern capitalist city that leads to urban-based social movements. In such cases, these movements need not be class-derived, since they are more likely to emerge from what a group sharing a common residential area perceives as a threat to its cultural identity or neighborhood autonomy. One cannot predict what form these nonclass movements will take in response to the pressures generated by the class structure; they are contingent, rather than determined. What is crucial is that whatever the value or interest or goal at the base of the nonclass movement, it has been precipitated by the workings of a particular mode of production on the shape of people's lives.

Castells thus presents us with a developed theory of the relationship between class structure, urban space and urban-oriented social movements. In the case of the late capitalist city, with its access to modern technologies of transportation and information flow, people's experience of surplus extraction is determined and shaped by the ways in which the spaces where they live and consume are separated from the spaces in which they work and produce. In this situation, social movements grounded in the experience of neighborhood, family or racial and cultural identity should be the expected norm. Thus, once Castells's insight is recognized, the significant question for students of social change shifts from whether class or community is the more fundamental source of collective action. Rather, one must try to discover the relation in which nonclass mobilizations stand to the class structure which shuttles through and environs them.

Based on the wide range of movements they researched and studied, Castells and his staff concluded that urban social movements in the era of late capitalism usually form around a cluster of three goals: collective consumption, community solidarity and citizen action. *Collective consumption* refers to the attempt to expand the social wage, to bring to localities such social services as housing, improved education and health and child care centers. Movements of *community solidarity* seek to protect racial or cultural identity, or resist perceived threats to the integrity of the family and neighborhood. *Citizen action* movements fight for local autonomy, decentralization and neighborhood self-management. These three types of movements are not class-based, as Castells points out, "for the very simple reason that they do not relate directly to the relationships of production but to the relationships of consumption, communication, power" (1983: 320).

John Logan and Harvey Molotch are correct in warning against a sort of "romanticism of the grass-roots" from which Castells's work suffers. He seems conveniently to assume that all neighborhood groups–including those that are service-oriented and "preservationist"–may be understood as activist and progressive (Logan and Molotch, 1987: 38; Molotch, 1984). Still, the three goals Castells selects as shaping recent community action are close to the mark: these are the concerns, specifically urban-based or not, that mobilized many neighborhoods in the decades following the War on Poverty. Critically, for our purposes, they are tied precisely to the issues which neopopulism sees as generated out of "the interests of the community." The problem is that neo-populism conceives of these goals, and the issues around which they are built, as the basic elements of social struggle. It does not understand the ways in which they are molded by the urban form of the capitalist class structure. It thus identifies the *surface expression* of the resistance to capitalist modes of domination as the essential substance of that resistance.

Neopopulism does not have to recognize the connection between constituency movements and the exigencies of capitalist control. But unless it does, and also makes such linkages explicit and manifest in its organizing activity, it will continually undermine itself and the organizational movements which follow from its principles. As Castells somewhat wearily points out near the conclusion of his work, "...urban social movements are not agents of structural social change, but symptoms of resistance to the social domination even if, in their effort to resist, they do have major effects on cities and societies" (1983: 329).[8]

We now critically examine the term "community" and locate it within the multilayered framework for analyzing class which has been developed by Katznelson. It will be shown that while community signifies too many different things to be useful as a unit, either for the analysis of power relationships or as the basis for democratic social change, once placed in a framework of class analysis it can be a helpful instrument for understanding and engaging in social action.

The Limits of the New Populist Concept of Community

> *When people find themselves unable to control the world, they simply shrink the world to the size of their community (Castells, 1983: 331).*

> *Lacking the ability to deal meaningfully with the large-scale organizational and institutional structures that characterize our society, many of those we talked to turned to the small town not only as an ideal but as a solution to our present political difficulties (Bellah, et al., 1985: 204).*

The authors of the above quotes are intimately associated with the discussion of community, as a unit of resistance and as a basis for social transformation. Both recognize the limitations of that concept as a tool for either understanding or changing a world dominated by multinational, corporate power. Like other social thinkers, Castells and Bellah use community in both its descriptive and utopian meanings–or, in the words of Joseph Gusfield (1975), its semantic and poetic meanings. The poetic or utopian meanings of community refer to the value that is placed on it as a normative concept, echoing the *gemeinschaft/ gesellschaft* debate of an earlier era.

As a value term, "community" refers to the relationship among persons as an end, rather than as a means. It stands in opposition to the notion of working people as "hands" or "costs of production." It challenges the idea that land, whether urban dwelling space or rural farmland, is a commodity the value of which is measured purely in exchange terms. It encompasses the idea that housing is a human need, to be met as such, and not merely a product to be supplied if the price is right. Clearly, the idea of community is powerful and draws upon deep human desires and commitments that are fundamentally opposed not only to the needs of the capitalist organization of production, consumption and reproduction, but perhaps even to industrial organization in general. However, the power of the concept as a value commitment does not in itself warrant our use of the term, either in an analysis of contemporary conditions or as a prescription of resistance to them and for transformation.

As was argued above, the concept of community as a basis for social activism is the product of the particular types of social changes and social movements that emerged during the post-World War II period. Theorists of this form of social change call it "New Populism." From the New Populist perspective, the major agent of social transformation must be "the community." For them, "the community" becomes a substitute for both the older Marxist notion of the proletariat as the agent of revolution *and* for the social democratic program of seeking state intervention in the market on behalf of human needs. For example, Bowles and Gintis (1987: 179) explain the feasibility of their image of "post-liberal democracy":

> ...by stressing workplace and community empowerment as opposed to state expansion, the vision of postliberal democracy avoids one of the great dead ends encountered in the expansion of personal rights and simultaneously addresses a key weakness of social democracy. By stressing that the extension of democracy is not synonymous with the extension of state power, postliberal democracy affirms the sentiment that neither the centralized state nor the capitalist corporation will be the vehicle of human liberation.

Without turning a blind eye to the manifest evils of state bureaucracy, we believe that the ease with which an idea such as "community empowerment" seems to avoid the "weaknesses of social democracy" is more a function of its ambiguity than of its superior utility as a concept.

There is an irreducible reality to the term "community" as it applies to the geographical units that constitute the American local political landscape. These units have taxing power, authority over schooling and power to zone for land use, thereby obtaining certain regulatory powers. However, most analysts (and activists) concerned with social change are not interested in community primarily as it exists at the level of the 650 separate taxing bodies on suburban Long

Island. Nor are they referring to the 73 Primary Metropolitan Statistical Areas in the U.S., each of which is economically integrated into one of the 21 Consolidated Metropolitan Statistical Areas (U.S. Census Bureau, 1986). The complexity of levels of governance and common interest is prohibitive. Rather, to the extent that its meaning is made explicit, community is viewed as a collectivity in need of empowerment, or as a relationship of persons in which we are ends (neighbors), rather than means (buyers and sellers). As such, community refers to a *process*, not a thing or place.

Joseph Gusfield's discussion of "community" emerges as the product of people consciously acting in common, defining themselves as "us" different from, and frequently opposed to, "them." Given the importance to homeowners of the power to exclude "them" through zoning (a political/community function), the different meanings obviously sometimes coalesce. However, the political patchwork of communities capable of legally exercising that power hardly exhausts the meaning of the term. As Gusfield puts it:

> The nature of the social bond and the selection of bondsmen is not a fixed and given fact; a part of the *essence of the group*. Instead it is a facet of historical situations; a part of the *existence* of acting persons (1975: 39, italics in original).

Leaving aside the use of the term "community" to mean "interest group" (as in the Jewish community, the gay community, or the community of scholars), it is fairly obvious that community membership is more or less voluntary and that the existence of a "community" capable of acting in common to achieve goals requires the conscious recognition of "bondsmen" and the deliberate forging of such a bond. However, even if we only look at those uses tied to a geographical location, we are using a term which has moral meanings attached to it. A community school, community hospital or community center, however bureaucratic and impersonal it may be, is nonetheless expected to "belong," on some level, to the people of the locality it is supposed to serve.

The type of community most frequently cited as the model of resistance during the past two decades is the urban neighborhood (Boyte, 1980; Castells, 1983; Plotkin, 1987). The emergence of urban communities, which self-consciously resisted efforts to remove poor and working-class residents from central cities in the name of urban renewal, is a function of the macro-economic trends of the 1950s through the 1970s. The rapid growth of community organizations during the 1970s was largely a response to what Castells calls "the reappropriation of urban space." Cutbacks in housing subsidies for the poor, "red-lining" of working-class areas to eliminate private mortgages and home-improvement loans, and diversion of public funds into "downtown development" and middle- and upper-income housing all served as mechanisms for making the central cities "safe" for investment and profitable construction. This process took place within the context of a shrinking public pot, as the corporate tax share of the national budget decreased from 23 percent in 1960 to less than eight percent in 1984. Gary Delgado summarizes,

> It was the resistance to this phenomenon, the reappropriation of urban space, that became the context for the formation of community organizations in the 1970s... Community organizations were set up to fight evictions, resist urban removal, control schools and police and address neighborhood safety, zoning and the threat of superhighways dividing the neighborhood (1986: 9).

The urban "communities" that were galvanized into collective action as a result of the pressures of urban renewal and redevelopment (including the pressure from central city black families to find housing in nearby, exclusively white neighborhoods) were not political subdivisions with taxing and zoning powers. Sometimes they had neighborhood designations (i.e., Chelsea, Dorchester, Southside, Washington Heights); sometimes the embattled community was a subsection of a larger neighborhood. Its self-identity as a "community" combined a sense of historical continuity with the immediacy of the threat from "them." In this case, "they" were city-hall planners advocating downtown development at the expense of low-cost housing and services, and financial interests eager to invest in desirable central-city locations once the land became available.

As veterans of innumerable public meetings during which the microphone was seized from city officials with the demand that "the community" be heard, we are reluctant to abandon such a politically powerful concept. At the same time, that experience brings home forcibly the degree to which "community" is in the eyes of the beholder. It includes those who agree to undertake collective action together to achieve some public goal–the modification or elimination of existing policy, the inauguration of new policy, the introduction or augmentation of public services or the elimination of a public nuisance. Other than as a convenient political slogan, the idea that power *ought* to inhere in communities is, to say the least, problematic. The upper-class "community" of Irvine, California, fighting to prevent further development of multiacre lots in the vicinity, is not the same as the working-class communities of Chelsea (Manhattan) or Cobble Hill (Brooklyn) fighting to hold on to affordable housing in the face of gentrification. The lower-middle-class white Brooklyn "community" of Canarsie, tightly organized to control the movement of black families into the area, is not the same as the neighboring "community" of East New York, which is trying to prevent the location of halfway houses and juvenile homes in a low- and middle-income black residential area. And, obviously, none of these are the same as the "community" of Pittsburgh, which has included business, the unemployed, service employees and practically all residents in efforts to reindustrialize the Monongahela Valley.

The fact that communities cut across lines of social stratification within a residential area (as, for example, in instances in which a community organizes to keep an industrial employer in the area, to control a polluting industry or to keep out a dangerous or polluting plant or dump) says little about the relationship between community and class. Many communities, especially those in suburbs, equate the values of community with the maintenance of their expensively purchased lifestyle. On the other hand, renters and homeowners sometimes join forces to exercise control over growth and development, as in the well-documented and closely watched case of Santa Monica.

In his recent book, Plotkin (1987) has shown the complex intertwining of class interests in any given land use conflict. Despite the complexity, however, it is possible and helpful to situate "community" itself, as a concept, within a framework premised on the central notion of class conflict in capitalist society.

"Community" Within the Framework of a Layered Class Model

Our focus is less on grand schemes of class or other relationships than on the ways in which class and community are articulating terms and ways of understanding the issues that may or may not mobilize people into collective action. We stress issues because mobilization for collective action takes place in response to a particular event or to achieve a particular goal, not to alter the general structure of the game itself. At the same time, the major grievances that mobilize people cannot be eliminated within the rules of the game of capitalism. As was shown in the first sections of this paper, the categories of class alone, however finely drawn, do not sufficiently articulate the kinds of grievances people experience. Although "community" is frequently the self-defined locus of the grievance and the vehicle for collective action, as a term it lacks sufficient clarity and explanatory power to serve the purposes some of the New Populist analysts would have it serve.

The urban social movements to which discussions of community organization and empowerment refer represent the community or residence side of the community/workplace dichotomy in American political life and social consciousness. This side of our lives is not insulated from class, however; it is merely not experienced in class terms but in the language and action of ethnicity and community, race, social status and political affiliation. It is not merely experienced as such, for these are the "trenches" (in Katznelson's [1981] terminology), of urban civic life through which struggles for change are channelled and contained.

Rather than try to read the breakdown of class fragments or strata within a community, or worse, simply dismiss class as irrelevant to struggles related to issues of consumption and distribution, it is desirable to use Katznelson's layered concept of class to clarify the function of community (with its penumbra of meanings) in a society whose essential characteristic remains that of class conflict over the appropriation of surplus value (Katznelson, 1981, 1986).

Katznelson argues that the notion of class suffers from conceptual overload: too many different meanings are packed into a single term. He seeks, therefore, to break the concept apart, to crack it open along lines of fault not visible until history is provided the opportunity to test the original Marxian formulations. Class is not a unified construct, he suggests, but is composed of "four connected layers" identified as structure, ways of life, dispositions and collective action (1986: 14). These four levels of meaning are summarized as he proposes them.

The first level, *structure*, is shared by all systems based on private capital investment. It refers to the fundamental organization of the economy, whereby collective capital exploits collective labor by appropriating the surplus value produced by the latter. Not only do most Americans not understand capitalism in this form, but it is not experienced in this form by the real people who participate in it. Although it shapes that experience, it lies, by definition, outside the realm of immediate perception and awareness.

What we experience, as workers and as consumers of what is produced, occurs at the second level of class. This is the *"way of life"* precipitated by the operation of capital and its continuous drive for profit as it has developed in our society. It is the job one holds, the hours and pay level and the degree of authority over others or submission to others' demands. It includes the type of neighborhood in which one rents or owns a home, the availability of public and private facilities for recreation and education and the degree of exclusionary control one exercises in that capacity to determine with whom one shares that way of life. As a "way of life" it includes the ways in which our children are prepared to take their place in the organization of society–as job holders, executives, citizens and parents. It includes the ways in which society is stratified, using race, ethnicity, educational level, gender and geography to allocate goods and services.

It has often been noted, with regret by the political left and with satisfaction by the right, that the class position held by persons in the terms described above does not offer much predictability as to what they feel, think and believe about their situation. There does not appear to be any determinate relation between class position and how people will act to preserve or alter that situation. What Katznelson proposes is that we accept that *disposition* or "consciousness," feelings and ideas, is a third level of analysis, related to class formations but dependent on many other factors. Katznelson further argues that, in the U.S., the off-work consciousness of working people developed in relation to community, understood primarily as the place of residence that is simultaneously the locus of political representation. Since residence, or geographical community, is historically tied to income strata and, especially within urban areas, to ethnicity and race, these identities are often coextensive with locally-oriented political-party activity and the exercise of citizenship. At that level of consciousness, then, Americans operate with non-class "mental maps" in their off-work lives (Geertz, 1973: Chapter 8). If the thesis developed in Katznelson (1986) is correct, the bad news is that this is a given of the American scene and is not likely to change, no matter what strategies for social change are developed.

The good news lies in the recognition that the fourth level, *collective action*, is no more rigidly determined by beliefs and ideas than those are wholly determined by one's position in a class structure. The error of generations of Marxists was supposing that disposition, or consciousness, could be deduced from a correct reading of class as "way of life." The trick, therefore, was to find members of the real working class, teach them the correct political understanding and values, and mobilize them into action. The error of the New Populists is to suppose that collective action is determined by ideology or disposition, rather than only limited or influenced by it. The trick for the New Populists, then, becomes identifying the real values and dispositions of "The People," and hitching collective action to those.

There are real structures and processes that are a function of capitalism, whether people have constructed the understandings to include them or not. These are the large-scale institutional structures and organizations which people find they cannot control, and that, in Castells's words, shrink down to the size of their community.

Obviously, people are more likely to mobilize for collective action in terms of familiar identities and beliefs. Any activist knows that, in the U.S., probably the easiest issue to mobilize people around is protection of their property rights. Next easiest is the demand that "the community" participate in decisions that affect the life situation (e.g., property values, child raising and educating, shopping, traffic patterns, environmentally determined health conditions, in-migration of lower-status neighbors due to government housing policy). Even racial solidarity, so powerful as an inspiration to collective action on behalf of black citizenship rights, may pale in the face of either of these types of issues. We also know, though, that in the absence of a commitment to some larger concept of social justice, mobilization for collective action based on these most readily accessible "dispositions" does not necessarily move people in the direction of greater equality or democracy. In fact, it is precisely these readily accessible, mobilizing sentiments that lead collective action into the "trenches," the preexisting channels, of competitive pluralism and communal defensiveness that assimilate protest into the structures of politics as usual.[9]

Our concern here, however, is not with predicting or planning social movements or upheavals. We are trying to see if it is even possible for collective action, in the off-work context of American politics, to be related to class issues and conflicts when it is known that the consciousness or disposition of the people whose "toes are pinched" by social conditions is non-class in nature. In particular, we are looking at those issues which are understood in terms of community–the rights of communities as political units and actors, and the privileges of those who dwell within them. We are trying to confront the dilemma posed by the fact that dispositions are oriented toward "community" in relation to many off-work issues, yet collective action that fails to include "class content" (for want of a better term) that is not directed at the class structures of appropriation consistently fails to address the roots of the problems people face.

The factors that have the possibility of reconnecting collective action to class structures and processes (in the absence of class consciousness) are leadership and organization. Since the link between the disposition, consciousness or identity of a collectivity of people and the type of collective action they undertake is not rigidly determined (although these two levels are obviously related), there are choices possible at the moment of transformation from a feeling or sentiment of collective grievance into collective action for redress of that grievance. This reconnection occurs in the formulation of program, the combination of explanation and proposed solution which gives direction to collective action.

Programs informed by class content tie local issues to the larger questions of the restructuring of policy at state and federal levels. In the sphere of environmental organizing, for example, the alternative NIMBY (Not in My Back Yard) has been posed against the demand for stronger and more democratically formulated state and federal controls on industrial production and waste. While these are not necessarily contradictory, the choice of whether to articulate the program primarily in terms of "community" (NIMBY) or "class" (public controls on private industry) is a matter of emphasis that will determine the overall direction of the collective action or struggle. The existence of these choices has to do with the reconnection of what are understood as community issues to the class processes of a capitalist society.

A similar example can be found in the conflict over control of the San Antonio aquifer discussed by Plotkin (1987). Collective action to protect the city's water supply can remain at the level of competing communal rights. Alternatively, the issue of water, like land use, as a resource that cannot be reduced to exchange value and property rights, can be moved to the federal level, where there is sufficient power to set limits on private development. Of course, the organization of people to address such an issue takes place at the level of the self-defined community, even though the social power to resolve it lies elsewhere.

Examples can also be taken from the women's movement, at those points at which it is engaged in the public arena. The need for day care, for example, may be experienced as a women's issue a community issue, a race issue, or even a work-related issue (as unions are beginning to include day care as an employer-paid benefit). The "class content" of a program demanding day care services or facilities, however, is related to the idea that child care and preschool education are social responsibilities. A class perspective rejects the notion that "you get what you can pay for," so that the children from lower economic strata and status groups are entitled only to what their individual parents can make possible. Again, this does not mean that other nonclass issues related to the care and education of children are unimportant (e.g., non-sexist, multiracial patterns of staffing, or curricular development), only that these do not reconnect what may be experienced as a nonclass issue (e.g., sexual or racial equality) to the class structures.

The strategy of collective action in a particular situation is contingent upon many factors, including the dispositions of those who have been moved to undertake the action. However, without "class content" of the kind described above, the struggle once again will be channelled through the existing trenches from which little change can be made. The question, then, is whether people whose history, experience and inherited values have rendered close to invisible the impact of class structure on their lives can be moved to organize themselves, not as a class, but at least in terms of class-oriented policy issues. These are issues that, in their programmatic formulation, specifically seek state re-ordering of priorities of both the process of private capital accumulation and the distribution of social surplus within a market economy.

Social Movements as Organized Publics

It has been argued in this paper that class and community are not opposing concepts, but different modes through which society organizes people's connection to the worlds of production and politics. Synthesis, therefore, rather than argument, is needed over which is foremost, or which is the more valid construct for promoting collective action. The most helpful idea is the old notion of the democratic public, as it had been reformulated, first by John Dewey in the 1920s and then by C. Wright Mills writing in the midst of the repressive, anxious, fragmenting America of the 1950s. Both Dewey and Mills sought social change, both were aware of the inadequacies of Marxist analysis to the complexities of twentieth-century capitalism, and both suggested that theorists and practitioners think of social movements as organized publics. This idea will be explored briefly and developed in this conclusion, for it seeks to transcend, at least conceptually, the splintered identities and interests which day-to-day life in the modern polity precipitates for working people.

Dewey (1927: 166) tried to determine the conditions necessary for the emergence of what he called "a democratically organized public." He took his departure

> from the objective fact that human acts have consequences upon others, that some of these consequences are perceived, and that their perception leads to subsequent effort to control action so as to secure some consequences and avoid others (1927: 12).

A public is open to formation, then, when a group of actors recognizes that it is being affected–in ways it considers undesirable–by a second group of actors, or by a set of institutions, that operate from a social realm in some manner distinct from those being affected. This is the "us-them" sense in which the experience of community itself becomes rooted.

Dewey further argued that there is a distinction between conditions which objectively create a public, and an aggregate's correctly perceiving itself as such. Publics, that is, may not fully comprehend the sources of their grievances. Here, he integrated into his theory of the democratic state the idea that members of a given population may have essential interests and concerns that are systemically generated, but of which they are plainly and simply unaware. Collective action and corrective social policy will not emerge, therefore, unless affected aggregates become conscious of themselves as a public (1927: 131). The organized public takes shape as people come together to take action to change the structures.

In the 1950s, Mills returned to the notion of publics. In those dark years of McCarthyism and the pronouncement of the end of ideology, those years of the happy suburban family and juvenile delinquency, social critics were fully confronting the phenomenon of mass society. Mills recognized even then that the search for community was a reaction to the sense of disconnection from larger societal institutions. "This loss of any structural view or position," he argued, "is the decisive meaning of the lament over the loss of community." He insisted that "[t]he political structure of a democratic state requires the public; and, the democratic man, in his rhetoric, must assert that this public is the very seat of sovereignty" (1959: 322, 323).

The recognition of social alienation–the sense of powerlessness and inefficacy–as a malaise more profound and general than that associated with "alienated labor" forced Mills to probe deeply into what the internal structures of a public were all about. This was a task for which history had provided Dewey, and the other American progressives of his era, neither the empirical social conditions (the full emergence of the bureaucratic state) nor the conceptual language to undertake.

In the world examined by Mills, public discourse over alternatives of social life had been displaced by conformist-oriented and corporate controlled mass media as the major source of public opinion. Labor unions and political parties had become unresponsive bureaucratic machines. The voluntary associations of local politics–the traditional publics of classic democratic thought–had been taken over by experts and the philosophy of professional administration. The "man in the mass" he wrote, "is without any sense of political belonging" (1959: 307-8).

The reconstituted public was the only possible form of social organization which could meaningfully reconnect people to their world and provide them with some degree of control over its political direction. A public, for Mills, had three decisive characteristics: it was "a context in which reasonable opinions may be formulated...an agency by which reasonable activities may be undertaken [and]...a powerful enough unit, in comparison with other organizations of power, to make a difference" (1956: 308). In other words, a public provided people with an arena in which to deal with ideas, to act collectively on those ideas and to develop a sense of effectiveness in the struggle to transform those ideas into reality.

Overall, the key to the fabric of the public, and what differentiates it from any other form of political or voluntary association, is that its members understand and experience social grievances as "public issues" rather than "private troubles."

> The knowledgeable man in a genuine public...understands that what he thinks and feels to be personal troubles are very often also problems shared by others, and more importantly, not capable of solution by any one individual but only by modifications of the structure of the groups in which he lives and sometimes the structure of the entire society (Mills, 1959: 187).

Organized publics emerge, and structures are challenged, only when people come to believe that what they first felt as personal grievances are in fact socially grounded, that others outside one's immediately identified peers suffer the same undue treatment; and that some form of broad-based, collective action may result in policies to regulate or redirect the sources of anxiety and frustration.

In the discourse being proposed here, organized publics function as social movements, but movements that link constituent- and community-based action groups to policies and programs that have class content and orientation. The term "organized public" describes social movements that seek to reshape political rules in broader democratic directions, and that have core structures rooted in any type of social base, whether class, constituency or community. The labor movement of the 1930s, and the civil rights movement of the 1950s and 1960s, may be understood as organized publics in this sense. Indeed, any mass-based group which has a program somehow aimed at extending the protections of the state to groups threatened by private and bureaucratic decisionmaking exhibits, to one degree or another, the elements of a public.

We are looking for ways to move from within the daily currents of life of a particular constituency, from dispositions rooted in the immediacy of inherited political experience, to policies and programs that tap into *the structures of class and state that set these movements within the context of market capitalism*. This task falls precisely to the political organizer, and returns to the notion that people must often be educated to the larger, structural sources of social grievance. Otherwise, public issues remain treated, if not as private troubles, then as localized ones.

People must *be* organized. "Social movements do not simply occur," Jo Freeman writes (1983: 26). The organizer cannot simply reflect the existing level of consciousness of a given constituency. The New Populists are correct in asserting that nonclass movements are essential in the building of social change. They are also correct when they trace the origin of social movements back to community networks and inherited cultural traditions. At the same time, though, it is myopic to lose sight of Dewey's and Mills' argument that the knowledge available to people and the ways in which their experience has been historically structured obscure the larger nature of the social forces at work on them. Reliance on inherited values and free spaces alone prevents constituencies that are organized as publics from arriving at informed understandings of what sorts of policies and programs will most directly attack the sources of their grievance. This is simply to recognize that societies do, in fact, mystify, and that the ability of people to control their world demands demystification. One of the key roles of the organizer, no matter the nature of the public to which he or she is attached, is to aid in that process, "continually to translate," in the words of Mills, "personal troubles into public issues, and public issues into the terms of their human meaning for a variety of individuals" (1959: 187).

There are no guarantees. Particularly in America, the holds of localism, family identity and racial and ethnic political consciousness may be so strong as to preclude constituent- and community-based publics from generally projecting programs aimed at state regulation of the social surplus. Even then, the hold of global capitalism over our resources and political structures might be too great for even class-oriented programs to make a significant difference in the quality of people's lives. The only alternative, though, is acquiescence to a set of political and economic arrangements that continually deny people economic dignity, pit them against each other and dehumanize social life in general.

Notes

1. Olofsson makes the same point using a more formalized language. He argues that "the field of operation and the validity of...culturally revolutionary activities are politically indeterminate. They can be articulated with very different politico-ideological formations, social groups and classes. As they are related to the constitution of individuals as subjects, and the microsocial relations, their transformative energy can coexist with very different macrosocial trajectories" (1988: 31).

2. For a classic statement of this argument, see Hartz, 1955.

3. Alinsky had begun to break with the Communists, and their vision of community organization as an extension of the class-party, sometime in the late 1930s. The Back of the Yards, which Alinsky referred to as "the first real People's Organization," held its founding meeting in July 1939; thus, Alinsky was developing the ideas on which it was based much earlier. In *Reveille for Radicals*, published at the beginning of the Cold War period, Alinsky made a formal statement of his theoretical principles regarding class-based organizing. "It is not just trying to deal with the factory manager," he wrote,

   > but with every element and aspect, whether it be political, economical or social, that makes up the life of the worker. This will mean a complete change in the philosophy of the labor movement, so that instead of viewing itself as a separate section of the American people engaged in a separate craft in a particular industry, it will think of itself as an organization of *American citizens*... (Alinsky, 1969: 36, italics in original, originally published 1946. For BYO founding, see p. 47).

4. Parks' decision not to get up was spontaneous, but the fact that she was a long-time member of the NAACP and no stranger to activism is important. The presence of organized movements may not always be obvious when social action takes place, but their role in preparing people for such action has proven itself again and again. This is one of the overlooked lessons of Thompson, 1963. For Parks' action see Sitkoff, 1981: Chapter 2; Raines, 1983: 37-51; and Parks, 1974: 276-80.

5. For some histories of the New Left, see Ferber and Lynd, 1971; Sale, 1973; and Unger, 1975. For two general histories of the 1960s, which include penetrating discussions of both the civil rights and student movements from differing political perspectives, see Hodgson, 1978; and Matusow, 1984.

   For the women's movement see Evans, 1980; Feree and Hess, 1985; and Freeman, 1975. For histories of the community organizing movement see Adamson and Burgos, 1984; Delgado, 1986; and Fisher, 1984.

   Environmentalism in America has never had the generalized activist base associated with these four; its concerns have most often been expressed through locally based community-action programs or consumer-protection interest groups such as PIRG. This is not true of Europe, however, where the Greens remain an autonomous and large-scale political presence.

6. For one of the best class-oriented studies of populism see Rogin, 1967. More classic works include Destler, 1966 (originally published, 1946); and Quint, 1953. The major neopopulist study of the agrarian movement is, of course, Goodwyn, 1978.

7. "Marxism," Castells continues, "has been, at the same time, the theory of capital and the development of history through the development of productive forces, while also being the theory of class struggle between social actors fighting for the appropriation of the product and deciding the organization of society."

8. "Major effects" in this context has an unclear meaning. Castells appears to be trying to have it both ways: urban social movements are not "structurally" significant, but they are significant.

9. See Katznelson, 1981, for the most cogent discussion of exactly this process in New York City (Washington Heights), during the "community control" and other communal uprisings of the late 1960s. See also Mollenkopf, 1983: especially Chapter 5. He argues that an eventual consequence of the revolt against urban renewal was cooptation of community organizations and their leaderships. Leaders came, Mollenkopf wrote, "...to view neighborhood needs in programmatic rather than political terms... In the most extreme cases, these tendencies have produced what might be called 'programmatic tribalism,' with fragmented clans, each with its own patrons and clients, maneuvering against the next." At the same time, Mollenkopf recognizes that once the Nixon Administration undermined the community action program, these leaders did not have much choice. Many of them, by seeking to "become more influential in city-wide decision-making," were

simply trying to do what they could to preserve "the values and visions with which they emerged on the political scene in the mid-1960s" (1983: 197).

References

Adamson, Madeleine and Seth Burgos (1984) *This Mighty Dream.* Boston: Routledge and Kegan Paul.

Alinsky, Saul (1969) *Reveille for Radicals.* New York: Random House.

Bellah, Robert, et al. (1985) *Habits of the Heart.* New York: Harper and Row.

Bluestone, Barry and Bennett Harrison (1982) *The Deindustrialization of America.* New York: Basic.

Bowles, Samuel and Herbert Gintis (1987) *Democracy and Capitalism.* New York: Basic.

Boyte, Harry (1980) *The Backyard Revolution.* Philadelphia: Temple University Press.

Castells, Manuel (1983) *The City and the Grassroots.* Berkeley: University of California Press.

Dawley, Alan (1976) *Class and Community, the Industrial Revolution in Lynn.* Cambridge: Harvard University Press.

Delgado, Gary (1986) *Organizing the Movement: The Roots and Growth of Acorn.* Philadelphia: Temple University Press.

Destler, Chester McArthur (1966) *American Radicalism.* Chicago: Quadrangle Press. Originally published 1946.

Dewey, John (1927) *The Public and Its Problems.* Denver: Swallow Press.

Evans, Sara M. (1980) *Personal Politics.* New York: Vintage.

Ferber, Michael and Staughton Lynd (1971) *The Resistance.* Boston: Beacon Press.

Ferree, Myra Marx and Beth B. Hess (1985) *Controversy and Coalition: The New Feminist Movement.* Boston: Twayne Publishers.

Fisher, Robert (1984) *Let the People Decide: Neighborhood Organizing in America.* Boston: Twayne Publishers.

Freeman, Jo (1975) *The Politics of Women's Liberation.* New York: Longman.

Freeman, Jo (1983) On the origins of social movements. In Jo Freeman (Ed.), *Social Movements of the Sixties and Seventies.* New York: Longman.

Geertz, Clifford (1973) *The Interpretation of Cultures.* New York: Basic.

Goodwyn, Lawrence (1978) *Democratic Promise: The Populist Moment in America.* New York: Oxford University Press.

Green, James R. (1980) *The World of the Worker.* New York: Hill and Wang.

Gusfield, J. (1975) *Community: A Critical Response.* New York: Harper and Row.

Gutmann, Herbert G. (1977) *Work, Culture, and Society in Industrializing*

America. New York: Vintage.

Hartz, Louis (1955) *The Liberal Tradition in America.* New York: Harcourt Brace Jovanovich.

Hobsbawm, Eric J. (1959) *Primitive Rebels.* Manchester, England: Manchester University Press.

Hodgson, Godfrey (1978) *America in Our Time.* New York: Vintage.

Katznelson, Ira (1981) *City Trenches, Urban Politics and the Patterning of Class in the United States.* Chicago: University of Chicago Press.

Katznelson, Ira (1986) Working-class formation: Constructing cases and comparisons. In Ira Katznelson and Aristide Zolberg (Eds.), *Working-Class Formation.* Princeton: Princeton University Press.

Logan, John and Harvey Molotch (1987) *Urban Fortunes.* Berkeley: University of California Press.

Luke, Timothy W. (1989) Class contradictions and social cleavages in informationalizing post-industrial societies: On the rise of new social movements, *New Political Science, 16/17* (Fall/Winter): 125-153.

Matusow, Alan J. (1984) *The Unraveling of America.* New York: Harper and Row.

Mills, C. Wright (1956) *The Power Elite.* New York: Oxford University Press.

Mills, C. Wright (1959) *The Sociological Imagination.* New York: Oxford University Press.

Mills, C. Wright (1967) *White Collar.* New York: Oxford University Press. Originally published 1951.

Mollenkopf, John (1983) *The Contested City.* Princeton: Princeton University Press.

Molotch, Harvey (1984) Romantic Marxism: Love is (still) not enough, *Contemporary Sociology 13*(2): 141-3.

Olofsson, Gunnar (1988) After the working-class movement? An essay on what's "new" and what's "social" in the new social movements, *Acta Sociologica, 31*(1): 15-34.

Omi, Michael and Howard Winant (1986) *Racial Formation in the United States: From the 1960s to the 1980s.* New York: Routledge and Kegan Paul.

Parks, Rosa (1974) "Montgomery Bus Boycott," interview with Myles Horton at Highlander Folk School. In Grant, J. (Ed.), *Black Protest.* New York: Fawcett Premier: 276-80. Mimeographed 1956.

Plotkin, Sidney (1987) *Keep Out: The Struggle for Land Use Control.* Berkeley: University of California Press.

Quint, Howard H. (1953) *The Forging of American Socialism.* New York: Bobbs-Merrill.

Raines, Howell (1983) *My Soul Is Rested.* New York: Penguin.

Rogin, Michael (1967) *The Intellectuals and McCarthy: The Radical Spectre.*

Cambridge: MIT Press.

Sale, Kirkpatrick (1973) *SDS*. New York: Vintage.

Sewall, Jr., William H. (1980) *Work and Revolution in France: The Language of Labor from the Old Regime to 1848*. New York: Cambridge University Press.

Sitkoff, Harvard (1981) *The Struggle for Black Equality, 1954-1980*. New York: Hill and Wang.

Thompson, Edward P. (1963) *The Making of the English Working Class*. New York: Random House.

Touraine, Alain (1981a) *Solidarity*. New York: Cambridge University Press.

Touraine, Alain (1981b) *The Voice and the Eye: An Analysis of Social Movements*. Cambridge: Cambridge University Press.

Unger, Irwin (1975) *The Movement: A History of the American New Left, 1959-1972*. New York: Dodd, Mead.

United States Bureau of the Census (1986) *State and Metropolitan Data Book*. Washington, D.C.: Government Printing Office.

Wilentz, Sean (1984) *Chants Democratic: New York City and the Rise of the American Working Class*. New York: Oxford University Press.

Wright, Erik Olin (1979) *Class, Crisis and the State*. London: Verso.

Wright, Erik Olin (1985) *Classes*. London: Verso.

RETHINKING THE SIXTIES LEGACY: FROM NEW LEFT TO NEW SOCIAL MOVEMENTS

Carl Boggs
University of Southern California

In contrast to the "total break" thesis characteristic of most New Left literature, which posits a collapse of 1960s radicalism in the period 1968-70 and therefore a gulf separating it from the future, this essay argues for a continuity from the 1960s to the contemporary phase of new social movements and the appearance of political formations such as the Greens. The themes that permeated and galvanized the New Left—participatory democracy, community, cultural renewal, collective consumption, and the restoration of nature—have been typically carried forward into the modern ecology, feminist, peace and urban protest movements that have proliferated since *the early 1970s. At the same time, whereas the New Left failed to establish durable organization, constituencies or even a theory of its own development, the new movements represent a far more mature and stable representation of local democratic struggles that grew out of the earlier period. The immense diversity of new social movements, which increasingly shapes progressive politics today, suggests an obsolescence of those global solutions and strategies that the left has historically embellished.*

As we enter the 1990s, that now-distant era of 1960s radicalism appears to be strangely alive and worthy of renewed attention. After nearly two decades of scorn or neglect, the New Left has reentered the American conscience, this time in a spirit of nostalgia and even celebration. Twenty years after the explosive upheavals of 1968-70, more than a dozen books on 1960s politics and culture have been published, most of them offering "fresh" insights into the peculiar energy and rhythms of that period.[1] The general thrust of such books, as well as the scores of magazine articles, musical tributes and films on the same topic, contrasts sharply with the hostile attitude toward the 1960s previously adopted by most academic and popular writers. The New Left was typically viewed as at best utopian, irrational and reckless; at worst crude, willfully destructive and violent. Most agreed that it was little more than a temporary childish phase of rebellion; an impetuous acting out of immature youths who, saturated with drugs, sex, rock music and mysticism, were destined to self-destruct in a frenzy of rage, hedonism and fanaticism.[2]

Participants in New Left politics and the counterculture were often described as self-righteous, dogmatic and narcissistic. Harsh verdicts of this sort permeated the observations of not only mainstream writers such as Lewis Feuer, Seymour Martin Lipset, Daniel Bell, Christopher Lasch and, more recently, Allan Bloom, but also of academic Marxists and traditional leftists who saw the 1960s as an infantile distraction from the "real world" of class struggle, economic crisis and contestation for state power.

The recent wave of contributions shows, if nothing else, just how truly mythological these verdicts were. Employing a combination of sociological, biographical and journalistic insights, they demonstrate that the familiar negative stereotypes, often constructed from a remote vantage point, do not hold up under close scrutiny. With rare exceptions, it has become clear that previous efforts to analyze New Left radicalism ultimately failed to grasp the complex interplay among cultural and political forces that shaped the deep currents of popular revolt.

This revisionist history of the New Left, however, has been marred by the so-called "total break" thesis: the notion that the popular struggles associated with the 1960s came to an explosive and sudden halt somewhere between 1968 and 1970, when the more apocalyptic visions held by activists were presumably dashed once and for all by an out-of-control drug culture, rampant street fighting and Marxist-Leninist sectarianism. This perspective is extremely distorted, confusing the collapse of SDS (Students for a Democratic Society) with the broader legacy of both the New Left and the counterculture rooted in some enduring oppositional processes at work in American society. This legacy, so poorly understood by progressive and mainstream analysts alike, gave rise to a vigorous (if still limited), independent radicalism throughout the 1970s, as well as to that historically significant phenomenon commonly subsumed under the label "new social movements."

The conventional notion that the various 1960s movements were fashioned from more or less the same ideological cloth does not really bear up under close scrutiny. Revisionist interpretations suggest that, on the contrary, the New Left was defined by only one overarching political theme from beginning to end, from the civil rights movement to the early SDS years to the Columbia University uprising to the Yippie phase: the commitment to participatory democracy. What galvanized all social forces was a passionately anti-authoritarian ethos, a preoccupation with direct action, community and self-activity that carried into virtually every arena of struggle. The period was shaped by a certain utopian revival of democratic, populist and even anarchist traditions that, despite their vagueness, appealed especially to youth, students and intellectuals. There was a consensus that democratic ideals could be established on a foundation of abundance and technological innovation. As Miller (1987) shows in his carefully developed study, the early SDS was the repository of two broad impulses: a grass-roots populism that would test the limits of liberalism and a dedication to civil rights empowerment in the South. The *Port Huron Statement*, the founding document of the SDS, thus embraced a Rousseauian fascination with the virtues of direct democracy and social solidarity that, from the standpoint of its very optimistic authors, could be realized without confronting the power structure itself. (In Western Europe, on the other hand, this theme took on a more clearly institutional expression in the form of such concepts as "autogestion" and "self-management.")

If democratic empowerment was the prime mover of SDS activism from 1962 to 1968, the reality was that SDS was only a small part of the 1960s panorama, contrary to much New Left historiography (see, for example, Sale, 1973). There was, of course, the counterculture, with its diffuse amalgam of cultural, political and even spiritual influences that unfolded on an altogether different terrain: Yippies, Diggers, communards, street people and other marginalized elements of a youth scene that championed alternative lifestyles, a theatrical politics and a revolt against leaders, heroes and organizers. For many, cultural insurgency was directed toward the realization of "collective peak experiences" (Stevens, 1987: 293). The Berkeley People's Park episode of May 1969 expressed these accumulated visions and sensibilities and more, including an embellishment of "nature" and a revival of public space consonant with the concerns of the later ecology movement.

Todd Gitlin's far-ranging account reveals in great detail how the New Left was in reality an uneasy agglomeration of crosscutting groups, interests and ideologies. Youth culture overlapped with, but was separate from, the student movement and its struggle for educational reform, academic freedom and a greater share of power within the university. The civil rights movement itself was divided between the liberal-reform outlook of groups such as CORE, SCLC and the NAACP and the militant strategy of groups such as SNCC and, later, the Black Panthers. Of course, there were the early voices of feminism associated with the Redstockings, and the Women's Liberation Front, and scattered protests by women against male domination within SDS and other New Left groups. The sometimes catalyzing role played by independent socialist organizations such as IS, SWP and YSA is generally overlooked; theirs was typically a "third-camp" socialism that rejected the Cold War politics of both Western capitalist powers and Soviet-bloc Communism. By the end of the 1960s, as is well known, rival Marxist currents surfaced along with the appearance of various movements, hero-figures such as Ché Guevara, Regis Debray, Fidel Castro, Rosa Luxemburg, Wilhelm Reich, Herbert Marcuse and, of course, Lenin and Mao.

The turn toward Marxism (and Marxism-Leninism) after 1969, identified with the rise of the Progressive Labor and Weather politics that doomed SDS, is usually characterized as nothing more than a misguided sectarian exercise or a reckless vanguardism. There is much truth to such depictions. At the same time, there was another dimension to this shift that has been overlooked by most observers: the discovery of issues related to class, power and the Third World that in fact opened up new avenues of theorizing about social change even as the framework within which such issues were posed—generally Third Worldist, often self-righteous—commonly sapped political energy. Many Marxist currents (often inspired by "Western" Marxist thinkers) that appeared within and around university campuses, and within a variety of grass-roots movements, moreover, were complex enough to resist facile characterizations of them as outdated, vanguardist sects. (In Western Europe, where Marxist groups enjoyed considerably greater popular support as well as theoretical influence, a dismissive attitude was even harder to sustain.)

The 1960s political reality, therefore, was a fragmentary, pluralistic and sometimes chaotic mosaic of rebellious impulses and currents that could never be incorporated into the rubric of a single, overarching "movement." This complexity is magnified even further once the global nature of the period is taken into account. Thus, in Western Europe, as both Fraser (1988) and Caute (1988) stress, the political complexities allowed for a rather different trajectory: an entrenched socialist tradition, where strong Social Democratic and Communist parties had long been fixtures of the system, meant that a far more coherent "extraparliamentary" opposition could emerge, making possible the coexistence (for a brief time) of old and New Lefts within the same orbit.

Given such social and ideological diversity, the New Left as a whole could not have been afflicted with the degree of anti-intellectualism (sometimes referred to as "hostility to theory") that the conventional wisdom assumes. Activists in 1960s movements have been characterized as antidemocratic nihilists with no regard for the pursuit of knowledge, whether in the university or in the arena of social change itself. A disrespect for authority, rife within the counterculture, carried over into all intellectual, political and cultural pursuits. Most of the New Left turned its back on the pretentious, arid theorizing of both academic social scientists and traditional Marxists; they were, understandably in the context of the Vietnam War, anxious to stress the primacy of action. The period still was undeniably one of acute intellectual ferment. SDS, the student movement and the youth culture were born of a deep alienation from technocratic education, cultural boredom and inherited political beliefs. The very notion of a "Great Refusal" that defined an entire decade of rebellion implied, more than anything, a widespread sense of critical and reflective opposition to the status quo; one that was abundantly articulated in books, magazines, music, poetry, films and underground newspapers.

According to Miller (1987), the final draft of the *Port Huron Statement* was woven together after many long and difficult exchanges among the authors, many of whom viewed the manifesto as the first salvo of a new American radicalism. In it one could detect the influence of a wide range of thinkers: C. Wright Mills, Paul Goodman, Albert Camus, Erich Fromm, Allen Ginsberg, Jack Kerouac and John Dewey. That the early SDS sought to transcend, however awkwardly, the confines of both liberalism and Marxism indicates a critical probing, an openness and a willingness to experiment with new ideas. Such an enterprise demanded a restless, eclectic intellectual style, that is, anything but the ritual acceptance of established beliefs or correct ideological lines.

Despite a tendency to glorify spontaneity, most activists within SDS and elsewhere (e.g., SNCC) respected intellectual work that was removed from the academic milieu; they hoped to reconstitute the educational process on a different, more critical basis that linked campus life to the larger imperatives of social change. Moreover, SDS had, from the outset, assigned a vital if not decisive role in the popular struggles of the time to students and intellectuals.[3] The *Port Huron Statement* is very clear about this (Miller, 1987: Chapter 9). In Western Europe, a school of radical theorists (Andre Gorz, Alain Touraine, Serge Mallet and others) insisted that the university was destined to be one of the dynamic centers of "new working-class" initiatives in an increasingly complex, advanced, capitalist order. Wedded to corporate and military priorities, yet home to a new generation of radicals, the university was seen as more a locus of ideological conflict and social transformation than a hostile institution to be smashed.

At the same time, the abiding emphasis on participatory democracy meant that intellectuals would not be assigned any sort of historically decisive (or "Jacobian") role; that tenet was too closely identified with the old left, with the Marxist tradition and, especially, with Leninist regimes. Thus, intellectual energy was absorbed into a broader totality of processes. As Gitlin observes, the New Left was fueled by a cycle of energy that was simultaneously intellectual and moral, political and sexual. SDS itself originated out of a sense of historical urgency and existential will that set in motion a series of explosive actions and events that, by the late 1960s, took on what Miller calls a nearly "mythic stature" (1987: 141). The year 1968 alone was more turbulent than any since World War II; from France to Mexico to Japan, from Berkeley to Chicago to Columbia, assaults on politics-as-usual rekindled the long-dormant radical tradition in the West. At the height of the May events in France, activists upheld the dictum that only the imagination could impose limits on what was possible. French sociologist Raymond Aron observed that "almost everyone was in the grip of a kind of delirium. The French people, and certainly the people of Paris, felt that the state had disappeared, that there was no more government and that once more anything was possible" (Caute, 1988: 239). Throughout the industrialized world, the proliferation of insurgent movements, however amorphous they were, signalled a legitimation crisis that was profoundly political and cultural as well as economic in origin. The 1960s, despite its many well known failures, did offer a glimpse of a truly radical opposition.

Of course, the New Left as such never developed into such a radical opposition, in the U.S. or elsewhere. There were several reasons for this: the inability to create durable forms of local organization, the absence of a coherent ideology that could link together the disparate groups and movements, a focus on momentary, demonstrative actions at the expense of building alternative forms, a fetishism of Third World liberation movements and their theories and a base of support largely confined to university campuses and college towns. The eclipse of the New Left came down to the collapse of its three main components: SDS as a national organization, the vision of revolutionary apocalypse and the idea of a youth culture (Flacks, 1989: 96-7). Thus, even to suggest that the turbulence of the 1960s posed the theme of "revolution" or challenged bourgeois hegemony seems far-fetched, especially from the vantage point of the 1990s.

Given this context, it should hardly be surprising that, as Miller, Gitlin and others have noted, the New Left scarcely attempted to develop a social theory appropriate to its own experience. (The Marxist-Leninist currents did offer a "theory," but one derived from external models.) Underlying the fiery rhetoric was a spontaneity so strong that strategic thinking about social change (as opposed to mere tactical maneuvering) was impossible. Nor did an imputed "global" solidarity furnish real answers: from issue to issue, from locale to locale, from country to country, each popular struggle essentially went its own way.

Beyond the "Total Break" Scenario

A full historical account of the 1960s legacy, however, cannot stop here; while some parts of the New Left died or were left to atrophy, others continued and even gained strength over time, although often in new guises. Most writers, sympathetic or not, agree that the New Left fell apart sometime between 1968 and 1970. Amid the chaos of left sectarianism, organizational impasse and a wildly self-indulgent counterculture, the "movement" is said to have disintegrated virtually overnight, giving way to cooptation, privatized escape, religious cults, novel therapies and, for some, the return to traditional lifestyles. The historical break was seen as abrupt and total.

In its cover story on the 1960s in January 1988, *Time* magazine wrote that "1968 was a knife blade that severed past from future," an epochal year that "stepped outside of time" (*Time*, 1988: 19). In his memoir of the period, Richard Goodwin laments the passing of "the heady days when we thought we were going to change the whole world." Such idealism, he says, was ultimately killed by greed and self-interest.[4] Most would agree with the proposition that the 1960s was a time that embodied great visions of change but which turned into a nightmare of adventurous violence, dogmatic posturing and a decaying drug culture. In 1968 the May Events in France, of Columbia, Chicago and Mexico City took place; 1968 was also the year of the Martin Luther King and Robert Kennedy assassinations and Richard Nixon's ascendancy to the White House. In David Farber's (1988: 263) view, it was the Chicago events outside the

Democratic Convention that framed the "breakdown of political discourse," after which the movement became a victim of its own distorted media image. George Katsiaficas (1987: 81), whose understanding of events is far less apocalyptic than most, nonetheless wrote that "a whole epoch ended in 1968." For Gitlin, 1968 was the time in which violence and fantasy finally triumphed over rational political discourse and action. "For the rest of the decade," he writes, "there was a lingering sense of playing in overtime, wondering when the game was going to end in sudden death." Chicago became the "Gotterdammerung" of the period because "all the protagonists thought polarization served their larger purposes" (Gitlin, 1987: 317-19). Reflecting on the wreckage of SDS in June 1969, Gitlin (1987: 408), in a candid personal statement, confesses that "(a)nxiety and despair were most of what I knew. My world had exploded, ten years of the movement. I had lost the ground I walked on."

For Caute, too, the end came in the wake of the SDS collapse, when the ultraradicalism of Progressive Labor and the Weathermen had destroyed political initiative just as popular mobilization against the war was reaching its peak. The Marxist-Leninist groups turned their wrath on everything from the campuses to the Yippies to the counterculture, resulting in alienation, burnout and, eventually, demobilization. Thus, "the campus insurrection that began at Berkeley in 1964 faded and was replaced by the reassuring contours of normality" (Caute, 1988: 449). According to Miller (1987: 317), the decade ended with the Weathermen's "Days of Rage" in Chicago in October 1969 when the original democratic spirit of Port Huron was lost in an orgy of random violence. What remained were little more than small oases of "cultural space" along with a "congeries of smaller single-issue movements." In this context the search for democratic renewal could only "swim against the tide of history" (Miller, 1987: 326).

By 1970, judging from Tom Hayden's personal account, the generation of idealists who, in the context of the antiwar movement, stood for life and against death, was haunted by the specter of hatred, egomania and death. The political culture of the 1960s degenerated into a kind of "radical claustrophobia" that in the end forced many activists out of the movement entirely. Hayden (1988: 415) writes that "(a)fter the Chicago trial ended in 1970, everything around me continued to decay, our lives spiralling toward some personal and political abyss." But Hayden, who eventually made the transition from grass-roots activist to California state legislator, came to revise his view both of the New Left and of the political order it sought to call into question: "It took me a long time to accept that, far from being a police state, the system had worked" (1988: xvi).

Gitlin, too, found that with the passing of nationwide campus upheavals in May 1970 an "exhausted movement had lost its moral edge" (1987: 415). Government repression against the student, antiwar and black movements hurt, but the left had collaborated in its own demise; the dialectic of defeat was largely internal, an "implosion." Above all, SDS failed to supply the organization and leadership needed to keep centrifugal tendencies under control. Thus, "the riptide of the Revolution went out with the same force it had surged in with, the ferocious undertow proportionate to the onetime hopes" (1987: 420). Breakdown gave way to an incoherent "grab-bag of movements," a penchant for conventional lifestyles and the ubiquitous "transcendence industry" (Gitlin, 1987: 425).

This "implosion" of the New Left, though clearly exaggerated by many observers, did reflect a building tension between the participatory impulse of the early SDS and the emergent vanguardism of Marxist-Leninist currents. For one thing, the Marxist-Leninist contempt for "petty bourgeois" values, individualism and formal democracy—not to mention the university setting itself—amounted to a dismissal of New Left experience *tout court*. The bankruptcy of 1960s radicalism meant that it would be necessary to undertake a new start, inspired perhaps by Cuba or China or, most likely, Vietnam. In fact, vanguardism represented a facile solution to the chronic 1960s impasse rooted in spontaneity and lack of strategic direction. The Marxist-Leninist response was to substitute organized cadres, party building and "scientific" theory for the frustrating amorphousness of local struggles that seemed to lack political focus. This desperate search for political certainty in a chaotic world, however, turned out to be illusory.

What Gitlin refers to as "pseudo-Leninism" was in reality a caricature of radicalism, indeed a flight from politics, insofar as it rested on a foundation of class guilt, name calling and prefabricated phrases borrowed from other contexts that served as a substitute for genuine theory and analysis. More than that, the Marxist-Leninist style of "desperado politics" was simply another expression of the elitist arrogance toward the common person that typifies vanguardist behavior.

Interestingly, the revisionist literature illuminates the extent to which virtually every 1960s current (i.e., Yippies, SDS, Marxist-Leninist groups, Weather underground) were afflicted with the same problems. In different ways they shared a romantic fascination with heroic vanguards, an organization dilettantism and a social rootlessness that gave rise to a roving style of politics, a detachment from local constituencies, a male-aggressive leadership and the use of ritual phrases strung randomly together in place of theoretical discourse.

It was therefore easy for activists to gravitate toward simplistic formulas readily available in orthodox Marxism, Leninism and Maoism, a temptation heightened by the weakness of American Marxism and the vast gulf separating the "old" and "new" lefts. At the same time, one is struck by the degree to which both 1960s radicalism and its Marxist-Leninist antithesis adopted a common political language ("smash the state," "smash monogamy," "off the pigs," etc.) and the inevitable self-righteous posturing that accompanied it. In each case, when it came to hard and precise questions about long-term strategy there were surprisingly few statements or manifestos that could furnish viable answers. What were the main features of a rapidly changing social structure in advanced capitalism? What was the character of state power? What were the main forms of ideological control? How could a truly New Left build a politically effective bloc of forces around distinctly radical objectives? Indeed, what were the radical objectives? Of course, theorizing along these lines could never have progressed very far in such a limited time span. The point, however, is that the New Left responded to such pressing questions with silence, whereas the Marxist-Leninist groups were content to apply formulas from another period (nineteenth century capitalism) or another geopolitical setting (Cuba, China or Vietnam).

Meanwhile, the ideology of Black Power advanced by the Panthers and kindred was likewise lacking in strategic potential. As a seductive myth and mobilizing tool, Black Power could be highly cathartic; as a framework for long-term political struggle, however, it was destined to bring only frustration, resting as it did on the charismatic appeal of leaders such as Bobby Seale and Eldridge Cleaver and the specter of ongoing violent conflict between black militants and local police. While the earlier civil rights movement, much like SDS, sought to incorporate its demands within the orbit of liberal democracy, the Panthers' own version of vanguardism turned out to be just as mechanistic and illusory as that of the white, Marxist-Leninist currents.

It follows that the unravelling of the New Left as a cohesive force was a process that went much deeper than the disintegration of SDS alone. What needs to be emphasized and what even the revisionist literature fails to recognize, is that SDS was but a small, distorted part of the entire 1960s scene, a kind of "young boys' network" increasingly cut off from the larger flow of energy and the pressing concerns of students, youth, blacks and women. The internal conflict within SDS was symptomatic of certain divisions within the New Left, but it was only a single act within the whole drama. Thus, any analysis that seeks to explain the demise of 1960s radicalism as a failure of SDS organizational resolve is highly misleading.[5] As Wini Breines (1988: 543) argues, critiques of the New Left that attribute everything to the failure of SDS have often come from former SDS leaders, typically male, who felt cut off from the growing militancy of local movements. More significantly, such critiques obscure the very rich multiplicity of realities that shaped insurgent activity during the 1960s and later. Breines points out that "(t)here were many centers of action in the movement, many actions, many interpretations, many visions, many experiences. There was no unity because each group, region, campus, commune, collective and demonstration developed differently, but all shared in a spontaneous opposition to racism and inequality, the war in Vietnam and the repressiveness of American social norms and culture, including centralization and hierarchy"

(1988: 543).

Such rebellious energy, moreover, did not disappear with the death of SDS, nor with the Chicago events or any other apocalyptic moment. Those obituaries which locate the end of 1960s radicalism in the 1968-70 period ignore the fact that peak expressions of militancy actually occurred between 1968 and 1972 rather than 1967-69. Thus it is often forgotten that the protests over the U.S. mining of Haiphong harbor in spring 1972 were quite massive, surpassed only by the May 1970 outbursts that followed President Nixon's bombing of Cambodia and the events at Kent State and Jackson State. Even leaving this aside, it is clear that the broader meaning of the New Left, including its failures and successes, cannot be grasped by the mechanistic "total break" thesis which insists that the "rebellious" 1960s was immediately followed by the "passive" 1970s, and that the failure of organizational resolve was at the center of this presumed collapse. This thesis obscures a sense of history as process rooted in the unfolding of social forces, where past is connected to future, the 1960s to the period that followed.

Despite the popular energy they were able to mobilize, 1960s movements were ultimately unable to consolidate anything resembling local power bases; the dynamics of spontaneity were far too powerful. A potential radical bloc existed, but lacking any clear political translation, ideologically or organizationally, it inexorably dissipated. The problem, however, was not lack of centralized organization or leadership, nor was disruptive sectarianism the critical obstacle. In the context of a New Left that glorified participatory democracy and local community, no centralized structure and no vanguard leadership could have salvaged the radical initiatives of the moment since the very effort to do so would have negated the essence of such initiatives. The disintegration of the New Left, if one can characterize it as that, was a function of much deeper problems at the level of theory and strategy: there was no overall sense of direction, in part because of the persistence of romantic fantasies and revolutionary visions unrelated to the actual forces at work.

Elements of Continuity

It would be a mistake to allow preoccupation with the themes of "collapse" and "decline" to obliterate our understanding of the historical legacy of New Left politics. It is impossible to read this new wave of literature on the 1960s without becoming persuaded of the immense novelty of what was going on. In a relatively brief decade, popular struggles ignited a phase of rebellion that touched the lives of millions in the U.S. alone.

What then were the novel and enduring features of 1960s politics? Beyond immediate achievements—helping to force the U.S. military out of Indochina, pressing for social reforms and affirmative action, democratizing many institutions—what was truly original and significant about the New Left? Hayden (1988) suggests that the period was unique precisely in its call for a politics of identity and authenticity that could no longer be realized within either the liberal or socialist traditions. Gitlin (1987) argues that the peculiar blend of politics and culture, especially the music but also the lifestyles, gave the New Left a distinct, nearly messianic, sense of mission. Miller (1987) and others stress the recurrent theme of participatory democracy. The most visionary account is probably that of Katsiaficas (1968), who situates the 1960s within the European radical traditions of 1848, 1905 and 1917, with 1968 symbolizing another phase of the universal struggle against domination. These and other accounts point toward an understanding of the New Left as the initial expression of explosive new social forces based in the knowledge industry, the new middle strata and marginal groups that are likely to reshape the contours of social change in the West.

To affirm the novelty of the New Left is also to stress the immense gulf that separated the old from New Lefts, the 1930s from the 1960s generation. While Maurice Isserman may be correct in stating that traditional socialist groups sometimes played a creative role in the formation of the New Left (especially SDS), this connection was always tenuous and strained at best. At least before the celebrated turn toward Marxism, the differences were sharp. The traditional left extolled the primacy of parties, unions, manifestos and programs; a search for ideological certainty cloaked in the garb of "scientific" theory; faith in social progress through economic growth fueled by science and technology; and attachment to conventional social and cultural norms. In contrast, the New Left was anarchistic in its quasi-existential desire for free self-expression and creativity, in its attack on elitism, personality cults and bureaucracy, in its passion for alternative lifestyles and in its willingness to break with established patterns and experiment with new social arrangements. The short-lived triumph of New Left ideology guaranteed a basic shift away from previous definitions of radical politics, at least those associated with the Marxist tradition.

From this viewpoint, it seems unlikely that such a novel phase of radicalism could have disappeared as abruptly as the conventional (and revisionist) wisdom assumes. Could the "mythic" struggles of the 1960s have come crashing down to earth so quickly, with so little trace of their historical influence? Put another way, was the break between the 1960s and 1970s really so total, so cataclysmic?

The "total-break" argument rests on a myopic view of how the 1960s generated enormous currents of social change that flowed into the subsequent two decades, beneath the conservative hegemony of national politics. A nostalgia for the specific drama of New Left forms—huge, unruly demonstrations, marches, sit-ins, street confrontations and dramatic cultural events—can easily obscure those elements of historical continuity that outlive such forms. An identifiable 1960s legacy has persisted and in some ways even expanded since the epochal events of 1968-70.

The legacy was one less of structural or policy changes than of shifts in popular consciousness, in the "rules" governing most facets of everyday life. Participants in New Left politics and the counterculture typically experienced, or at least anticipated, a sense of cultural renewal. What was the long-term impact of such renewal? The total break scenario assumes that the vast majority of activists either turned away from this conversion (akin to the "God is Dead" thesis) or simply renounced their progressive commitments in favor of careers, consumerism and privatized lifestyles. The general thrust of both conventional and revisionist literature notwithstanding, it now seems clear that the main trajectory from 1960s to 1980s does not fit either pattern. Ronald Fraser, for example, interviewed a large number of New Leftists from several countries and found that most are still politically active; while few could be defined as "socialists," most remain dedicated to some vision of social change while many are described as "independent leftists" (Fraser, 1988: 367). Most ex-activists, especially in the U.S., continue to adhere to broadly libertarian values, even where ideological self-understanding may be lacking.[6] The exhaustive study conducted by Daniel Yankelovich (1982) and associates found that many 1960s beliefs, most notably a distrust of authority, persisted in large sectors of the American population throughout the 1970s.

More revealing insights into the post-1960s dynamics abound in an important study by Jack Whalen and Richard Flacks (1989). They undertook the difficult task of analyzing shifts in ideology and lifestyles among a leading group of student radicals who were involved in the burning of the Bank of America building in Santa Barbara, California in February 1970. Comparing activists with nonactivists from the same milieu, the authors found a surprising continuity in both sets of respondents: the militants, for their part, were able to sustain the idealism that had inspired the commitment of their student years through their adult working lives.

In dozens of interviews, Whalen and Flacks construct fascinating portraits of young people who were consumed by "revolutionary" identities in 1970 and who, when faced with the erosion of the student movement and its various supports, had to search for a new world of meaning. Despite often severe dislocation, most ex-activists somehow managed to integrate New Left themes (participation, autonomy, creativity) into their work, careers, family and community lives (Whalen and Flacks, 1989: Chapter 6). Fifteen years after the bank burning, former participants still viewed themselves as "progressives" or "left liberals"; in contrast, nonactivists were more likely to be "conservatives" with comfortable, suburban lifestyles tied to the nuclear family, career mobility and material affluence. Ex-activists typically worked in the public sector or in social service occupations, while most non-activists had good-paying jobs in the corporate sector.

The 1960s militants, of course, were no longer involved in the demonstrative politics of their youths. They were either active in the more routine world of popular movements and community service, or they had become "disengaged." Many were what Whalen and Flacks call "passive radicals." Here the response of one former activist is worth repeating at length:

> I don't think my political beliefs that I had and was acting on in 1970 have changed. I'm not suddenly ready to register with the Republican Party and I'm not into the idea of getting a job at the top of a corporation. I think that capitalism is collapsing right before our eyes...And Ronald Reagan—it's a living nightmare. And I'm against the death penalty. I don't want to put up a new parking lot across the street. [But] I'm not doing anything to make those things happen. I know my life is very insular, but it's the one I'm living" (Whalen and Flacks, 1989: 210-12).

Whalen and Flacks demonstrate, against all received wisdom, that the 1960s legacy has had a durable impact on the consciousness of those who were most engaged. Their findings might have been even more suggestive had they chosen to interview participants outside the inner circle, so that ideological impact could be measured according to levels of involvement. Their study has put to rest the myth that New Leftists were simply affluent students whose "alienation" soon gave way to high-powered careers, large incomes and conservative beliefs. What emerges instead is a continuity, however partial and uneven, of ideas and even commitments, despite a profound change of political milieu. Most ex-activists still distrust authority, reject conventional lifestyles and question materialistic values. The contours of progressive politics in the 1980s were thus probably shaped less by the limits of personal conviction than by various contextual factors that, at least during the Reagan years, encouraged more low-key forms of activity. It might even be argued that the continuity described by Whalen and Flacks reflects a political maturing insofar as a sense of "realism"—despite its overall reformist implications—has replaced the earlier New Left eschatology with its naive faith in total, imminent change, its glorification of marginalized strata and its romantic attachment to "armed struggle."

Post-1960s Radicalism

The implications of the Whalen-Flacks study can be carried a step further:

ideological continuity of the sort identified here may suggest other, more concrete and structural, linkages between the 1960s and what followed later. Like most other observers of the period, the authors never fully explore the intricate connection between New Left radicalism and the proliferation of new social movements in the 1970s and 1980s. The rhythm of grass-roots feminist, gay, peace, ecology and urban protest movements that have mobilized millions of people *since* 1970 clearly has its pulse in the 1960s. In the most global sense, as Katsiaficas (1968) argues, the New Left and the new movements have roots in the assault against the same general conditions: bureaucratization of authority relations, industrial and urban decay, the ecology crisis, the arms race, widespread social anomie and so forth. Surely the collective forms of action that have evolved mainly outside the sphere of production, and that have certainly grown in numbers since the 1960s, would seem to affirm the validity of this argument.

As is shown elsewhere, the new movements embrace themes that were already present, in less developed form, in 1960s radicalism: a popular, grass-roots insurgency centered primarily outside the existing (pluralist) public sphere; an emphasis on qualitative goals, cultural radicalism, collective and consumption-oriented demands and nonclass-based identities (Boggs, 1986: Chapter 2). At the same time, while such thematic commonality lends historical meaning to the period, the very modalities of popular struggles have shifted dramatically. The 1960s phase was characterized by a diffuse, rapidly shifting, more or less rootless politics with apocalyptic ideologies and exhibitionist style. The later appearance of social movements, however, signalled more durable, stable patterns of activity that were grounded in concrete, ongoing work in patient efforts to build coherent organization. With the new movements there is less attachment to externally derived ideologies, and also less reliance on the campuses as sources of mobilization. (Indeed, the very idea of "mobilization" seems far less appropriate to the new phase of activism.)

During the 1970s and 1980s, contrary to prevailing opinion, local movements actually became more numerous and differentiated; thus the feminist, ecology and peace movements each gave expression to a diverse range of groups, ideologies and strategies. There is a uniformity, however, that seems irrepressible; new social movements are located at the core of social contradictions (class, bureaucratic, patriarchal, ecological and racial) that permeate advanced capitalist societies. The New Left was perhaps the first, and clearly the most explosive, glimpse of cumulative struggles around these contradictions, which were not anticipated by liberalism or Marxism.

New movements expanded at a time when the growth of centralized power and the bureaucratization of public life led to a closure of political discourse, to a massive gap between a remote, national state and a more dynamic, local life.

In this context an independent radicalism implied more than anything the struggle for empowerment, though one confined essentially to civil society (Bookchin, 1989: Chapter 4). The feminist and ecology movements take on particular significance here, insofar as they both represent, in different ways, efforts to overcome alienation, a sense of imbalance and domination. These movements ideally embellish not only democratization but a recovery of the self in a world in which politics has been deformed. Not coincidentally, both feminist and ecological sensibilities intersect with, and are reinforced by, the progressive side of the holistic revolution in therapy, healing and health care stemming from the counterculture. As Bookchin (1989: 157) stresses, both feminism and ecology demystify the role of power in all spheres of life; both carry forward the strong antiauthoritarian impulses of the 1960s and both cut across class lines, status issues and parochial interests. Further, there is within feminism and ecology alike a prefigurative dimension which rejects a purely instrumental approach to politics typical of liberal pluralism and the productivism inherent in Marxism.

New social movements in the U.S. have survived into the 1980s, often even extending their local presence at a time when the right has had a strangle-hold on the national agenda. Surely this phenomenon owes much to the absence of leftist parties and the relative closure of the two-party system, the partial inroads of the Rainbow Coalition notwithstanding. New movements have been at the center of public protests around an infinite variety of concerns: apartheid in South Africa, nuclear reactors, the arms race, violence against women, abortion rights, gay rights, homelessness, U.S. intervention in Central America, affirmative action, animal rights, oil drilling, toxic wastes and tenants' rights, to name only the most visible. In this context, new movements have catalyzed the formation of alternative institutions (cooperatives, alternative media, bookstores, clinics, etc.); they have helped sustain electoral coalitions with progressive agendas; they have given rise to a new critical discourse and a radical intelligentsia both within and outside of the universities, and they have stimulated the rebirth of student activism in the late 1980s (Vellela, 1988).

The growth of a radical, intellectual subculture is the sometimes forgotten legacy of the 1960s. Many elements of this subculture—feminism, Western Marxism, post-structuralism, social ecology, critical political economy—converge with the themes of the new movements, which permeate not only the universities but also the high schools, media, art world, trade unions and even some municipal governments.

In higher education, the discovery of neo-Marxism and the various offshoots of critical social theory by a generation of students and scholars, a process that really did not begin until the late 1960s, was inspired by the New Left preoccupation with ideology and consciousness, culture, social relations and the larger problem of domination that extends not only to institutions but also into the very interstices of civil society and the natural habitat. Creative theorizing, while often dull and abstruse, has, on the whole, transcended the limits of mainstream academic work, the New Left and traditional Marxism. As for the stale formulas of Marxist-Leninist thinking, they seem increasingly archaic in the dynamic, pluralistic world of postmodernity and the new social movements, not to mention the disintegration of the Communist world itself. The presence of a sizeable critical intelligentsia alongside the popular movements underpins the renewal of student political involvement. Beneath the surface manifestations of social conservatism and careerism on most campuses has unfolded a surprising amount of ferment and protest. Student mobilization at dozens of schools has been fueled by some familiar issues (such as racism, affirmative action, CIA recruiting, U.S. intervention abroad), along with newer priorities such as gay rights, toxic waste and animal experimentation. Vellela (1988: 249-56) lists hundreds of progressive organizations, programs and protest actions on major American campuses, most of which (in 1987) achieved expression through nine umbrella student groups.

The immense diversity of social movements makes it difficult to generalize about their bases of support, organizational styles, strategies or trajectories: some look to direct action, others are more inwardly focused, and still others are content to pursue moderate reforms. During relatively quiet periods, as in the 1980s, movements, regardless of their ultimate goals, commonly lose their subversive energy. At the same time, Katsiaficas (1968) is correct in emphasizing the radical potential of new movements insofar as they can be located within emergent global forces of social transformation. Thus, while the New Left was more explosive and was guided by greater revolutionary pretensions, the new social movements have probably carried forward a more deeply oppositional theory and practice. This is especially true in Western Europe where, for example, the Greens movement achieved a dramatic breakthrough of sorts in the mid-1980s, laying the basis of a radical strategy that had always eluded the New Left (and the diffusion of movements that followed). Constructed on a unique convergence of citizens' initiatives and local movements, the Greens movement has sought to incorporate essentially New Left themes within a coherent party structure and electoral framework.

As post-war capitalism moved to stabilize itself on a foundation of centralized state power, Keynesian social policies, a militarized economy and the institutionalization of class conflict, the new social movements made their own indelible imprint on the political landscape. Like similar movements in an earlier era, these modern incarnations of popular struggle have run up against the immense power of national and multinational economic and political institutions; power that has restricted their autonomy and, in many cases, absorbed, isolated or marginalized them. For most movements, however, some form of insurgency persisted throughout the 1970s and 1980s, shaped more often than not by the historic concerns set in motion by the 1960s: the recovery of community, direct action, personal politics and consciousness transformation. As Bookchin writes: "No radical movement of any importance in the future could ignore the ethical, aesthetic and anti-authoritarian legacy created by the New Left and the communalist experiments that emerged in the counterculture" (1989: 151).

Conclusion

The historical lineage connecting the New Left and new social movements has been obscured, if not completely ignored, in the bulk of writing on the period, which has adhered to the total-break scenario. The notion that the New Left came to a sudden, convulsive ending around 1970 or earlier blurs not only this connection but also obliterates the historical meaning of the 1960s as such. To postulate two distinctly separate moments in time—the turbulent 1960s vs. the quiescent 1970s and beyond—not only ignores the remarkable diffusion of new movements but, perhaps more significantly, over-idealizes the New Left. Thus, of the post-1960s period, Gitlin concedes the "formidable success of popular movements, local projects and reform efforts," but quickly adds that it would be naive to believe that history has moved forward and upward when, in fact, "left victories" really dwindled over time (Gitlin, 1987: 433). As we have seen, Miller (1987) views the "congeries of movements" that followed the disintegration of SDS with contempt. Whether seen in a positive light or not, scattered references to New Left residues in whatever form do not amount to a serious analysis of the 1960s legacy.

As for the New Left itself, Katsiaficas conjures an image of "revolutionary politics" that may be only slightly more exaggerated than the revisionist norm. For him, the 1960s was an historical watershed of a "synchronized world-historical movement" directed against far-flung networks of domination (1987: 27). He argues that the New Left brought a renovated idea of revolution to the industrialized countries through the "praxis of millions" tied to an "insurgent culture" that is not limited to material concerns (1987: 22). Moreover, "As the practice of the New Left went beyond the existing categories of experience, so its theory transcended the established forms of social thought (1987: 220). Such sentiments agree with the apocalyptic visions trumpeted by a good many 1960s activists, but after two decades one can only ask, "What theory? What transcendence?" The implications of such an overdrawn picture should be obvious: in claiming too much for the New Left it winds up claiming too little for what followed.

This is not to denigrate the immensely powerful and enduring radical legacy that grew out of the New Left. The point is that the 1960s were merely a beginning. As an embryonic and youthful movement, it often affirmed the drama of the spectacle and a discourse of inflated rhetoric over political substance; the idea that the turbulence of the 1960s was somehow "revolutionary" could be entertained only as fiction. Despite its often grandiose self-conception, New Left politics was never more than a series of disparate, chaotic revolts against authority; there was no transformative project, no systematic challenge to bourgeois hegemony. Probably the most that can be established is that it anticipated, in multiple ways, the likely future shape of political opposition in the West. If the later social movements have become more routine and less attractive to the mass media, they also embody a theoretical depth and practical grounding that was rarely visible in the 1960s. Perhaps for this reason, feminism alone has, since the early 1970s, shaped popular consciousness, daily life and public policy to an extent greater than all New Left struggles combined.

Notes

1. See, for example, Caute (1988); Farber (1988); Fraser (1988); Gitlin (1987); Hayden (1988); Isserman (1987); Katsiaficas (1987); Miller (1987); Goodwin (1988); Stevens (1987); Vellela (1988); and Whalen and Flacks (1989).

2. A notable exception to this dismissive attitude toward the New Left is Breines (1982).

3. On the role of students and intellectuals as agencies of change in New Left ideology, see Breines (1982: Chapter 6).

4. Goodwin expressed these ideas in an interview with the *Los Angeles Times* (1988).

5. Sale (1973) was the first of many to argue for the decisive role of SDS organizational collapse in the decline of the New Left.

6. The response of Black Panther co-founder Bobby Seale, based on a 1988 interview, may not be typical but is nonetheless suggestive. Seale, who works at Temple University in Philadelphia, has been working to help build grass-roots movements around the issues of racism and literacy. "I'm still a political revolutionary," said Seale. "The fire never went out of me, but perceptions and realizations change" (*New York Times*, 1988).

References

Boggs, Carl (1986) *Social Movements and Political Power.* Philadelphia: Temple University Press.

Bookchin, Murray (1989) *Remaking Society.* Montreal: Black Rose Books.

Breines, Wini (1982) *The Great Refusal: Community and Organization in the New Left, 1962-68.* New York: Praeger.

Breines, Wini (1988) Whose new left? *Journal of American History* (September).

Caute, David (1988) *The Year of the Barricades: A Journey Through 1968.* New York: Harper and Row.

Farber, David (1988) *Chicago '68.* Chicago: University of Chicago Press.

Flacks, Richard (1989) What happened to the new left? *Socialist Review* (January-March).

Fraser, Ronald (Ed.) (1988) *A Student Generation in Revolt.* New York: Pantheon.

Gitlin, Todd (1987) *The Sixties: Years of Hope, Days of Rage.* New York: Bantam.

Goodwin, Richard (1988) "A Different View of the Sixties," *Los Angeles Times* (14 September), Section C: 1.

Goodwin, Richard (1988) *Remembering America: A Voice from the Sixties.* Boston: Little, Brown.

Hayden, Tom (1988) *Reunion: A Memoir.* New York: Random House.

Isserman, Maurice (1987) *If I Had a Hammer: The Death of the Old Left and the Birth of the New Left.* New York: Basic.

Katsiaficas, George (1968) *The Imagination of the New Left: A Global Analysis of 1968.* Boston: South End Press.

Miller, James (1987) *Democracy is in the Streets.* New York: Simon and Schuster.

New York Times (1988) "Bobby Seale: Legacy of a Revolutionary Revisited," 20 August: 19.

Sale, Kirkpatrick (1973) *SDS.* New York: Basic.

Stevens, Jay (1987) *Storming Heaven.* New York: Harper and Row.

Time (1988) "1968: The Year that Shaped a Generation," Special Issue, January 11: 19.

Vellela, Tony (1988) *New Voices: Student Political Activism in the '80s and '90s.* Boston: South End Press.

Whalen, Jack and Richard Flacks (1989) *Beyond the Barricades: The Sixties Generation Grows Up.* Philadelphia: Temple University Press.

Yankelovich, Daniel (1982) *New Rules.* New York: Bantam.

SOCIAL HOUSING AND THE 'SOCIAL QUESTION': EARLY HOUSING REFORM AND ITS LEGACY[1]

Michael Harloe
Department of Sociology
University of Essex

...differentiation of the great mass...of working people is a necessary preliminary to the statement of conclusions. In the first place there is the artisan element. Members of this class are in receipt of fair wages. As a rule, they are steady, thrifty and socially ambitious. They are good tenants...They can pay sufficient rent for good houses, and for them builders, whether private individuals or model companies ...can and usually do make satisfactory provision...

The next step in the gradation is occupied by individuals who have not mounted quite so high in the social scale. One section has been unfortunate, and...has become discouraged in the effort to maintain a fair standard of existence. The other includes those prone to be lazy or careless, and those who are not particularly intelligent or ambitious or are possessed of bad habits. Both sections...are not desirable tenants. The first section of this class is generally that which model enterprises of a philanthropic character have attempted to deal with, though the greater number of model agencies have designedly left them out... They need looking after, and they are the class with which lady rent collectors should establish reciprocal relations of business and sympathetic interest...

The third section includes the incorrigible, the drunkard, the criminal, the immoral, the lazy, and the shiftless...as Lord Shaftesbury significantly remarks, they have hardly any domestic or civilized feelings. There must be an entire change of policy on the part of governing bodies towards this class. Lord Provost Russell of Edinburgh goes so far as to say that they should be driven from their hiding places into municipal lodging houses, where they could be under police control, the sexes separated, and the children placed in institutions where they might grow up useful members of society...

The slum must go. Not only is it a menace to public health, but it is a moral fester wherein character is being continually debauched and the evils which afflict civilization recruited.

Eighth Special Report of the Commissioner of Labor, The Housing of the Working People. 1895: 439-42

Throughout Western Europe and North America housing has been edging its way back into the public agenda. The complacent assumption of the 1960s and 1970s–that housing deprivation was no more than a marginal and declining feature of these "postshelter" societies–is being challenged by the evidence of a reversal in the long postwar trend of improvement in housing conditions and accessibility. Increasing numbers of households find themselves unable to afford decent housing, even unable to afford *any* housing. At the same time, governments are failing to respond to these new needs. Indeed, the main thrust of most national housing policies is in the opposite direction. Direct housing subsidies have been slashed and many governments are actively seeking to privatize social rented housing by sales to individual owners or to private landlords or property speculators.

How are we to understand this failure of governments to respond to rising housing needs? Clearly there is some link between contemporary policies and the rightward swing in the political systems of most advanced capitalist countries in the past 10-15 years. Clearly too the collapse of the postwar economic boom has had severe implications for housing, increasing the level of unmet needs and reducing the public resources available to meet these needs. There are at least two reasons, however, why such apparently obvious explanations should be questioned and qualified. First, there is no necessary connection between right-wing politics and reducing governmental concern with housing. For example, in Europe, after both world wars and at other times right-wing governments actually increased their support for housing. Second, there is no necessary connection between recession or economic crisis and reductions in public expenditures on housing. Again, the history of the immediate postwar years and the Depression in the 1930s tell us otherwise.

These historical counter-examples raise a further and more fundamental objection to an implicit assumption that underpins much contemporary analysis of housing and housing policies. This concerns the initial question, "Why are governments failing to respond to housing needs?" The question assumes that it is failure that has to be explained, that it would in some way be normal or natural for there to be a response. This assumption, if little else, has been a common characteristic of most housing-policy analysis. For some, policy has been motivated by the pressure of public or elite opinion; for others, the state has been operating as an arm of capitalism, reproducing labor power, for example. Such assumptions tend to be associated with an evolutionary perspective of governmental involvement in housing becoming ever more extensive over time. However, the contemporary situation has challenged this perspective, along with the assumption that the current "failure" to respond is an historical anomaly, caused above all by recent political and economic events.

The inability of such evolutionary theories concerning the state's role in housing to account for the recent situation requires us to reexamine why state involvement has occurred in the past. A clearer understanding of the circumstances that led governments to intervene in housing provision, and the reasons why such intervention took particular forms, provides, at the very least, some powerful insights into why, in the current era, there is an apparent failure to respond. If one examines the housing histories of the advanced capitalist societies it is evident that there have been several key periods when major changes occurred in the role of the state, some of which have already been referred to. It will be argued in this paper, however, that a reexamination of the history of housing reform, the role of proposals for social housing within it and state action (and inaction) in the period from the late nineteenth century to 1914 is particularly revealing.

Looking Back at Housing Reform

There are dangers in looking back at the origins of social reform from the vantage point of the late twentieth century. We tend to see the past through a frame of reference shaped by our contemporary concepts, theories and concerns. We can misinterpret history as teleology, selecting evidence to demonstrate the inevitable progression of social policy development. We often assume too simple and direct a connection between the social needs to which reform was purportedly a response, the campaigns of reforming elites and the actual development of policies.

In reconstructing the history of social housing (state subsidized non- or limited-profit housing), we face all these difficulties. First, there are problems of meaning. For example, "public health" now refers to the control of physical disease, whereas in the nineteenth century it referred to moral and social "health" too. More precisely the concern was with the "health" of the new working class, and was motivated by the actual or presumed consequences of this class's condition for the dominant social order. In fact, housing and public health reformers were concerned with a more basic issue, variously described as "the social question" or, in a telling phrase, "the dangerous classes."[2] They were not simply responding to narrowly conceived housing or health needs. These issues were not yet treated as distinct fields of social policy, overseen by bureaucrats and specialists, divorced from broader questions about the reproduction of capitalist society. It is thus inadequate and misleading to view the early history of, for example, housing reform as if it had a logic and meaning related purely to conceptions of housing needs and policies that later became institutionalized within academic and political discourses.

Teleological explanations of the emergence of social housing, seeing it as an inevitable outcome of the failure of other solutions to the "housing problem," pervade conventional housing histories.[3] Such accounts abstract "housing" from the broader context noted above. They often falsely privilege one, frequently minor and highly contentious, aspect of housing reform in the years before 1914, suggesting that social housing had a central role in reformist debates and proposals. They also tend to perpetuate the myth of a benevolent governing elite, which, having recognized that the housing needs of the working class could be met in no other way, responded accordingly. However, teleology is also to be found in accounts that explain housing developments as the inevitable outcome of working-class struggle or the need to reproduce labor power (for example, CDP, 1976; Ginsburg, 1979). The problem here is not that class struggle or the interests of capital were irrelevant, but that the relationship of these to housing was complex. These links varied temporally and crossnationally, their nature has to be established by research, not just assumed *a priori.*

Finally, there is the problematic relationship between housing needs, reform proposals and state policies. The simplistic model, which assumes a humanitarian response to needs by reformers followed later by government action, does not match historical reality. The reformers did not simply respond to need, they had their own perceptions of working-class housing conditions, why they existed and why and how they should–or should not–be addressed by the state. Empirical evidence and humanitarian language were deployed by reformers, but their basic purpose was to sustain material and social interests that were rarely those of the working class. There were equally problematic connections between the concerns of reforming elites and the factors which motivated state action. For example, it has been pointed out that the late-Victorian Parliament often legislated when the London housing market was relatively oversupplied (Foster, 1979). Increased regulation then reduced slum housing, raised rents and benefitted major property owners. A similar relationship between increased tenement-house regulation and the property market occurred in New York (Jackson, 1976: 72).

Points similar to these have been explored recently by Topalov (1985). He criticizes fragmented and narrow studies of social policy. Such approaches developed as reformers decomposed the "social question" into a range of specific problems and policies designed to address specific "needs" and are now entrenched in academic analyses and in practice. Conventional and many Marxist studies take as the object of research one or another of these fragmented fields of enquiry, seeking, without much success, to trace direct causal links between specific policies and their effects on social and economic contradictions. However, in reality "all these piecemeal state actions act together on the reproduction and transformation of the working class as both a labor force and as a danger to the capitalist order in the production process, as well as on society at large" (Topalov, 1985: 267-8). Despite this, many recent writers have sought a functionalist short-cut, assuming a unique connection between specific policies and, for example, the resolution in practice of problems of labor-power reproduction or social integration. Topalov argues that the mistake is to start from, and be contained within, the confines of social policy as defined by the state itself. We must instead examine the broader field of social practices and their determinations, the real object with which social policies as a whole have been concerned.

Although Topalov criticizes the narrow approach of much social-policy research he is not suggesting that research into social policy and reform should be abandoned. In fact, especially in relation to the early history of social policy and social reform, we can provide a more adequate analysis even if we remain largely within the confines of an examination of state policies and social-reform movements themselves. This is because, although Topalov is correct in noting the eventual reduction of "the social question" to a set of piecemeal problems and policies, the connections between specific reforms and the broad project of controlling the "dangerous classes" and sustaining hegemony was often clearly expressed in the early reformers' discourses.[4] Even though we cannot, simply by reconstructing these discourses, say much about their consequences for the working class, we *can* remove the distorted understanding of the housing-reform movement that has been produced by "reading" history in ways that ignore the fact that the explicit object of reform was the "condition of the working class" and that reform proposals were motivated by more than a recognition of "needs" or by humanitarian impulses. We can also explore some aspects of the response of the organized working class to these reforms.

Reinterpreting Housing Reform

In his paper, Topalov outlines some of the key features of early social reform. As is shown below, many of these typified early housing-reform movements. For example, organized labor was often indifferent or hostile to early reforms. When working-class organizations did make demands, they were often transformed and displaced by actual state policies. Topalov also notes the similarities among reform proposals in many industrializing countries in the late nineteenth century. He writes,

> (t)hey express the realization that repressing working class revolts is not enough, they have to be prevented....Everywhere the same kind of tasks are identified as necessary to fulfil this aim. Progressive employers will more effectively enforce their rule within the firm by "rationalizing" production, that is by increasingly depriving producers of any control over the work process. Social reformers and the state will try to reshape workers' habits outside the workplace, especially through far-reaching changes in the urban environment.

This project led to many inquiries into the state of the object to be transformed, the worker and the imposition of a framework of analysis on this data which

> hardly shed light on workers' actual practices...(t)hey cannot comprehend the rationality of the latter, which is determined by the reality of

and resistance to exploitation and to accompanying discipline outside the workplace. Workers' practices are indeed observed and disguised in ways which fragment social reality in order to yield manageable objects for social policies (Topalov, 1985).

Central to this analysis was a classification of workers that linked position in the labor market (or outside of it) to an imputed level of morality and what might be called a "potential for salvation" (i.e., for social integration). Topalov writes that workers were classified as

> skilled, deskilled, or unskilled; permanent or casual; factory, workshop or home working; native or immigrant; poor to be relieved or outcasts to be locked up [he could have added 'deserving or undeserving']. The problem at hand is to give some intelligibility to these various classifications. This can be done by identifying which moral tendencies, or cultural systems... accompany the material conditions, so as to discriminate between three populations. Standing between adapted workers and undeserving poor are those who may be saved or civilized. Repressive policies deal with outcasts who are to be if possible eliminated, driven into workhouses or ousted through immigration. Reform policies...are chiefly targeted towards those who might be reshaped so as to comply with the norms of a swiftly changing industrial capitalism (1985).

Topalov also refers to the role that the extended notion of "public health," discussed above, played in the reformers' discourses; "(a) key word characterized one of the main ways to reform: cleansing–that is, transforming the physical environment of working-class life in order to change its social reality." This hygenism gave rise to an urban-reform plan involving architects, urban planners and housing reformers, based on environmental determinism. He could have added that once this movement became entrenched in the bureaucracy and in professional organizations, what began as means to a broader end–environmental reform as a method of redetermining social reality–soon became, for its supporters and those it employed, an end in itself, thus helping to fragment and obscure what was originally a unified approach, not to urban reform *per se* but to social reform and the problem of the "dangerous classes."

Finally, Topalov notes that despite some common features, reformist movements were often in conflict. There were arguments among reformers and opposition from industrial and property interests, organized labor and politicians. A key issue was the relative role of state and private initiative. This observation underlines the point that the socio-economic and political context of reform has to be examined to understand its content and development. Comparative studies are invaluable in this respect, highlighting the nationally specific ways in which a broadly similar project of social reform, arising from a broadly similar process of capitalist industrialization, urbanization and the creation of a working class, resulted in nationally specific institutions and practices. Furthermore, this exploration of early crossnational variations is crucial to the understanding of later policy development because, although these developments were responses to some distinctively new conditions, the institutions and practices that evolved before 1914 and their associated social interests had an influence on how later policies were formulated.

Key aspects of housing reform in the Netherlands, Denmark, Britain, France, Germany and the U.S. are discussed below. Although the "social question" arose in each country in response to broadly similar developments, there were some important differences in these developments and the attitude of reforming elites to housing, compared, for example, to issues of workplace regulation, the extension of suffrage or education. The scale and pace of capitalist industrialization and urbanization also varied, thus affecting the salience of the housing issue. In addition, there were important differences in social, economic and political structures that affected, for example, the level of resistance to reform, the role of the private market and the ways in which state action could be made politically acceptable. Such considerations helped to determine the nature and range of acceptable "solutions" to the housing problem. Finally there is the question of what role, if any, working-class pressure played in shaping early housing reform.

The Netherlands[5]

In the first half of the nineteenth century the Netherlands was in decline. Industrial development lagged and the rural population increased faster than the urban population. From mid-century, industrialization accelerated but the urban population, centered in Amsterdam, Rotterdam and The Hague, increased rapidly only from about 1870. Even by the end of the century, though, only about a third of the population lived in towns of any magnitude and the rural-to-urban transition was completed only after 1945. Nevertheless, by the late nineteenth century concern with "the social question" was evident.

Political development was also slow in comparison, for example, to Britain or France. Absolute monarchy lasted until 1840 and the liberal middle class was also somewhat slower to develop. The 1848 constitution, based on a limited franchise, led to liberal dominated governments until the end of the century. In this period key religious divisions emerged in Dutch politics which have significantly affected social policy. In the 19th century the major division was between secular liberals and the Protestant-dominated conservatives, although in comparison with Belgium, liberalism was less extreme in Holland. Organized party politics began in the late 1870s when the conservative Anti-Revolutionary Party developed the first party program to include references to protective legislation for the working class. Labor organization also evolved slowly; trade unions developed after 1865 but tended to be anti-socialist, and there was also a Calvinist-based workers association.

In the Great Depression, which lasted from the early 1870s to the 1890s, the Dutch economy stagnated while unemployment and social tension increased. A social democratic workers' party was founded in the 1890s as large-scale industrialization took off, but it was not until just before World War I that organized labor became a significant industrial and parliamentary force. It rejected, however, the possibility of governing in alliance with the radical/liberal movement; thus, the impact of organized labor on social-reform politics before 1914 was minimal. The conflict over social reform was fought out, instead, among the bourgeois parties, which underwent several important transitions. As elsewhere, following the liberal triumph in establishing parliamentary government, there was a gradual breakup of this political grouping. In the 1880s a radical/liberal movement developed, supporting a universal franchise and other developments such as expanded municipal services. It had some dealings with the early socialists and some local successes, especially in Amsterdam where the municipality took over public transport and other utilities. Unlike in some other countries, though, even mainstream liberals adopted a considerable reform program in the early 1890s.

There were also developments in the conservative parties. Religious divisions created a Catholic and a Protestant party but they were often allied, especially over social legislation. They were antagonistic to social reforms that involved direct state intervention; they saw this as an attack on religious freedoms and on the institutions, especially the schools, that sustained their faiths. The need for some reform was accepted, but these parties argued that state power should be filtered through their organizations. A combination of state aid and "private initiative" was acceptable; direct "public initiative" was not. In 1888 the two parties formed their first coalition government, the education issue being the major reason for this alliance. The Catholics were also influenced by the 1892 papal encyclical *De Rerum Novarum*. This encouraged Catholic parties in attempts to coopt and integrate the working class by social policies that stressed sustaining family life (and fertility), religious observance, self-discipline and self-help.

As elsewhere, concern about social legislation temporarily peaked in the 1880s, as protests caused by the Depression intensified the apparent threat of the "dangerous classes." The coalition government legislated to support "free" schools and to regulate child and female labor, the first social legislation since

1874. In 1891 the liberals returned with their reform program, they ruled until 1901 and the first major Housing Act was one of the final measures of this last purely liberal government. There were also limited tax reforms, an extension of the franchise (to cover about 30 percent of the adult population), social insurance and health legislation.

From 1901 to 1914 there was often no clear governing majority. By 1914 the social democratic party was firmly in the reformist camp and was not regarded even by its strongest opponents as a revolutionary menace. The confessional (religious) parties, however, had a parliamentary majority and this grouping, supported by some of the working class and with a commitment to social reform beyond that normally found in conservative politics, remained the dominant political force up until the current era. Its emphasis on state aid for "private initiative" has influenced how social policies, including housing policies, have been structured. This involves the so-called "pillarization" of society, in which the major socio-political groupings developed their own social service, as well as cultural and other organizations, aided by, but retaining some independence from, the state.

As elsewhere, a few philanthropic housing organizations developed from the 1850s.[6] Thus, one typical housing reform "solution," the paternalistically managed model dwelling, aimed at "educating" better-paid skilled workers who could afford rents set by "five percent philanthropy" was present in the Netherlands. However, a second, working-class-based form of organization began to appear, the cooperative building societies. These were supported by a few better paid and more securely employed workers and, as with some philanthropic foundations, often built for owner occupation. A third "solution," again on a very limited scale, was employer housing, in which a direct attempt to mold the worker to the new regimes of industrial and social discipline was apparent. All of these housing "solutions" were influenced by foreign experience. For example, as elsewhere, model housing built by Protestant industrialists at Mulhouse from the 1850s, as part of a project of social reform and self-help leading to owner occupation, inspired similar proposals. A further "solution" advocated in the Netherlands was inspired by Octavia Hill in Britain, who attempted by strict management to police the morals and behavior of working-class tenants, thus making commercially run housing profitable. A Hill-influenced "Association for Dwelling Improvement" was founded in 1893. An alternative approach first appeared in 1874 when the progressive liberals in Amsterdam provided indirect municipal support for workers' housing.

These developments all accompanied a growth of concern about "the social question" by governing and intellectual elites, especially after 1870 when several investigative and promotional organizations and journals were founded. According to van der Schaar, the "social question" encompassed housing, child labor, the right to strike, working-class suffrage and poor/unemployment relief, and statistics were deployed to link bad housing to social and physical pathologies and to workplace conditions.[7] In the 1890s, proposals for housing legislation were influenced by French, Belgian and British reforms. Attention focused on slum clearance and increasing the supply of working-class housing; these were seen as ways of manipulating the environment to support a broader reform project. In 1896 an influential report advocated aid to housing to "enable the worker to keep his foothold in the struggle for existence," to keep away from the bar and crime, to rehabilitate family life and to increase health and labor-force participation.

As in other countries, housing reform was much debated. Some reformers argued that high land prices, the product of speculation, led to rents that were unaffordable by the working class. They demanded land-use regulation by "extension planning" and the building of garden cities. A second issue was whether the regulation of private housing and building alone could solve the housing problem. A third issue concerned the type of housing to be built, "barracks" or "cottages" (i.e., rental apartments in the cities or owner-occupied, single-family housing in rural areas). In Holland as elsewhere the dispersal of the working class to rural home ownership was the ideal of many reformers; it might inhibit collectivism, strengthen individualism, self-sufficiency and family life and tie workers to the social order through petty property ownership (this was the key target for Engels's attack on German housing reformers and was central to conservative housing-reform strategies in many countries). This was difficult to achieve, however, especially in countries with low wages and centralized production, such as the Netherlands. (Suburban, single-family housing *did*, however, provide a significant "solution" for the labor aristocracy and the rapidly growing clerical labor force in the countries with the highest standards of living, the U.S. and Britain, from this period.) Another key issue was how the state should support housing. In the Netherlands, as elsewhere, there were objections to using subsidies for reducing the price of housing below a cost-covering level. Apart from ideological concerns about fostering working-class "dependency," there was the desire to avoid competition with private enterprise. It was argued that subsidized housing would drive out private investment, thus increasing subsidies and state intervention. To the bourgeois governments in the Netherlands and elsewhere, this degree of intervention in the free market was unacceptable.

The 1901 Housing Act, which set the framework for much subsequent Dutch housing policy, reflected these general reformist concerns and some of the specific features of the Dutch political and social structure noted earlier (for detailed accounts of the Act see van der Kaa, 1935; Ministry of Reconstruction and Housing, 1948; Hetzel, 1983). It enabled municipalities to regulate housing, building and planning and the state to provide loans for working-class house-building. The lending risks were not borne by the government, however, as loans had to be guaranteed by municipalities. Municipal building was not envisaged; this would be state socialism. Instead the loans would go to "private initiative," nonprofit housing corporations, approved by government and municipally regulated but not controlled, and not operated in the direct interest of employers, unions or other producer/consumer organizations. This allowed the major politico-social groupings to establish corporations linked to their own interests, and was one reason a polarized "politics of tenure" did not develop in the Netherlands (Bommer, 1934; Harloe and Martens, 1985). State support for ownership was, interestingly, prohibited, apparently to prevent working-class housing from being speculatively sold off. The 1901 Act, a broadly drafted enabling law with wide and flexible powers to be detailed later, did allow for strictly limited subsidies in circumstances where there was no alternative (i.e., for slum clearance and rehousing slum dwellers) the poorest sections of the working class, seen as a potent source of social danger yet unable to pay for the improved housing essential for their social reform. These would be temporary subsidies, however; with better housing the reformed poor would participate more effectively in the labor force, gain higher wages and in time pay economic rents. In such a manner were reformism and liberal, free-market principles reconciled.

The Housing Act easily passed in Parliament; other aspects of the "social question" caused greater divisions. Legislation did not automatically lead to policy implementation, however; property interests were powerful at the local level. Few municipalities were eager to regulate housing, and where this did occur property owners resisted strongly. The Ministry of Finance also limited the application of the financial provisions of the act. It tried to impose economic rather than historic cost rents, as the latter was seen as unfair to private enterprise. Cheap rents would unfairly favor a few, so the real solution to the housing shortage was to raise wages or build more private housing; subsidies were a short-term and inadequate palliative. Against this version of liberal economics, the reformers merely argued for some flexibility in rent setting, not for a general regime of below-market rents. As van der Schaar comments, both sides accepted that nonprofit housing would only accommodate better off workers, despite reformist rhetoric that drew on revelations about slum conditions and the "subproletariat" to make its case. In fact, the real "solution" envisaged to housing poorer workers was for them to filter into the somewhat better housing vacated by the artisans for whom, in practice, social housing was intended. In the Netherlands, as elsewhere, early social housing was not for those in the greatest need, it was for the first and some of the middle group of the threefold classification of the working class to which Topalov referred. Most other "solutions" that involved increasing housing supply (for example, model dwellings, employer housing and suburban development) were also aimed at these groups. As noted below, a more punitive approach was often proposed for the "residuum."

Denmark[8]

There were some similarities in Dutch and Danish nineteenth-century urban and economic developments. Both were heavily dependent on agrarian production linked to the British market, retained a substantial rural population and only completed the urban transition after 1945. In fact, late nineteenth-century Denmark was even less urbanized than the Netherlands. There was heavy urbanization in Copenhagen which, with adjacent Frederiksberg, contained almost 25 percent of the national population; thus, much early housing-reform activity was located here. However, industrialization was spread widely, as it was linked with the highly successful agricultural development, especially from the 1870s, when conversion from cereal to dairy and pig production occurred. This followed an earlier transition from feudal agriculture to one based on larger landowners and small, independent farmers. Out of this came a strong tradition of rural producers' cooperatives. Cooperatives later spread to the cities and influenced the organization of social housing.

The growth of small-scale farming had a major impact on party politics, which emerged after the end of the absolute monarchy in 1849. As in the Netherlands, liberalism accompanied the rising middle class and this group pressed for constitutional reform in alliance with the small farmers. The 1849 constitutional reform, however, was limited and the monarch ruled with conservative ministers (representing large landowners and capitalists) until 1901, using the royal prerogative to appoint the executive even after the liberals and their allies gained control of the lower house of the legislature (which about 15 percent of the population elected). This conflict dominated politics until 1901, when the king was forced to recognize the changed balance of power and appoint the first liberal government. As elsewhere, once it had gained power the liberal bloc split and a radical/liberal party (supported by the intelligentsia and professionals) was formed in 1905. This was never a large party, but was a key political power broker for much of the twentieth century. The main liberal party then became a more conservative agrarian party and eventually formed governments with the old right-wing grouping that, by World War I, had accepted parliamentary democracy, becoming a modern conservative party, although given the existence of the agrarian liberals it remained urban based. In contrast with the Netherlands, the fragmentation of the nonsocialist parties was based on the rural/urban division, not religion.

The transition to modern industrial organization was retarded by a lack of natural resources and a preindustrial relic, the guild system. This ended in the

1860s, and was followed by considerable industrial growth, urban migration and the growth of a labor movement. A social democratic party, founded in 1871, soon moved from Marxism to reformism and the relations between this party and the unions, on the one hand, and industrial capital and its political representatives, on the other, rapidly became accommodative. In 1899 a system of collective bargaining was established, which has survived and has limited industrial conflict. Labor's reformism was encouraged by the restricted size of the industrial work force (the Radical Liberals have attracted significant rural working-class votes). More generally, the structure of the Danish economy and society prevented absolute domination by any single political/economic bloc and encouraged a politics based on coalition building (proportional representation, introduced with universal suffrage in 1915, reflected and reinforced this situation). In 1905 the pattern of political alliances which had dominated politics for 50 years emerged. The Radical Liberals formed their first government with social democratic support (the latter rapidly gained parliamentary seats after 1884). In 1913 the social democrats could have taken power with radical support but they chose to wait until, it was hoped, they would gain an absolute Parliamentary majority (socialists joined the wartime government and the party formed a minority administration in 1924).

With its distinctive pattern of economic development, the growth of the working class in Denmark apparently created less anxiety than it did elsewhere. The "social question" took a less acute form, even in Copenhagen where working-class housing was probably less squalid than, for example, in German, British or French cities (Boldsen, 1934). At the beginning of the century, the private market provided working-class housing in Copenhagen at comparatively low rents, although the situation worsened after 1907 when the market collapsed, leading to demands for state intervention to clear slums and to meet rising needs caused by inmigration. Small-scale philanthropic efforts began in the 1850s, but by the 1880s were eclipsed by self-build associations. These were, however, as elsewhere, for the "respectable" working class and usually for ownership (later many of these were sold to speculators) (Greve, 1971). State loans for working-class dwellings built by the associations or by local authorities became legally possible in 1887. From the 1890s there was an upsurge in cooperative building organizations. In Copenhagen these later built much social housing (Umrath, 1950: 24-7). However, the cooperatives, like the self-build associations, housed better paid, more securely employed workers. Interestingly, the garden-city solution also had some influence; a "garden city association" was founded in 1911.

Pressure for increased state intervention grew after the 1907 housing crisis (Madsen and Devisscher, 1934). The 1887 law, which involved loans for slum clearance and rehousing, was used only by a few cooperatives (Department B

School of Architecture, 1971). In 1897 loans were provided for local authorities and co-ops building for working-class owner occupation (unlike under the earlier act, the state now assumed the lenders' risk). This stimulated some building. After 1907 a more regulated system of state loans emerged, with set standards and government supervision. The loans were for housing people of "moderate means." In fact, the local authorities mainly passed the loans on to the societies. Although the need for slum clearance played an important role in housing-reform arguments, as elsewhere, problems of compensation were considerable. Much of the societies' building was for owner occupation (and white-collar and better-paid working class) in the single-family housing that began to develop around Copenhagen before 1914. However, rental cooperatives linked to the labor movement, which became very active after 1918, began to build in the capital from 1912.

Britain[9]

The Netherlands and Denmark were small countries with relatively slow urbanization and a limited working class located mostly in a few large cities. Britain was, of course, very different–the first industrial nation, 80 percent urbanized by 1900, with a large working class and strong craft unions. Unlike in the other countries reviewed in this paper, the fastest period of urban concentration in Britain occurred before 1850. Consequently, by 1900 there had already been a considerable history of housing reform. As elsewhere, the regulation of housing on public-health grounds could most easily be reconciled with the liberal state, although resistance to regulation by local property interests was widespread. Model housing began in London in the 1840s; later, the model-dwelling companies obtained public capital and land at reduced costs. The need for slum clearance, justified for reasons discussed earlier, was the main argument for housing reform (English and Norman, 1974). Employer housing was limited, although a few projects were built. Model housing was rarely affordable by less skilled workers, and it was eventually accepted that filtering was the main possibility for this group, although Octavia Hill, as already described, attempted to provide cheaper but profitable housing for some.

In fact, there was some scope for private housing for the better-paid working class. Despite mass urban poverty, there were some workers with reasonably secure and high wages by the 1880s. There was a long history of limited working-class owner occupation based on cooperative building societies. By the late nineteenth century, these were becoming large-scale organizations, no longer with any real cooperative basis, collecting working- and lower-middle-class savings and providing home ownership loans. Aided by cheap transport legislation, suburban living attracted such groups. Conservatives encouraged this, seeing the creation of a mass of small property owners as an "outer defense" against attacks on landed property (Offer, 1981). Interestingly, Howard's garden-cities proposal, first published in 1898, which linked urban development to cooperative and public ownership of property and industry, was adopted by conservative and business interests (Fishman, 1977: 62). The resulting garden cities and suburbs largely ignored Howard's wider social objectives.

Housing reform was almost entirely a matter for debate by Conservatives and Liberals, the two main political parties. Franchise extensions in 1867 and 1885, however, meant that the artisan and lower middle classes gained a potential political voice. The wish to coopt these workers by providing paternalist reforms rather than full political rights influenced Conservative social reforms in the 1860s and 1870s. The Conservatives' main priority was to defend rural land-owners. They had no doctrinaire objection to limited state intervention if this was necessary to protect property. The Liberals, of course, represented industrial capital and the middle class, strongly committed to *laissez faire* and the "night-watchman state." However, by the 1880s there was competition for the new working-class voters and, in this decade of economic depression, a concern among ruling elites about social unrest. In fact, an article by the Conservative leader Lord Salisbury led to a Royal Commission on the Housing of the Working Classes in 1885. This demonstrated that none of the popular "solutions" to the housing problem would provide affordable accommodation for the mass of work-ers. However, subsidized housing was not acceptable. A consolidating housing act in 1890 reenacted powers which allowed local authorities to build unsubsi-dized housing linked to slum clearance and to provide "working class lodging houses" (now defined to allow the construction of single family houses and apartments). It was not envisaged, however, that these powers would be greatly used. Moreover, public building was to be a temporary expedient and the local authorities were required to sell such housing after ten years.

Two factors stimulated housing reform in this period. As we noted earlier, Parliament often passed regulatory acts when the housing market was slack. Social unrest also created a fear that the "respectable working" class might ally with the "residuum," the old specter of the destabilizing "dangerous classes." In the 1890s, as such fears faded, discussion about reform diminished (Stedman Jones, 1971: 322-6; Sutcliffe, 1981: 55). In fact, the expansion of cheap transport and working-class suburbanization was, especially in London, increas-ingly segregating the two sections of the working class. The problems of casual, ill-paid labor, the root causes of the earlier social conflict, however, were not solved; now the poor were increasingly seen, partly under the influence of Social Darwinism and imperialism, as a problem which weakened the British Empire and should be eliminated (Semmel, 1960). Punitive attitudes toward poverty, that slums and overcrowding should be solved by clearance and dispersal, increased. Some argued that, in London, cheap housing would inhibit industrial outmigration, thus reducing industrial efficiency. Fit workers should also move out, leaving only the poor whose plight was a product of criminality and fecklessness. Such punitive attitudes were widespread well into the 1900s. Advocacy of "solutions" to the problem of the residual poor, such as deprivation of citizen and parental rights and incarceration in labor "colonies," was shared by many welfare reformers, including Beveridge, the Liberal architect of the post-1945 "welfare state."

Such attitudes were shared by many labor leaders (Englander, 1983: 184-9). The skilled trade unions were socially and politically quite conservative. By the 1890s a few working-class representatives had been elected to Parliament as Liberals, starting a collaboration between the Liberals and organized labor that lasted until 1914. The Independent Labor Party, formed in 1892 and dominated by the unions, rejected Marxism and socialism and had only very limited support. This was the respectable and patriotic face of labor (Halevy, 1961). Its main concern was to ensure that union rights to organize were protected. Up to 1914 it seemed that labor might be incorporated in the radical wing of liberalism (which, as elsewhere, had recently emerged). Unlike in Germany or France, but like in Denmark, by the 1900s organized labor was rarely regarded as a threat to the social order. Integration rather than repression of this sector of the working class, by modest social reforms and fairly conciliatory industrial relations, was clearly evident. It was not until the early 1900s, when for a time union rights seemed threatened, that the modern Labor Party was founded. Its leaders supported free trade, increased trade union protection and some limited industrial and social reforms; housing was not significant among these. A few localities built unsubsidized rental housing, but this was really an expansion of so-called "municipal socialism," supported by some Conservative and Liberal as well as Labor politicians. Most building occurred in London, where the London County Council began in the 1890s to build apartment blocks on slum-cleared sites and later suburban single-family rental housing (Greater London Council, 1980).

The national politics of urban reform was dominated by a conflict over who should pay the costs of urbanization (Offer, 1981). The main source of revenue for the rapidly rising costs of local-authority infrastructure and services was the local property tax (rates). The Conservatives argued for central government grants to relieve the rate burden on property interests. The Liberals opposed increased central spending that would raise taxes on industry. Just before 1914 Lloyd George, the leader of radical liberalism, developed a program to attract rural votes (Swenarton, 1981: 33-4), which combined land taxation, minimum income legislation and other social reforms. High land prices, it was believed, caused high rents; land reform would lower working-class rents and solve the financial problem. Interestingly, some Conservatives pressed, unsuccessfully, for limited subsidies for workers' housing before 1914 (Wilding, 1972). Their motives were clear: in rural areas this housing would reduce the pressure to raise rural wages. In towns it would aid slum clearance and the profitable reuse of land. The Liberal government, however, in power from 1906 until the war, rejected housing subsidies, instead passing weak town-planning legislation in 1909. The strategy was to control peripheral land use and tax land profits, thus opening up the "suburban solution." Liberals also supported cheap suburban transport and garden cities (Sutcliffe, 1981: 47-87).

Various "solutions" to the housing problem were thus canvassed before 1914. Subsidized housing was advocated only by a minority. Conservatives supported a strategy that would protect property interests, especially by encouraging petty property ownership by the "respectable working class." Liberals wanted land reform and planning to open the private-market solution to more of the working class. Organized labor tended to support Liberal policies, although less so in the period just before 1914. Meanwhile, no version of housing reform offered much to unskilled labor except the possibility of filtering into the housing vacated by skilled workers moving to suburbia or, for the "undeserving poor," a variety of punitive solutions.

France[10]

The political and economic contexts of French housing reform differed significantly from those of the countries discussed so far. While industrialization and urbanization did occur in the nineteenth century, by the 1890s the level of urbanization was only a little higher than in Denmark and below that of Britain and the Netherlands. It was also concentrated in Paris. The national population increased slowly, although rural-to-urban migration was considerable. Most industry was small-scale, and there was a large and politically important peasant-based agriculture (as elsewhere, the urban transition was completed only after 1945). The politics of housing and perceptions of the housing problem largely centered on the situation in Paris.[11] There was an extensive renter- and small-business-based petty bourgeoisie that strongly resisted state intervention (unlike Britain, for example, where such interests had less national political influence). Working-class housing conditions, especially in Paris, were appalling. In 1909 a British Board of Trade report on the French cost of living found that in France, in comparison with Britain, there were higher death rates and overcrowding and much poorer sanitation, and workers worked longer hours for lower wages yet paid similar levels of rents (Board of Trade, 1909).

Nineteenth-century French politics was marked by great conflict and severe working-class repression, especially in 1848 and after the Paris Commune.

Republican government was not firmly established until 1875, but even then the secular/religious conflict continued. The Third Republic was dominated by industrial capital and the professional middle class in uneasy alliance with a large part of the petty bourgeoisie and peasantry. Historical and religious divisions crosscut class divisions, though, so there was a succession of coalition governments. Despite internal conflicts, the ruling elites had a strong adherence to liberal principles and severely limited government intervention. Fear of the "dangerous classes," a factor encouraging limited social reform elsewhere, was particularly strong among the French bourgeoisie. Repression, though, rather than any integrative strategy, appears to have been the dominant response. Working-class organizations were suppressed, industrial relations were extremely exploitative or at best paternalistic and property interests fiercely resisted housing and public-health regulation. Most social reformers were clear defenders of the status quo, unwilling to consider more than marginal incursions on liberal principles in the workplace or in the urban arena. The British model–rapid industrialization and urbanization with increasing state regulation of industry and social life–was regarded by many as an example to be avoided. Thus, little attempt was made to integrate or coopt the working class by reform policies. Often the bourgeoisie expressed extreme antipathy towards the working class. For example, one historian of housing reform suggests that the working class was widely regarded as barbaric; a dangerous, immoral and inferior race (Guerrand, 1967: 17-21). There was a great sensitivity to the dangers of immorality and revolution presumed to be lurking in the slums. One illustration of this was the debate about apartment versus single family housing. This debate occurred in many countries, and many reformers believed that the latter housing would encourage working-class "respectability." In France, though, the preference for such housing and opposition to "collective solutions" was especially evident. Here, too, Catholic social reform doctrines, which encouraged petty property ownership as a means of protecting existing society, strongly influenced some reformers.

In contrast to the situation in the countries already discussed, where the mainstream labor movement soon developed a reformist character, there were deep divisions and a stronger revolutionary current in France (the secular/religious division also affected the movement). Apart from some support for municipal socialism in the 1890s, early socialists opposed most social-reform proposals, including the first cheap-housing legislation. Given the history of state repression plus the hardly disguised motives of the social reforming elites, such hostility is not surprising. As elsewhere, liberalism developed a radical wing toward the end of the century. But this radicalism rejected any alliance with working-class politics. Supported by the petty bourgeois professions (teachers, lower-status officials, etc.) plus some peasants and workers, the

Radicals were anti-big business and strongly individualistic. By 1900 it was a central party of government but was quite conservative in practice. Magraw notes that the radicals used anticlericalism to gain working-class support, but when this ran out they chose immobility rather than social reform. In general, all liberal factions united to oppose Catholicism, socialism or more than very limited state intervention in freedom of contract and the market.

Opposition from property owners to housing and public-health regulation prevented much improvement in conditions. An ineffective public health law was passed in 1852, but no further legislation occurred until 1902. Even then communal powers over slum housing were much more limited than in Britain, for example.[12] There were a few model-housing experiments in the 1850s, part of Louis Napoleon's attempt to build a political coalition by supporting large-scale industrial and urban capital and coopting the working class; the latter project was soon abandoned. There were also several employer-provided housing schemes from mid-century, but these were viable only in rather isolated locations. At any rate, employers hardly needed such housing in urban labor markets, which were fed by immigrant workers who could be employed cheaply and replaced easily. The Mulhouse development did influence later reform proposals, however. Its emphasis on working-class owner occupation was reinforced by Le Play, whose writings stressed the need to encourage family-centered life and small-scale property ownership to ensure social integration and to counter socialism.

There were also some developments in cooperative and limited-dividend housing. Cooperatives (legally sanctioned in limited liability form in 1867) expanded in the 1880s, but a split occurred between those allied to the socialists and those, supported by the reformers, who relied on elite patronage and working-class self-help for home ownership. Limited-dividend housing began in the 1850s, but as elsewhere, capital for such ventures was limited. Many reformers were also critical, as has been noted, of the apartment blocks which such organizations built. The suburban "solution" was hardly significant in France, unlike in Britain or the U.S., though, due to lower wages and the lack of cheap transport or industrial decentralization. Especially in Paris, however, many poorer workers, excluded from the center by rising rents, lived on the periphery in self-built shacks, lacking urban infrastructure and remote from their low-paid jobs in the city. The problems of these *lotissements*, suburban shanty towns, were ignored by government.

The leading housing reformers, who founded the Societé Française des Habitations à Bon Marché (SFHBM) in 1890 and promoted the first cheap housing law in 1894 (Loi Siegfried), favored severe limits on the role of the state and were hostile to anything that might encourage collectivism, such as apartment blocks or genuine cooperatives. Siegfried regarded even the very limited British

1890 Housing Act as state socialism. It is therefore not surprising that when the Loi Siegfried was enacted, after much opposition, it was minimal in nature, aiming to foster working-class cooption through petty property ownership. The law provided cheap loans and limited tax privileges for limited-dividend housing societies and for individual borrowers. Rental housing was not prohibited, but there was a strong preference for owner occupation. The law defined no housing role for the local authorities; this was absolutely unacceptable. The housing was to be sold or let at economic prices/rents so as not to compete with private enterprise. As elsewhere, this housing was affordable only by better-off workers; in fact, much of it was probably occupied by the lower-middle class.

The law achieved little as the state organism which was supposed to provide loans was reluctant to do so. By 1905, the largest organization to benefit from the act had built only 200 units. In all, only 7,000 to 8,000 units were built and other aspects of the law had also been unsuccessful (Read, 1985: 485-7). In 1906 communes and departments were allowed to provide limited assistance to housing societies and cooperatives but not to take them over. Pressure for increased government intervention was centered on Paris, where socialist councillors now pressed for municipal building. Mainstream housing reformers, led by the SFHBM, strongly opposed this proposal, as did the major political parties. After 1910 the share of working-class housing in new building fell sharply, and rents rose sharply in relation to incomes; middle-class housing was a much more profitable investment (Topalov, 1987: 107-228). Intense overcrowding continued and evictions and homelessness caused social agitation, demonstrations and an atmosphere of crisis among governing elites, but opposition to publicly built housing remained strong. In 1912 a new law compromised between the necessity to make some response to the crisis and the desire to limit state intervention. Local authorities were allowed to promote independent public-housing agencies (an idea based on recently formed Italian housing institutes). These were nationally regulated and controlled by committees nominated by the prefects, local housing related organizations and the local authorities. This structure aimed to prevent local authorities from controlling rent levels to unfairly compete with private enterprise or buy votes. The public-housing offices had to build on the same terms as the private groups using the 1894 act, to prevent unfair state competition. Interestingly, the law provided rent subsidies for large families in cheap loan housing–the product of Catholic social philosophy and the general concern about the low birth rate, seen as a source of national weakness in an imperialist age.

Thus, housing reform was narrowly conceived and very limited in practice in France before 1914. The rather slow industrialization and urbanization and the limited urban working class may have contributed to this, but the nature of class relations and ideologies meant that the widespread fear of the "dangerous classes" encouraged repressive, rather than integrative, policies. At any rate, labor was deeply divided and to some extent manipulated by anti-clericalism and republicanism. State intervention that might have threatened the freedom of the *patron*, landlord or the landowner was strongly opposed. Even the skilled workers, however, unlike their British and American counterparts, did not move to improved suburban housing. Given this, and the lack of effective housing regulation, conditions remained appalling up to and beyond 1914.

Germany[13]

The urban transition in France occurred relatively slowly, under bourgeois political control and a dominant liberal ideology. Germany differed in each respect. For several reasons, including lack of a national state before 1870, industrialization was retarded, but it then increased rapidly and involved large-scale enterprises. Modernization occurred under a monarchical and authoritarian political regime, an alliance of the Prussian landed aristocracy and industrial capital. This regime, especially under Bismarck, pursued an explicit strategy of excluding the liberal middle class and the working class from power.

The urban population in Prussia–the dominant state in the German Reich–stagnated up until 1850, then grew rapidly. Thus, by the 1890s Germany was more urbanized than France, while 50 years earlier the reverse had been the case. This rapid population concentration occurred not only in cities such as Berlin, but also in rural areas, notably the Ruhr, where natural resources were located. The problem of housing the new labor force was acute and in Germany, more than in any other country discussed here, there was a major development of employer housing, especially in locations such as the Ruhr. Accounts of this housing show that it was seen as a way of reducing turnover and enforcing discipline, especially among skilled workers, whose opportunity for mobility in an expanding economy was considerable. The situation was different in established cities, especially Berlin, where massive land and property speculation occurred, supported by banks. Rents rapidly escalated and over-crowded *Mietkasernen* ("rent barracks") became the main form of working-class housing.

The Prussian aristocracy ruled through a strong state bureaucracy. There was little principled objection to state control of social development, and authoritarian and paternalistic methods were employed. The governing elite remained narrow and closed; the substantial but politically weak liberal middle class relied on state power to counteract the emerging working-class threat. It was not able, unlike this class elsewhere, to capture the state apparatus, establish a liberal parliamentary system and limit state intervention. The Prussian parliament was dominated by property interests. Parliamentary institutions, moreover, had only weak powers; the real government was retained by the Kaiser and the aristocratic/industrial elite up until 1918. Aggressively imperialistic and nationalistic policies provided a basis from which the elite manipulated mass opinion and stifled discontent (and the "threat" and repression of the workers movement also helped ensure middle-class acquiescence).

Several countries already discussed here had features that encouraged sections of the bourgeoisie into an accommodation with reformist socialism. This was not so in Germany, where bourgeois parties were divided by religion (Catholic/Protestant), location (rural/urban) and occupation (professional/commercial-industrial) and were competing for influence in the authoritarian political system. Moreover, the ruling elite itself had little desire for such compromise up until 1918. The worker movement was heavily repressed and excluded from any access to national political power. Socialism took root in Germany earlier than in Britain, and in 1875 a unified, social democratic party with strong Marxist influence was founded, although later there were internal struggles between Marxists and reformists (Fletcher, 1987). By 1914 this had become the leading mass socialist party and the largest German party, but it was initially based on the artisan work force; support from unskilled workers, let alone the "*lumpenproletariat*," was very limited. The rise of the party and trade unions was perceived by the ruling elites and the middle class as a considerable threat. From 1878-90 antisocialist laws repressed the workers' movement. Repression was also the norm in the workplace. One consequence was that the workers' movements developed an enclosed subculture with many social, cultural and community organizations. This was on a greater scale than in the other countries discussed in this paper. Some historians, noting the unwillingness of the ruling elite to come to any accommodation with the working class, have described this subculture as a form of "negative integration."

The history of social reform in Germany is well known (see, for example, Rimlinger, 1971; Ritter, 1986). Bismarck promoted social insurance legislation to coopt skilled workers and the lower middle class to the social and political order. He soon abandoned this strategy, however, which was viewed with suspicion and hostility by the liberal middle class and the workers' movement. Industrialists opposed further reform, as the failure of the policy seemed apparent. Ironically, the legislation did in fact lead to some integration as working-class representatives became involved in the social insurance apparatus, seeing it as a basis for working-class mobilization. This reinforced the drift to socialist reformism from end of the nineteenth century. Revolutionary beliefs, however, remained strong, as there was no opportunity for thoroughgoing collaboration with bourgeois political groupings.

Social reform movements, involving conservative, liberal and Catholic ideologists, developed from the 1870s. Bismarck responded to their influence at first, but after abandoning social reform he argued that conditions could be improved only by industrial expansion, leading to an increase in workers' wages. Meanwhile, discontent must be repressed. As elsewhere, the earliest housing experiments date from mid-century, when the conservative writer Huber helped form a Berlin building society.[14] This aimed to promote cooperative owner occupation among skilled workers, for the same reasons that led conservatives to support petty property ownership elsewhere. This was an isolated experiment; interest in housing reform revived among liberals only in the 1870s. Using social reform as a protection against revolution ("to prevent a Paris Commune in Germany") was a key objective (Bullock, 1985: 52, 68), but the reformers were divided. For example, conservatives supported forms of cooperative housing but liberals opposed such collectivism.

As in other countries, the reform debate intensified when the perceived threat from the "dangerous classes" rose. A revival of social reform in the 1880s coincided with social unrest and was influenced by contemporary British reform debates. Demands were made for increased state regulation, for educating the workers to want better housing (influenced by Octavia Hill) and for promoting owner occupation over tenement housing. There was less universal opposition in Germany than in France to some government involvement in housing, reflecting the general attitude toward state-civil society relationships in Germany and a tradition of civic involvement in those urban service functions deemed essential for the public good (Dawson, 1914). The extreme speculative pressures in cities made land reform an important topic. Liberal economists opposed any intervention, but from the 1890s some cities bought land and sought to control its development.

The first sanitary reforms and building and housing regulation occurred in the late 1860s, with some limited-profit and cooperative housing being built. As in France, there was a split between genuine cooperatives and Huberist exercises in paternalism. As elsewhere, opposition to reform from property interests intensified when shortages of supply and profits were greatest. By 1914 a few cities had built a little housing, and there was a modest amount of non- or limited-profit housing for better-off workers (Local Government Board, 1919). Opposition to state-supported building for general needs remained strong, however, because it might compete with the private market. As noted below, most assistance was for forms of "tied" housing provision, an extension of employer housing. From the late 1880s reformers pressed for national regulatory legislation and later for state aid for provision. This was seen as necessary to circumvent opposition from local property interests. The imperial bureaucracy, though, made no more than token concessions. Most socialists were inimical to state intervention, influenced by revolutionary theories and the cooptative nature of existing welfare policy. By the 1900s, however, some socialists supported reform, especially where they had gained local electoral victories. In 1900 the national party considered voting in the Reichstag with the center parties on housing reform. An added complication was resistance from city and state governments to imperial interference with their autonomy.

In the early 1900s, in a time of relative prosperity, interest in national reform languished. It revived later as the housing crisis again increased. As in the previous crisis, though, the government made only a token response. This lack of national housing legislation was not the whole story for, apart from the local developments noted earlier, the social-insurance funds provided loans for cooperative and limited profit housing. This development contrasts with the record of minimal national housing legislation and requires explanation. Cooperative housing expanded after an 1889 law made it viable (Umrath, 1950: 29-34). There were three types of cooperative: the traditional ownership form; those renting to the skilled working class, often linked to the labor movement; and those founded by white-collar workers, which expanded before 1914. Direct government support was small-scale, although some cheap land was provided by city governments. What made their growth possible from the 1890s were social-insurance-fund loans.

Two factors encouraged this development (U.S. Bureau of Labor Statistics, 1914: 157-281; Local Government Board, 1919). The funds initially paid out few benefits and accumulated considerable reserves. Housing built for better-off workers and the middle class was a secure investment. This situation changed as claims on the funds grew, and just before the World War I the government increased the interest on its loans and restricted their availability. Also, the housing had to be occupied by social-insurance contributors in most cases (the better-off working- and lower-middle class). The rationale was that better housing would improve contributors' health and limit claims for insurance benefits. Most housing was linked to specific industries or occupations (for example, central, state and local governments sponsored building societies to house their workers). Nearly all building was tied to specific sources of employment, so this growth of workers' housing may be seen as a form of employer housing, though less directly controlled than that provided in the first phase of industrialization.

Housing reform thus remained a fairly marginal phenomenon before 1914. Unlike in France, there was less universal and deep-rooted, principled resistance to state intervention, but there *was* a distinctive combination of political and economic forces and an approach to the "social question" that attempted to repress and isolate the working class rather than bring even skilled workers into the system. This encouraged a "negatively integrated" labor movement in which self-help housing cooperatives accompanied other cultural and social institutions. A distinctive feature was the use of social insurance funding for workers' housing, but access was restricted.

In 1908 the British Board of Trade reviewed German housing conditions, noting that rents were very high and overcrowding extreme (Board of Trade, 1908). Compared to Britain, rents were about 25 percent higher but wages 20 percent less; food costs and hours of work were also higher. The majority of the German working class lived in poor housing and was heavily exploited. Cooperative and nonprofit building was largely "middle-class housing," as it was far too costly for most workers. There were a few Octavia Hill-type schemes, but no reference is made in the report to suburban housing, and there is little evidence that this was a feature of working-class housing in Germany at this time.

The United States[15]

The possibility of national housing reform in the U.S. was absent before 1914, as constitutional responsibility for housing lay with state and local governments. To a considerable extent the early history of reform centered on New York City. The approach that evolved there had a major influence on many other cities. Urbanization linked to industrial growth did not take off until the 1860s, when it occurred rapidly as the economy boomed and large industrial agglomerations formed. A distinctive feature of this growth was the wave of European migrants, especially from rural areas. One consequence was that the problem of the "dangerous classes" involved a concern about whether immigrants, with their "alien" cultures, could be assimilated to the "American way of life" and its presumed values, which included self-reliance, sobriety and individualism. The myth of a "golden age" of rural and small-town independence was drawn upon in this context. European developments were often disliked, especially when they involved any hint of collectivism or "state socialism."

From 1800 to 1890, the urban population increased from about 300,000 to more than 18 million, and the number of major cities from six to about 450. This population was concentrated in the North Atlantic and North Central states. New York grew from about 60,000 in 1800–smaller than Philadelphia and minuscule compared to the major European centers–to 2.7 million in 1890, second only to London in size. By the 1860s those features of the "social question" that so concerned European social reformers were present in New York. There was no public health or housing regulation. The growing slum population was viewed with anxiety by the middle class, because of the threat of disease and social unrest. Early reformers believed that slum living inevitably degraded the morals of the poor. Their control was also necessary to integrate the alien mass of immigrants into the American way of life. These reformers, supported by some larger-scale business interests, were opposed to a corrupt city government that obstructed reform. As elsewhere, though, reform pressure fluctuated. Thus, the 1866 Draft Riots helped bring about the first tenement-house regulations, but these were later not enforced.

There was some interest in British "philanthropy at five percent." From the 1870s on, a few "model dwellings" were built. Alfred White, the leading model-house builder, stressed that his housing was not "charity"; this would weaken self-reliance and encourage unhealthy dependence. Model projects must be based on sound business principles, charging market-level rents but providing better quality than the private landlord. But capital could obtain much higher returns from private housing, so few wished to fund model dwellings, although this "solution" continued to dazzle reformers for many years, according to Lubove.

Rapid economic growth in the 1880s was followed by renewed immigration and an agricultural depression in the 1890s, which contributed to increasing industrial and social unrest and unemployment. There was a heightened social and urban crisis and a growth in pressure for anti-immigrant legislation. Racist and nativist sentiments divided the working class, setting the (often) skilled "American" worker against the "un-American" alien masses. Using social policies to integrate these masses became central to the Progressive reform movement and its proposals for housing, education, social work, the provision of parks and so on. This social engineering assumed that changing the environment would modify behavior. It was conservative, aiming to sustain the existing economy and society and rejecting more than very limited state regulation. For example, in 1895 the federal government published a report on European housing, stating that municipal housing, especially that built in Britain, was a mistake (Commissioner of Labor 1895). Decent housing for most workers could be provided commercially and in model dwellings. For those who could not afford such housing, Octavia Hill felt that government should regulate only private-market conditions; state-supported building would destroy the market. In the longer term, cheap suburban housing, aided by improved transport links, would be an important solution for better-off workers.

In 1900, partly in response to the social and urban crisis in New York, a Progressive-controlled Tenement House Commission was established, setting a basis for housing reform that dominated New York and other major cities for the next 20 years. Lawrence Veiller, the secretary to the Commission, played a central role in campaigning for the approach adopted. There were three possible approaches to housing reform which seemed potentially acceptable: model dwellings, Octavia Hill "improvement" and increased tenement-house regulation. Veiller regarded the first two as of limited applicability and opted strongly for regulation. In some of his writing he indicated that the removal of the working class to rural settlements and encouragement of home ownership would be desirable in the long term, but the only immediate possibility was regulation (Robbins, 1966).

The Commission's report rejected municipal housing as benefitting only a "favored few" at the "sacrifice of self-dependence." It would be inefficient "under the necessarily cumbrous and mechanical methods of the government system," could be used corruptly "if tenanted with a view to votes" and, above all, would compete unfairly with private enterprise (quoted in Lubove, 1962: 180). Even tax concessions for cheap housing would be unfair. A new tenement-house law was passed in 1901 and was later copied in other cities. By 1914 a few reformers questioned regulation, but their proposals for public housing had no practical impact. A more significant development was land-use zoning, begun in New York City in 1916. According to some, it would improve housing affordability by controlling land values. In practice, it helped preserve high land values, excluding housing for the poor.

One notable feature was the lack of any working-class activity in relation to housing reform. Of course, the failure of mass socialism and the conservative attitudes of the craft unions to social reform have been widely analyzed but, according to Marcuse, housing was absent from the populist reform programs that gained working-class support around the turn of the century, nor was housing an issue in the Presidential campaigns of the Socialist Party candidate, Debs (Marcuse, 1980; personal communication, 1985). One reason for the lack of pressure for reform from skilled labor, the core of the European labor movement, was that the American workers were better off than their European counterparts and therefore able to obtain private housing. This was aided by relatively cheap suburban land, the rapid growth of suburban transport and some industrial decentralization beginning in the 1890s. Furthermore, although conditions among the immigrant slum dwellers may have been as bad as those in Europe, there was considerable upward mobility to better working and living conditions in a rapidly growing economy. Thus, the duration, if not the intensity, of housing deprivation may often have been less than in Europe.

These suggestions are supported by a 1910 British Board of Trade survey of U.S. living conditions and wages (Board of Trade, 1911). The report refers to a degree of prosperity among many workers that tended to increase housing standards and to the importance of rapid transit systems in encouraging sub-urbanization. Rentals per room tended to increase for larger dwellings, the reverse of the European experience (i.e., there was a strong demand for better working-class housing). There was a considerable amount of working-class owner occupation, rarely found in European cities. Recent migrants and blacks, however, were in very poor housing. The report notes that in the U.S. "American" workers were doing well compared with "negroes and immigrants"; in Europe the division was between "organized and efficient labor" and "unorganized and inefficient labor." In most cases, it was suggested, the standards of U.S. immigrants soon improved. The report also provides evidence for the greater ability of many American workers to afford private housing. Comparing skilled American and British workers (the best paid in Europe), the former earned about 230 percent more than the latter for similar hours worked. Housing cost about twice as much in the U.S., but its quality and size was superior. The cost of food and rent was about 50 percent more in the U.S., but the wage differential was far greater.

Housing reform in the U.S. was much more limited than in the industrializing European nations, amounting to little more than some private-housing regulation. As in Europe, the pressure for reform came from a bourgeoisie fearful of the new, alien, mass working class. Such pressures were relieved by economic, not political, means, however, through mobility in an expanding urban and industrial system. Tenement-house reform had a marginal impact but it was an approach that suited what were seen as the core values of this, the "first new nation." As Lubove points out, there were also more prosaic reasons why tenement house reform was attractive to the Progressives. First, in an era of rapid immigration and urbanization, any alternative might have involved large-scale public expenditure. Second, commercial landlords provided reasonably acceptable housing for many the working class. Finally, restrictive legislation seemed a cheap solution to the slum problem (Lubove, 1962: 182-3).

The Social Construction of Housing Reform

As has been shown, there was no inevitable progression toward greater state involvement in housing before World War I and no general recognition, as other "solutions" failed, that directly subsidized provision was necessary. At the same time, accounts that stress the role of organized labor or of capitalist requirements for labor force reproduction are, at best, oversimplistic. There are two aspects to reexamining the historical record. First, housing reform must be placed in the context of the real object of most reformers' concern–the defense of property and class privilege from the presumed threat posed by a large, urban-based proletariat. Second, the actual nature of this threat must be examined because it was this which largely determined policy formation, not the exaggerated arguments and appeals to bourgeois fears used by reformers who often had little independent political or economic power.

The early history of reform was underpinned by the issue of how the new working class was to be controlled, disciplined and socially integrated. There are several variables to consider here. First, there is the extent of the problem, the potential or actual ability of the working class to mobilize against its economic and urban exploitation. On the whole this ability was limited; even the organized, working-class contribution to housing reform was marginal. Prototypical working-class, self-help housing institutions, which became more significant in the interwar period, did develop in some European countries, however. Second, the strategies adopted by dominant groups regarding the "social question" varied. Political and economic relations were differently constituted. The importance of industrial-versus-property interests, rural-versus-urban interests and secular-versus-religious interests differed, and these influenced the balance between repression and reform, as well as attitudes towards state intervention. A third issue concerns the link between housing reform and labor-force supply. This was important in Germany but rather less so elsewhere (although industrial capital *did* provide some support for the improvement of worker housing elsewhere). Finally, there is the frequently ignored variation in the extent to which working-class housing could be provided by the market. It is often assumed that the private market was a universal failure in this respect. This was not so as, even before 1914 the "suburban solution" in the U.S. and Britain was viable for a part of the better-paid working class and the lower middle class.

This highlights the need to consider the whole range of housing-reform "solutions," linking them to the reformers' perceptions of the segmentation of the working class. Many reformers divided the working class into three sections (for example, see Commissioner of Labor 1895, 439-41). First were the skilled and "responsible" workers, a key target for reforms as it was felt essential to ensure that they were securely integrated within the existing social and economic order. Their potential for spearheading opposition, in the workplace or in civil society, was frequently noted, and this group did provide the leadership and core membership of working-class organizations. Conservatives often advocated owner-occupied housing, seeing it as a way of binding this group to the existing social order. A second reason why this group featured largely in reform programs, such as model housing, was more narrowly economic. Only this sector of the labor force could hope to afford the levels of unsubsidized housing costs involved.

A second section of the working class was the "deserving poor." Solutions to their plight were less apparent apart from frequent references to "Octavia Hill" methods: a regime of paternal control, encouraging thrift, sobriety and other virtues which, it was felt, would make minimal, commercially-run housing affordable. Some faith was also placed in housing and public-health regulation as a means of improving conditions. Moreover, as the working-class elite moved into better housing, the accommodations it left would, it was believed, filter down to the deserving poor.

Last, there was the "undeserving poor," the residuum for which repressive and punitive solutions were often advocated. This group was usually regarded, more or less overtly, as beyond salvation; the only solution was its eventual elimination from the urban scene. This attitude was widespread even among more socially progressive reformers (and was probably shared by many skilled workers). For example, Aronovici, a critic of Veiller who advocated wider government intervention, divided the population into seven classes (Aronovici, 1914: 2). The top three covered the middle and upper classes. The bottom four were "skilled wage earners" and "well paid unskilled wage earners" (these the private market could serve); "wage earners capable of paying rentals on the basis of a minimum standard of housing," the "deserving poor" to be served by filtering and "Octavia Hill" methods; and, finally, "the *subnormal* (my emphasis) who are unable to pay a rental that would yield a reasonable return on a home of a minimum standard of sanitation." Aronovici offered no solution for this group, but the implications of this omission and his language seem clear. Other, more conservative minds provided some suggestions. Thus Veiller advocated the forced relocation of ex-peasant migrants in rural settlements and racially segregated dormitories to keep alien masses under close control. Such ideas are similar to the punitive solutions to the problems of housing and controlling the "residuum" proposed in late Victorian Britain.

Of course there were divisions among the reformers; there was no neat and universally agreed-upon relationship between a categorization of the working class and housing "solutions." Some regarded model housing as the key reform and some dismissed it as insignificant, backing regulation or "Octavia Hill" methods, for example. Some looked to control of land prices and development, others to state assistance. In part these contending proposals reflected differing perceptions concerning which part of the working class should be targeted for reform. They also reflected broader social and economic interests, a good example being the differing reform proposals advanced by British Liberals and Conservatives.

What role did proposals for state subsidized housing play in all of this? Mostly it was very limited. Few reformers placed much emphasis on this solution, but there was some support in Europe for initiatives to increase long-term and reasonably cheap loan capital (and in some cases cheap land). This was a response to the problem that hindered model housing; the lack of investors prepared to accept limited profits when better opportunities existed in the private-housing market and elsewhere. Such reforms were not seen as rupturing the broad principles of liberal political economy, however. Limited intervention to correct excessive speculation and profiteering ("market imperfections") was acceptable, but rents must not be lowered beneath what they would be in a reasonably functioning private market by extensive direct subsidization. In practice, "cheap" capital usually meant borrowing at interest rates close to those paid on government borrowing, i.e., the lowest possible commercial rate (the other problem which "cheap" loans aided was that individual private loans covered only low proportions of capital costs).

Objections to subsidies took many forms–they would privilege a few unfairly, breed dependence, inhibit thrift and self-reliance, be open to political abuse and encourage bureaucratic and inefficient state provision (all arguments still familiar today). Many believed that with reforms, such as regulation, land reform and planning, the private market could meet working-class needs. Some even argued, perhaps sincerely, that the real answer was to raise wages, not subsidize rents. The central concern, however, was to avoid providing serious competition for the private market as the main source of working-class housing, so there was a general reluctance to advocate housing subsidies except in special circumstances. In France, as was noted, subsidies were provided for some large families. This was justifiable in terms of the national interest in increasing the birth rate and sustaining family life. In Germany assistance was tied largely to the needs of employers and the interests of the social insurance funds. The most common basis for legitimating subsidies, however, was slum clearance. The inability of slum dwellers to afford replacement housing was apparent, yet it was argued that without replacement housing they would recreate slums elsewhere in the city. Some slum clearance was also in the public interest, especially when it eliminated physical, social and moral contagion. Last, clearance could provide valuable redevelopment sites and sustain rent levels by reducing supply–provided, of course, that any replacement housing was in practice limited.

The case for subsidized housing was thus normally made by seeing it as a limited supplement to other reforms and to the continued centrality of the private market. It was rarely seen before 1914 as a mass solution to housing the working class. Ironically, the reluctance to interfere with the private market meant that the assisted housing which was built was usually too expensive for those in whose cause it was often justified. It was occupied instead by better-off workers and the lower middle class, who became the main beneficiaries of social housing after 1918. This contradiction, between the social arguments for subsidized housing and the economic realities which govern its actual provision, is central to understanding its later evolution.

The Legacies of Early Housing Reform

World War I overturned the social context within which housing reform existed before 1914. There was a massive extension of state intervention in civil society that could not simply end in 1918 (although in the U.S., which entered the war late and suffered relatively little, the reversion to minimal state intervention occurred rapidly). Inflation and political and social conflict reestablished the connection between periods of housing reform and wider threats to the established order. In Europe in 1918 it was apparent to many governments that working-class organization and militancy posed a severe threat, and that the lack of housing was a major basis for mobilization, even–as Russia had shown–for revolution. In addition, the private market could not immediately meet these needs. The rent controls and regulated access to housing adopted in wartime could not just be abolished because, even if sufficient private housing capital had been available, the massive inflation that had occurred resulted in market rents well beyond the means of the working class and large sections of the middle class (for a contemporary account, see International Labor Office, 1923).

In these circumstances European governments were forced to respond. In France, the main response until the late 1920s was to retain strong rent controls. Elsewhere, while controls continued, direct subsidies were also provided. This was not an inevitable extension of a trend apparent before 1914, though; it was a product of specific social, economic and political forces existing at the time. The continuities linking the pre- and immediately postwar years lie elsewhere. Most important was the continuing presumption that working-class housing would normally be provided by the unassisted private market and that subsidies were justified only in special circumstances. Before 1914, the limits related above all to slum clearance. After the war, the need was to provide, as a temporary exception, assistance for more of the population until economic recovery reestablished a normally functioning private market, or until the potential threat from those in need of housing abated (see League of Nations, 1939). The subsequent ending or curtailment of subsidies in Britain, Denmark and the Netherlands, where functioning private markets were reestablished in the 1920s, illustrates this point.

A second continuity concerns the institutional structures by which subsidized housing was provided. Needing to act quickly in the postwar crisis, governments adopted established institutional structures to develop and manage the new housing when possible. Often, as in France and the Netherlands, these structures were developed before 1914 as a compromise between unacceptably direct state intervention in housing and the necessity for a minimally accountable and controllable means of assisted provision. In Denmark and Germany there was a stronger element of working-class self-organization in some prewar cooperatives, which expanded after the war. In Britain the government would have preferred to support independent "public utility societies" but these were virtually nonexistent, so it relied on the local authorities. In these respects, and in relation to the overall concept of the role of the state versus the private market, there were links between the pre- and postwar periods. These influenced social housing development after 1918.

Returning briefly to the current housing situation, there are several issues to which this examination of the early history of housing reform and state housing policies directs our attention. Some have already been noted, such as the contradiction between the social arguments for, and the economic realities of, social housing. Above all, it is clear that the precise nature of the connection between housing needs, on the one hand, and state policies, on the other, must be closely examined. Particularly in the case of social housing we need to ask why this form of provision emerged, in some countries at least, on a significant scale. The existence of unmet housing needs alone will not suffice as an answer. In different places, and at different times, large-scale state support for social housing has been a response to particular housing needs whose continued existence posed (or was thought to pose) some threat to the achievement of broader social, economic or political objectives. As these needs cease to be significant obstacles to the achievement of such objectives, the state commitment to meeting them also fades. In Western Europe this point had been reached by the late 1960s, and in America some twenty years earlier. Quite simply, in many countries the postwar expansion of social housing was intimately tied to the project of economic reconstruction and modernization. As this succeeded, resulting in economic growth, full employment and rising real incomes, the conditions were created for the reassertion of "normality," that is, for private rather than semisocialized, provision for the mass of housing consumers (see Ball, Harloe and Martens, 1988 for a more detailed discussion of this history).

Although recent economic developments, in the general economy and in the housing market, have undermined the ability of the private market to provide decent and affordable housing for an increasing proportion of the population, there are several reasons why such a situation has not resulted in a reversal of state disengagement from housing provision. Put very crudely, the fact is that the growth of unmet needs involves, above all, sections of the population that are now marginal to the labor market and which have little capacity for posing any significant threat in political or social terms. Hence the rationale for extensive state action to meet such needs is absent. The fact that governments have been notably loath to reduce (mainly tax) subsidies to those groups of the population which are politically and economically stronger is consistent with this analysis.

This conclusion places recent events in a longer-term perspective. The policy "failures" of the past few years are not simply the product of recent economic or political developments. They are also deeply influenced by more fundamental and historically persistent features of the structures and social relations that constitute housing provision in capitalist societies. Comparative and historically based studies have much to offer in this context. The contribution that such work can make to a more satisfactory, critical analysis of the contemporary situation has, as yet, been all too infrequently recognized. The unfortunate divide that tends to exist between much urban history, on the one hand, and contemporary urban analysis and research, on the other, unnecessarily limits our understanding of the past and the present. Perhaps more importantly, it impedes our ability to make sensible predictions about what may happen next.

Notes

1. Among those who have helped greatly with this paper, although they bear no responsibility for its final contents, are Maartje Martens, Peter Marcuse, Christian Topalov and Jan van der Schaar, as well as the librarians of the University of Essex and of the Avery Library at Columbia University.

   The research on which this paper is based was supported by the UK Economic and Social Research Council and the Fuller Fund of the University of Essex.

   An earlier version of this paper was delivered at a conference sponsored by the International Sociological Association Research Committee on the Sociology of Urban and Regional Development *Trends and Challenges of Urban Restructuring*, Rio de Janeiro, September 1988.

2. The phrase first appeared in a book on slum dwellers in New York in 1880 (quoted in Lubove, 1962: 44-5).

3. See Daunton's recent critique of "Whig" versions of housing history (1983: 1-8; 1984: 2-8) and Englander (1983: ix-xviii).

4. An early, longer version of this paper contained a number of quotations from reform writings in which this motive was evident. Some good examples are reproduced in Bullock (1985) and Read (1985).

5. The following discussion draws especially on Daalder (1987) and Kossmann (1978). Data on population growth and urbanization in all six countries is derived from Weber (1969).

6. Useful discussions of early housing developments can be found in Bauer (1934) (who also reviews other Western European countries); Commissioner of Labor (1895) (also reviews Britain, France, Denmark and the U.S.); Searing (1971); and Grinberg (1982).

7. I am indebted to Jan van der Schaar for providing me with a number of translations (from Dutch) of various of his published papers from which these and the following details of early housing reform movements and debates are taken.

8. The following discussion draws especially on Daalder (1987); Glyn Jones (1986); Fitzmaurice (1981); Elder, et al. (1981); and Miller, (1968).

9. Major accounts used here are Tarn (1973); Gauldie (1974); Wohl (1977); Burnett (1978); Englander (1983); and Holmans (1987).

10. The following discussion draws especially on Landes (1969); Kemp (1972); Kuisel (1981); and Magraw (1983).

11. Major accounts used here are Dennery (1935); Guerrand (1967); Sutcliffe (1981); Butler and Noisette (1983); Read (1985); and Shapiro (1985).

12. According to Read (1985: 356) an 1894 law that made the connections to sewers of all Paris houses compulsory was opposed by Paris landlords. By 1925 one-third of the houses in the city remained unconnected.

13. The following discussion draws on Landes (1969); Rimlinger (1971); Berghahn (1982); and Ritter (1986).

14. Major accounts of German housing used here are U.S. Bureau of Labor Statistics (1914); Dawson (1914); Local Government Board (1919); Sutcliffe (1981); and Bullock (1985).

15. The following account draws especially on Lubove (1962); Friedman (1968); Jackson (1976); Fish (1979); and Marcuse (1980).

References

Aronovici, C. (1914) Housing and the housing problem. In American Academy of Political and Social Science, *Housing and Planning*. Philadelphia: AAPSS, 1-7.

Ball, M., Harloe, M., and Martens, M. (1988) *Housing and Social Change in Europe and America*. London and New York: Routledge.

Bauer, C. (1934) *Modern Housing*. Boston and New York: Houghton Mifflin.

Berghahn, V. (1982) *Modern Germany: Society, Economy, Politics in the Twentieth Century*. Cambridge: Cambridge University Press.

Board of Trade (1908) *Cost of Living in German Towns*. London: HMSO.

Board of Trade (1909) *Cost of Living in French Towns*. London: HMSO.

Board of Trade (1911) *Cost of Living in American Towns*. London: HMSO.

Boldsen, F. (1934) Development of housing in Denmark. In *The Social Importance of Housing Now and in the Future*. Stuttgart: Verlag Julius Hoffmann, 100-104.

Bommer, J. (1934) Holland. Building by public utility building associations. In *The Social Importance of Housing Now and in the Future*. Stuttgart: Verlag Julius Hoffman, 335-6.

Bullock, N. (1985) The movement for housing reform in Germany 1840-1914. In Bullock, N. and Read, J., *The Movement for Housing Reform in Germany and France 1840-1914*. Cambridge: Cambridge University Press, 13-276.

Burnett, J. (1978) *A Social History of Housing 1815-1970*. Newton Abbott: David and Charles.

Butler, R. and Noisette, P. (1983) *Le Logement Sociale en France 1815-1981*. Paris: La Decouverte/Maspero.

CDP (1976) *Whatever Happened to Council Housing?* London: CDP Information and Intelligence Unit.

Commissioner of Labor (1895) *The Housing of the Working People*. Washington, D.C.: Government Printing Office.

Daalder, H. (Ed.) (1987) *Party Systems in Denmark, Austria, Switzerland, the Netherlands and Belgium*. London: Francis Pinter.

Daunton, M. (1983) *House and Home in the Victorian City*. London: Edward Arnold.

Daunton, M. (Ed.) (1984) *Councillors and Tenants: Local Authority Housing in English Cities 1919-39*. Leicester: Leicester University Press.

Dawson, W. (1914) *Municipal Life and Government in Germany*. London: Longman, Green and Co.

Dennery, E. (1935) *La Question de l'Habitation Urbaine en France*. Geneva: Societe des Nations.

Department B, School of Architecture (1971) *The Housing Problem in Denmark*. Copenhagen: School of Architecture Copenhagen.

Elder, N., Thomas A. and Arter, D. (1981) *The Consensual Democracies? The Government and Politics of Scandinavian States*. Oxford: Martin Robertson.

Englander, D. (1983) *Landlord and Tenant in Urban Britain 1838-1918*. Oxford: Clarendon Press.

English, J. and Norman, P. (1974) *One Hundred Years of Slum Clearance in England and Wales–Policies and programmes 1868-1970*. Glasgow: University of Glasgow.

Fish, G. (1979) *The Story of Housing*. New York: Macmillan.

Fishman, R. (1977) *Urban Utopias in the Twentieth Century*. New York: Basic.

Fitzmaurice, J. (1981) *Politics in Denmark*. Hurst: London.

Fletcher, R. (Ed.) (1987) *Bernstein to Brandt*. London: Arnold.

Foster, J. (1979) How Imperial London preserved its slums. *International*

Journal of Urban and Regional Research 3, 93-114.
Friedman, L. (1968) *Government and Slum Housing*. Chicago: Rand McNally.
Gauldie, E. (1974) *Cruel Habitations*. London: Allen & Unwin.
Ginsberg, N. (1979) *Class, Capital and Social Policy*. London and Basingstoke: Macmillan.
Glyn Jones, W. (1986) *Denmark: A Modern History*. Beckenham: Croom Helm.
Greater London Council (1980) *A Revolution in London Housing*. London: Greater London Council.
Greve, J. (1971) *Voluntary Housing in Scandinavia*. Birmingham: Centre for Urban and Regional Studies.
Grinberg, D. (1982) *Housing in the Netherlands: 1900-40*. Delft: Delft University Press.
Guerrand, R-H. (1967) *Les Origines du Logement Sociale en France*. Paris: Editions Ouvriere.
Halevy, E. (1961) *Imperialism and the Rise of Labour*. London: Ernest Benn.
Harloe, M. and Martens, M. (1985) The restructuring of housing provision in Britain and the Netherlands. *Environment and Planning A 17*, 1063-87.
Hetzel, O. (1983) *A Perspective on Governmental Housing Policies in the Netherlands*. The Hague: Ministry of Housing.
Holmans, A. (1987) *Housing Policy in Britain: A History*. Beckenham: Croom Helm.
International Labor Office (1923) *European Housing Problems since the War: 1914-23*. Geneva: International Labor Office.
Jackson, A. (1976) *A Place Called Home*. Cambridge and London: MIT Press.
Kemp, T. (1972) *The French Economy 1913-39*. London: Longman.
Kossmann, E. (1978) *The Low Countries 1780-1940*. Oxford: Oxford University Press.
Kuisel, R. (1981) *Capitalism and the State in Modern France*. Cambridge: Cambridge University Press.
Landes, D. (1969) *The Unbound Prometheus*. Cambridge: Cambridge University Press.
League of Nations (1939) *Urban and Rural Housing*. Geneva: League of Nations.
Local Government Board (1919) *The Housing Problem in Germany*. London: HMSO.
Lubove, R. (1962) *The Progressives and the Slums*. Pittsburgh: University of Pittsburgh Press.
Madsen, O. and Devisscher, C. (1934) *Reports on Housing in Denmark*. New

York: Columbia Housing Orientation Study (mimeo).
Magraw, R. (1983) *France 1815-1914: The Bourgeois Century*. London: Fontana.
Marcuse, P. (1980) Housing policy and city planning: The puzzling split in the United States, 1893-1931. In Cherry, G. (Ed.), *Shaping an Urban World*. London: Mansell, 23-58.
Miller, K. (1968) *Government and Politics in Denmark*. Boston: Houghton Mifflin.
Ministry of Reconstruction and Housing (1948) *Housing in the Netherlands: The Relevant Acts and Regulations from 1900 Onwards*. The Hague: Ministry of Reconstruction and Housing.
Offer, A. (1981) *Property and Politics 1870-1914*. Cambridge: Cambridge University Press.
Read, J. (1985) The movement for housing reform in France 1840-1914. In Bullock, N. and Read, J., *The Movement for Housing Reform in Germany and France 1840-1914*. Cambridge: Cambridge University Press, 277-522.
Rimlinger, G. (1971) *Welfare Policy and Industrialisation in Europe, America and Russia*. London and New York: Wiley.
Ritter, G. (1986) *Social Welfare in Germany and Britain: Origins and Development*. Leamington Spa, N.Y.: Berg.
Robbins, I. (1966) Housing achievements. In Wheaton, W., Milgram, G. and Meyerson, M., *Urban Housing*. New York: Free Press, 9-13.
Searing, H. (1971) *Housing in Holland and the Amsterdam School*. Ph.D. thesis, Yale University.
Semmel, B. (1960) *Imperialism and Social Reform*. London: Allen & Unwin.
Shapiro, A-L. (1985) *Housing the Poor of Paris, 1850-1902*. Madison: University of Wisconsin Press.
Stedman Jones, G. (1971) *Outcast London*. Oxford: Clarendon Press.
Sutcliffe, A. (1981) *Towards the Planned City*. Oxford: Blackwell.
Swenarton, M. (1981) *Homes Fit for Heroes*. London: Heinemann.
Tarn, J. (1973) *Five Percent Philanthropy*. London: Cambridge University Press.
Topalov, C. (1985) Social policies from below: A call for comparative historical studies. *International Journal of Urban and Regional Research 9*, 254-71.
Topalov, C. (1987) *Le Logement en France: Histoire d'une Marchandise Impossible*. Paris: Presses de la Fondation Nationale des Sciences Politiques.
Umrath, H. (1950) *European Labour Movement and Housing*. Brussels: International Confederation of Trade Unions.

U.S. Bureau of Labor Statistics (1914) *Bulletin 158*. Washington, D.C.: U.S. Government Printing Office.

van der Kaa, H. (1935) *La Question de l'Habitation Urbaine aux Pays-Bas*. Geneve: Societe des Nations.

Weber, A. (1969) *The Growth of Cities in the Nineteenth Century*. New York: Greenwood Press.

Wilding, P. (1972) Towards exchequer subsidies for housing 1906-1914. *Social and Economic Administration 6*, 3-18.

Wohl, A. (1977) *The Eternal Slum*. London: Edward Arnold.

THE EFFECTIVENESS OF COMMUNITY POLITICS: NEW YORK CITY

Susan S. Fainstein
Rutgers University

Norman Fainstein
Baruch College
City University of New York

The overall political and ideological context and the convergence of bases for activism that stimulated the urban social movements of the 1960s have largely disappeared. We now see a politics of interest groups rather than movements. In New York City, despite a rich history of civic activism, white reaction to racially based militancy combined with economic recession and fiscal crisis to produce a conservative regime antagonistic to neighborhood groups. Community activism based on ethnicity, client status and geography nevertheless persists, and we examine instances of each type. New York is then compared to Boston and Chicago, where mayoral administrations have been more supportive of community demands.

My whole theory of urban change...is based precisely on what I call the productive fading away of social movements, which have been "betrayed" and fulfilled at the same time (Castells, 1985: 61).

Nearly 20 years have elapsed since urban social movements reached their apogee in American cities. Both betrayed and fulfilled, their organizational progeny have become part of regular urban politics, routinely consulted but offering little promise for large-scale transformation. Contemporary grass-roots activism is better captured by the term "community politics" than social movement, as citizens' groups have become more modest in their aims and less threatening to established power. Nevertheless, in many places they continue to articulate the interests of urban communities and bureaucratic clients. Thus, they affect the character of urban regimes and the quality of community life, albeit with great variation in effectiveness from city to city.

In a previous work we defined a social movement as "an emergent group which proposes to innovate and depends for its success on the conversion of a social collectivity into an action group" (Fainstein and Fainstein, 1974: 238). A movement differs from routinized political organizations in that it exists almost entirely through its actions rather than through a coherent structure, never assuming permanent form. In other words, it can be identified by its transformative goals and its efforts to attain them through raised consciousness and non-routinized activities rather than through its infrastructure and predictable mode of operating. While a movement may use all the tactics of normal politics, including lobbying, supporting electoral candidates and raising funds, its objective is always to transcend normal politics to affect underlying social and political structure, that is, to change the rules and boundaries of normal politics.

In contrast, the term "community politics" refers to normal politics operating below the city-wide level. Participants are not usually organized through partisan frameworks, groups are oriented around policy rather than personnel, they are frequently single-purpose and community groups in most large cities typically aim at benefiting low- and moderate-income residents.[1] Their involvement in governmental decision-making is usually through established institutions and routine consultative mechanisms; they are poised to press for programs serving their constituencies, but their primary energies are not directed at major social or political change.

The last four decades have encompassed three major phases in the development of community representation in American urban politics: 1) an almost sole reliance on elected officials operating through city-wide institutions (1950-64); 2) a period of social militancy aimed primarily at increasing the power of low-income and minority groups (1965-74); and 3) the present phase of nonmilitant community activism.[2] In this third phase the resemblances among cities in the relative muting of social conflict as compared to the earlier period must be explained through a general theory of the relationship between the national political economy and localities. But the variation among cities in the ability of community groups to influence policy must be examined in terms of the political coalitions, strategies, history and institutions of each particular city.

In this paper the rise and decline of urban movements in general are briefly described. The history of community action in New York City is then examined, first, to determine the character and effectiveness of community politics there, and second, to explore the differences between New York and some other cities. Policy effectiveness depends on the ability of community groups to penetrate the electoral system to the degree that they become incorporated into the governing coalition (see Fainstein and Fainstein, 1982). We attribute the incapacity of New York's community groups to organize a powerful electoral coalition and their consequent exclusion from the governing coalition primarily to racial and ethnic division as mobilized in the political system, and secondarily to the city's great size, to characteristics of its institutional structure and to its economic position.[3]

Economic Restructuring and Local Political Conflict

The post-World War II restructuring of the American economy to one of mass consumption enlarged the role of government in meeting the needs of business firms for infrastructure and citizens for subsistence. Local governments assumed crucial functions in providing for collective consumption (Castells, 1977; Preteceille, 1981). This enhancement of local governmental responsibilities, however, produced instability within urban bureaucracies and political structures, as different elements competed to define urban goals and to dominate a vastly expanded flow of funds. More significantly, it destabilized the relationship between urban government and its constituencies, with neighborhood groups and bureaucratic clients seeking to control the programs directed at them (Cox, 1984). The national civil rights and black power movements infused local conflicts with heightened meaning, so that their implications exceeded urban boundaries and were construed in terms of the overall struggle for racial equality (Fainstein and Fainstein, 1976). Urban social movements in the U.S. ultimately foundered on the racial divisions that had given them their primary impetus and were further diminished by the urban impact of the economic crisis of the mid-1970s.

That crisis stimulated a new round of restructuring. Along with the reconstitution of production to exploit locational differentials in costs, there was pressure on local governments to counteract the contraction of investment in places abandoned by capital. Response was twofold: reduction of expenditures for collective consumption and the development of incentives to attract capital. The redefinition of urban crisis as one of productivity rather than social welfare set the ideological context for a withdrawal of resources from community-based programs (Smith and Judd, 1984) and consequently a serious loss of resources for urban social movements (Jenkins, 1983; Fainstein and Fainstein, 1974: appendix).

Under the previous definition of crisis, community activism derived from and exacerbated structural contradictions displaced from the realm of production into that of consumption (Castells, 1977).[4] Racial and class inequality, which originated in labor market differentiation, played itself out in spatial segregation and differential access to services. Collectivities rooted in their common relationship to the means of consumption (neighborhoods and public services) attacked the public agencies that had authority over urban planning and service delivery. The stake of lower-income people in increasing and reconstituting collective consumption seemed reasonably clear.

In the present period, however, municipal governments successfully resist community demands for increased consumption by predicting capital flight if business is taxed to pay for social welfare. At the same time, the interest of low- and moderate-income urban residents in economic development activities is somewhat obscure. Without economic growth they are deprived of both jobs and tax base. With it they face the threat of employment mismatch and residential displacement. The issue for community groups is not simply a matter of supporting or opposing growth but getting the right kind of growth. Yet they cannot readily affect the nature of growth, since the decisions that shape investment remain in the purview of private businesses at distant command centers rather than within the discretion of local government. Thus, community groups have mostly limited themselves to asking for a share of the gain by pressing for various linkage programs.[5] Nevertheless, efforts to attract manufacturing industry or achieve worker ownership of firms threatening to flee localities have formed the basis for organizing in some places. Local governments have sometimes responded by participating in attempts to gain funding for these endeavors; where local organizations have succeeded in gaining such government involvement, we have some of the few recent examples of the combination of work and community in an effort to achieve social transformation (S. Fainstein, 1987a; Fitzgerald, 1987).

For the most part, though, community organizations act as interest groups calling for improved services and opposing large redevelopment programs. Interest group is taken here to mean an association concerned with a narrow range of policies whose aim is primarily to influence the content of public policy rather than the results of elections (see Key, 1963: 500). Most of the urban interest groups that currently compete for public resources did not exist before the militant period of the late 1960s and early 1970s. Thus, the present epoch is not simply a replay of the 1950s and early 1960s, when the much-celebrated pluralist arena had far narrower boundaries. It is instead a conservative phase in the cycle of reform and stagnation that has historically characterized urban political life (Shefter, 1985; Pecorella, 1987).[6]

The impact of the social movements of the 1960s and the neighborhood movement[7] of the 1970s was primarily to cause an elaboration of modes of political representation in most cities. Community planning boards, local development corporations, social service organizations and block associations, many of which had been formed in response to the participatory admonitions of federal programs or the demands of local citizens, became institutionalized within municipal government. Despite the absence, under the Reagan administration, of a federal mandate for community participation, city governments routinely continued to consult citizens' groups even while cutting back on the programs that formed their *raison d'etre*.[8] In cities such as Boston, Chicago during Harold Washington's administration and San Francisco, community organizations rather than party structures formed the electoral underpinnings for city council members and mayors and were more effective than their counterparts in other cities in seeing their programs enacted (see Browning, Marshall and Tabb, 1984). They have assumed many of the functions of the old political machine, including a role in the distribution of patronage; nonetheless they differ from the machine in their programmatic orientation. In these cities, as in New York, community groups have been integrated into normal politics; in none of these places, therefore, does their activity constitute socially transformative action. Nevertheless, within the spectrum of commonly accepted legitimate political activity, we can detect significant differences in the extent to which issue-oriented citizens organizations play an overtly political role.

New York presents an important contrasting case to municipalities in which community-based coalitions have succeeded in mounting an economic development program or in forging an electoral base capable of capturing the government.[9] The remainder of this paper will describe citizen politics in New York, compare it with that in other cities, discuss the reasons for its resemblances and deviations and analyze its future prospects. We will not try to explain why community groups have fared better in other cities, but will identify the specific confluence of factors that has caused the New York situation.

The History of Citizen Politics in New York

New York has a rich experience of civic activism.[10] Even before the protest movements of the 1960s, it had a history of community resistance to urban redevelopment and highway projects (see Davies, 1966; Lowe, 1967). It harbored the country's most successful rent-control movement (Schwartz, 1986), and in the United Housing Foundation it possessed a unique institution that, backed by organized labor, developed working-class housing on a large scale. By 1958 a reform movement within the Democratic party caused Mayor Robert Wagner to break with the regular party organization and pressed the leadership to become more concerned with community issues.

In the mid-1960s, minority groups in New York mobilized through a multifaceted political movement. The Ford Foundation and the Kennedy Administration, responding to the political and economic demands of the national civil rights movement, established a number of antipoverty, community-action agencies in the city (Clark, 1965; Marris and Rein, 1967). These included HARYOU-ACT in Harlem, Mobilization for Youth on the Lower East Side of Manhattan, the citywide Council against Poverty and the Model Cities program. They were involved in tumultuous contests for political control, becoming targets of community mobilization as well as providing resources that could be used by popular movements. Mobilized community residents forced the government to abandon all highway schemes that would physically divide the city and to jettison urban-renewal plans aimed at transforming lower-class neighborhoods; they obtained a civilian review board over the police (ultimately blocked in a referendum); and they mounted a welfare-rights movement that added thousands of recipients to the rolls as well as increased their benefits.

The most significant mobilization in terms of its immediate impact developed around education. A series of school boycotts and other protest activities forced a commitment to integration from the Board of Education (Rogers, 1968). The board's failure to implement that commitment, though, caused black communities to shift their objective from integration to control of their local schools. In 1968, the movement for community control of education precipitated a three-month teachers' strike and polarized the city along racial lines. In the end, white opposition resulted in "compromise" school-decentralization legislation in Albany, which restored power to school officials and the teachers union (Fantini, Gittell and Magat, 1970; Fainstein and Fainstein, 1974).

A combination of national and local factors caused the ebbing of minority-based, urban social movements in New York. The demise of the national civil rights movement and the reelection of Richard Nixon in 1972 isolated New York's activists. Locally, white ethnic reaction and fiscal problems forced Mayor John Lindsay to withdraw from his previous high level of support for minority aspirations. The recession of 1973-75 and the fiscal crisis of 1977-78 reinforced the new conservative balance of political forces. Edward Koch was elected mayor in 1977 by a coalition of the city's Jewish and Catholic communities. Watched over by business-dominated bodies entrusted with restoring the city's financial integrity, the Koch administration proved inhospitable to the formation of new progressive movements.

Despite a housing crisis and, until very recently, the growing poverty of the lower economic sectors of the city's population, militancy has been at most sporadic (see Katz and Mayer, 1985). Minority leadership has largely chosen to work within the regular political system, and community groups have received only limited concessions in response to their demands. Community activists, except for those working in neighborhood economic development corporations, have not sought to influence the composition of industry in the city. Rather, they have restricted themselves mainly to the traditional realms of collective consumption, turf defense and crime control, and they have operated largely in isolation from the electoral arena. Their role in shaping the character of the city has consequently been more limited than their capacity to mobilize participation would suggest.

In an article analyzing community politics in New York, we concluded:

> Decentralization and the creation of new linkage structures enlarge the number of groups participating in the policy-making process and increase the legitimacy and bargaining power of the relatively deprived. In other words, deprived minorities in many urban areas have now been absorbed into the pluralist bargaining system. Where once their impact on the political marketplace was no more substantial than that of the impoverished consumer on the economic one, they may now participate on a level analogous to the individual with some money to spend but

little to invest. The predictable result is compromise, an occasional gain, but no major redistribution across social classes (Fainstein and Fainstein, 1976: 922).

At that time the city had not recovered from the effects of two recessions, was suffering from a major outflow of population and was undergoing a fiscal crisis. More recently New York has experienced a high level of economic growth, low unemployment, population increase and the infusion of new revenues into the public treasury. Measured by economic indicators, its situation resembles that at the peak of community militancy and influence during the late 1960s under the administration of Mayor Lindsay. As it had under the Lindsay regime, the city government has embarked on a number of major redevelopment projects and has expanded the city payroll. Once again, the political atmosphere is racially charged, in part because of a number of widely publicized incidents involving police action against blacks as well as the Howard Beach case (when a white mob attacked three black men, resulting in the death of one). Nevertheless, our 1976 description of the character of community politics remains descriptively valid.

Dimensions of Contemporary Activism

Among the reasons for the potency of the movements of the 1960s was the convergence of their social bases. In particular, the movement for community control of schools combined the dimensions of racial identity, client status and geography (Fainstein and Fainstein, 1974: Chapter 1). These bases for activism now tend to be disaggregated. Each, however, has given rise to mobilization; examination of groups according to these dimensions gives a picture of community politics today.

Race and Ethnicity

Despite the salience of race as perhaps the major issue dividing New Yorkers, the prominence of racial and ethnic organizations as mobilizing forces has largely faded.[11] During the 1960s the Congress on Racial Equality (CORE), the Black Muslims, the Black Panthers and the National Association for the Advancement of Colored People (NAACP) played important roles in organizing protests, particularly around the issues of education and police brutality. While demonstrations reminiscent of earlier times have occurred in response to recent racially-charged incidents, they have not been carried out under the auspices of recognizable organizations and have not signalled the development of a coherent movement with specific aims.

The most significant of the incidents was the death of a black man as he was fleeing the attack of a group of white youths in Howard Beach, Queens, in December 1986. More than a thousand marchers walked through Howard Beach to protest the fatal assault in an event echoing the civil rights marches (*New York Times*, 1986). Attorneys C. Vernon Mason and Alton Maddox, representing the survivors of the attack, refused to let their clients cooperate with investigators of the case until a special prosecutor was appointed; this strategy ultimately attained its objective. Maddox declared that his responsibility extended beyond "just practic[ing] law in order to serve my clients. I have to try to change the basic power equation of New York" (*New York Times*, 1987a).

The two attorneys and other black leaders subsequently sought to use the case as the basis for organizing a new movement to combat racism. On the day of the verdicts, in which three defendants were convicted of manslaughter, the two lawyers, along with the Reverends Al Sharpton and Herbert Daughtry, headed a "Day of Rage." By severing subway and bridge links between Brooklyn and Manhattan, demonstrators disrupted rush-hour traffic for hundreds of thousands of people (*New York Times*, 1987b). The arrests of 69 protestors caused a further demonstration by hundreds of black supporters in the Brooklyn Criminal Courthouse (*New York Times*, 1987c). In the following month Maddox, Mason, Sharpton and Daughtry again led marches through Brooklyn against racism.

The series of protests has unquestionably heightened racial consciousness within the city and stimulated efforts by mainstream clergy and political leaders to promote interracial harmony. Even with the further impetus of Jesse Jackson's presidential-primary campaign, however, it has not so far spawned an identifiable social movement. While the leadership has sought to imitate the style of Martin Luther King, unlike King it has largely failed to win much sympathy within the liberal white community.

Client Status

The citywide movements for community control of schools and health care and the welfare rights organizations have long since vanished. The remaining significant mobilization based on client status aims at gaining housing for low- and moderate-income people. Housing advocacy groups operate primarily at the neighborhood level, as will be discussed below. They do occasionally join together, most prominently in the Metropolitan Council on Housing, in lobbying the city for additional resources and opposing costly redevelopment schemes.

The most important, genuinely citywide group is the Coalition for the Homeless. This organization has been extraordinarily effective in forcing the city government to respond to the situation of the homeless. It is not, however, based in the constituency it serves but rather consists of care providers and their supporters. It was founded in 1982 by Robert Hayes, an attorney. While still an associate in a major Wall Street law firm, Hayes successfully sued the city in 1979, requiring it to provide clean, safe shelter to every man who sought it. Subsequent litigation extended the right to women and families. By 1985, the coalition consisted of a ten-person staff and active members in 40 cities around the country (*New York Times*, 1985: sec. 4). Its primary activities are bringing lawsuits on behalf of its constituency and operating food and recreation programs for homeless people. Its lobbying and legal efforts have been directed at obtaining improved services, a ban on the destruction of single-room-occupancy hotels, the upgrading of shelter programs and the development of permanent housing to replace temporary quarters. In 1987 the coalition, which relies on corporations, foundations and government subsidies for its funding, had a $1.2-million yearly budget, and with *pro bono* assistance from major firms had brought more than a dozen lawsuits against public agencies on behalf of the homeless (*New York Times*, 1987e).

The Coalition for the Homeless resembles the National Welfare Rights Organization of the 1960s in that it too was founded by a committed professional. The welfare rights group, however, while also pursuing litigation aimed at increasing benefits to its constituents, focused mainly on developing a mass movement. Its staff time was devoted to organizing its membership rather than litigation and service delivery. It sponsored numerous demonstrations to bring attention to grievances and demand improved benefit levels (Cloward and Piven, 1974). The participants in these demonstrations were primarily welfare recipients, in contrast to the mostly middle-class, liberal marchers in a 1987 rally on behalf of the homeless (*New York Times*, 1987d).

In sum, the Coalition for the Homeless derives from New York City's long tradition of urban progressivism in which middle- and upper-class elements have worked for improved social services. It has as its constituency the most needy of the city's population, and it can demonstrate remarkable achievements in attaining its aims. But it remains an advocacy and service organization, not a mass movement.

Neighborhood

The most visibly mobilized groups in New York continue to be neighborhood based. Their issues are local—the improvement of neighborhood conditions. Virtually all neighborhood leaders identify drugs, crime, housing and education as the major problems of their areas. They address these problems by pressuring established authority to take action and seeking to raise funds from government, private donors and investment institutions. While protest actions such as sit-ins and marches remain part of their repertoire, they do not voice Alton Maddox's objective of changing the basic power equation of New York. Rather, they seek to gain a hearing and to attain the capacity to operate community programs.

The most important multi-issue neighborhood organizations are the community boards. Fifty-nine in number, they were established in their present form under the 1975 revision of the City Charter to encompass districts ranging from 100,000 to 200,000 in population. Their members are appointed by the borough presidents and city council members. They have advisory power over planning decisions and are consulted on questions of service delivery and budgeting. Their formal powers are weak, and their mode of appointment guarantees that their members will not be the most militant elements of the community. Nevertheless, they do serve as advocates of community interests, usually defending small businesses and low-income households against the expansionary ambitions of real estate developers (Marcuse, 1987).

Community board meetings offer a forum, attended by administrative and elected officials, in which other neighborhood organizations raise issues of concern on topics ranging from police to housing to sanitation. A community leader we interviewed in the North Bronx commented, "The main link between the city and the district is the community board. It has become the mediator between politicians, city officials and local residents." Nevertheless, community organizations, which include block associations, merchants groups, housing and economic development corporations and police precinct councils, also pursue their agendas through whatever additional political or bureaucratic path they can locate. These alternative routes include direct contacts with officials in the state legislature, borough president's office, city council and the service bureaucracies. Consequently, neighborhood politics has a rather disjointed character and varies considerably from one community planning district to another. The effectiveness of neighborhood organizations depends on the entrepreneurial abilities and political connections of their leaders. It depends also on general community characteristics to the extent that a particular district has a population containing activists. But no district manifests a highly mobilized general constituency.

The Crown Heights Neighborhood[12]

We have studied in some depth one neighborhood in central Brooklyn to describe the quality of community activism in contemporary New York. Crown Heights has not felt the pressures of major real estate developers that have stimulated strong counter-mobilizations in Manhattan. Despite having a population that is predominantly poor and almost entirely nonwhite, it is at the high end in level of participation and ideological commitment to community improvement for the benefit of low-income people. Examination of the neighborhood therefore shows the possibilities for community activism by an impoverished population under ordinary circumstances in the present period.

Crown Heights has a long history of community participation, with many of the same individuals remaining active for decades.[13] When in 1972 the city set up an experimental Office of Neighborhood Government in Crown Heights (a precursor to the present community-board/district-manager system), community organizations responded by joining together in the Crown Heights Board of Community Affairs (CHBOCA). This body, unique in the city, was composed of representatives of 35 organizations. Its chairperson, who is now the head of the community board, stated CHBOCA's goals:

> We see CHBOCA as the policy-making body for ONG. CHBOCA has as its goal sign-off power over programs and priorities of ONG; we want the goals of the office to be interpreted through CHBOCA; we want to have a veto over who is on staff. We also wish to have a working relationship with the agencies of the city government that allows us to have sign-off power over the programs, personnel and budgets of the decentralized agency offices (S. Fainstein, et al., 1973: 47).

As the quotation indicates, leaders in the early 1970s were continuing to demand community control of neighborhood institutions. But CHBOCA also reflected a crucial shift toward the present system of regularized community input. In the words of CHBOCA's chair:

> We need an orderly interpretation of the feelings of the community... We need to get away from street rhetoric and have a formal mechanism for community input (S. Fainstein, et al., 1973: 60).

Crown Heights's present neighborhood groups concern themselves almost entirely with collective-consumption issues. The only exception is the businessmen's association, which meets monthly to discuss common problems and which helps members seeking financing or technical assistance. The community board, which has "drawn in new people as well as old warhorses," holds well-attended monthly meetings. Its committees, which include non-board members, focus on specialized areas like housing and economic development and do most of the board's work.

Housing is the major issue on which the community board has attempted to affect city policy. Despite the existence of many streets with handsome brownstones, Crown Heights has not yet experienced gentrification. It has, however, begun to feel the interest of real estate speculators; consequently, city-owned property, acquired through tax foreclosure, has risen in value and is sought by private developers. Until recently the city's policy was to auction such property to the highest bidder, thereby both obtaining a lump-sum payment and returning the property to the tax rolls. The new purchaser usually holds vacant property, awaiting the propitious moment to either resell or develop it.

Community housing advocates have objected through the board to the deleterious effects on neighborhoods of maintaining derelict buildings as well as to their being priced beyond the reach of not-for-profit developers. The city has temporarily halted auctions but has not officially announced a change of policy. The community board has proposed an elaborate housing plan for the area, but it has received no indication as to whether the city government will make use of it in implementing its $4-billion housing program. The board also has pressed local banks to fulfill their obligations under the federal Community Reinvestment Act.

The most effective proponents of housing programs have been church-affiliated. One community leader noted: "If it wasn't for the churches, nothing would be happening. This is the only really hopeful group in terms of development. The rest are fragmented, kept quiet, coopted." The Brooklyn Ecumenical Council (BEC), consisting of 25 churches throughout Brooklyn, sponsors a housing development corporation. It currently has a city commitment of 1,800 units of "in rem"[14] housing which it is rehabilitating. So far, it has completed 24 moderate-income condos and is working on 113 cooperative units under a cross-subsidy plan. Financing has come from a variety of public, private and philanthropic sources, including the Roman Catholic Archdiocese and the Local Initiative Support Corporation (LISC).

BEC spent five years working to get approval and financing for its program. Since it had no track record in development, it experienced difficulty in attracting funds and political backing. Its tactics, developed in a program called "Denunciation and Annunciation," reflected a combination of protest actions against the city's housing auction system, conventional and unconventional uses of influence and bureaucratic organization. Its staff worked through the Brooklyn church leadership to gain the support of Brooklyn Union Gas, the state AFL-CIO, the city's Public Development Corporation and the New York City Partnership, a business-sponsored group oriented toward social improvement. It took over the office of Jonathan Rose, a prominent developer, to enlist his support; it obtained 10,000 names on a petition. Once it attained financing for its projects, it had to develop an organization capable of building them. The words of one of its officials summed up the kinds of calculations engaged in by this and many other community organizations: "We must say 'no' and 'yes.'"

The district's elected officials have responded to demands from community groups by acting as a higher-level lobby at the mayor's office and in state government. While Mayor Koch was regarded as abrasive and opposed to community interests, the borough president, the state senator and one of the city council members were universally rated as helpful. But, as one respondent put it, "The elected officials aren't leaders. The community has to put pressure on them." Another declared, "Elected officials are ineffective except as allies to neighborhood people, and what they push for. But there's a feeling on the part of residents that politicians' promises are not kept." A long-time activist explained:

> The active civic organizations are not political. I used to be the district co-leader. But I got out of politics because it was too dishonest, there were too many elections to prepare for, it was too distracting. There is so much infighting among the Democratic leaders that it defuses community interest.

Thus, there is little integration of community groups into the governing coalition, even though there is considerable access.

Crown Heights, then, presents a picture of active, stable community organizations playing a customary role. One hears little rhetoric demanding community power, and the division between community and electoral politics is maintained. Groups restrict themselves to consumption issues, where they have been reasonably successful in achieving investments in housing and infrastructure and improved services.

Current Status of Neighborhood Groups. While service improvement and especially better housing are obviously important in poor neighborhoods, they can do little to better the economic position of residents. There have been some efforts at fostering community economic activity, but their impacts are modest. The most significant such program in the city is Bedford-Stuyvesant Restoration. Its present situation reveals the limits on production-oriented community organizations in New York.

Founded in 1967 by Senator Robert Kennedy, Bed-Stuy Restoration, located in central Brooklyn, enlisted numerous corporate sponsors (Powledge, 1976). Using federal and city funds as well, it developed a shopping center, backed local, minority-owned businesses, attracted an IBM branch plant, constructed and rehabilitated housing and provided health, employment placement and other social services.

Since its peak, Restoration has lost two-thirds of its staff due to funding cuts. It is still large, though, relative to other such programs in the country, with a core staff of 38. In addition to government funding, it receives revenues from its various commercial and residential projects, including a supermarket and a Burger King. While having made some impact on the community, its continued dependence on shrinking public support prevents it from expanding its programs.

Bed-Stuy Restoration is essentially a staff-run group; New York contains few if any grass-roots mobilizations aiming at industrial or commercial development or employee ownership.

The effect of the recent decade of large-scale immigration on community activism is not yet clear. Asian groups, especially Koreans, have formed strong commercial associations. As well as providing mutual assistance, these groups have been lobbying for commercial rent control. In districts where there has been a major influx of immigrants, they have also gradually become involved with broader community groups, although they are less prominent than older residents. A *Newsday* poll of Brooklyn residents indicated that immigrants voted in city elections at a much lower rate than either first-generation, U.S.-born citizens or other respondents (35 percent versus 72 percent and 64 percent respectively). Surprisingly, though, they claimed to have participated in community board and school board meetings at a level comparable to first-generation Americans and only slightly less than the rest (*New York Newsday*, 1987). Different nationalities vary considerably in their level of participation, depending on their language abilities, legal status and native culture.

New York City's communities have sustained their activism over many years despite hostility from the mayor's office, declines in funding, ideological counterattacks and population change. They can point to a number of visible achievements: the halting or revision of a few large projects, most notably Westway and Columbus Circle, the commitment of a major portion of the city's capital budget to housing programs for at least the next decade and the stabilization and reinvigoration of many neighborhoods. They have not, however, maintained the influence they once had nor taken some of the paths followed elsewhere. We now examine some of the routes community organizations have traveled in other cities, then discuss the reasons why New York has differed and their implications.

Comparisons with Progressive Regimes in Boston and Chicago

Like New York, Boston and Chicago have experienced downtown booms and consequent residential pressures as a result of their roles as financial centers in the restructuring U.S. economy. In both cities active community groups have argued that municipal government must direct a share of the proceeds from commercial expansion to neighborhood improvements and housing for the benefit of working-class people. They have therefore made linkage programs one of their major objectives.

Boston (unlike Chicago) has actually adopted a linkage ordinance.[15] The success of neighborhood groups in achieving this objective occurred simultaneously with the election of Mayor Raymond Flynn, who backed the program.

Flynn based his campaign on a neighborhood alliance that supported his populist, confrontational style; he portrayed his predecessor, Kevin White, as the creature of real estate interests (Swanstrom, 1988). A white man who played on the traditional antagonisms of Boston's working class toward Brahmin corporate elites, Flynn was able to attract the white ethnic groups that in New York supported Edward Koch's very different orientation. More surprisingly, perhaps, he has managed to incorporate blacks into his governing coalition, despite his earlier record of opposition to school desegregation and his defeat of black candidate Mel King in the primary. Boston's community groups have not shown the reluctance of their New York counterparts to involve themselves in electoral politics. This is the case in part because they had a candidate who spoke to their cause. Conversely, the candidate was a product of the neighborhood movement, as was his opponent.

Harold Washington's victory in Chicago as a progressive candidate presents a probable model for the recently elected Dinkens Administration in New York, but his difficulties in attaining a supportive city council majority indicated the problems of a minority mayor's seeking redistributive policies in a racially polarized city. Washington resembled Flynn in the platform on which he ran for election in 1983; he differed, however, in his electoral base. With his support coming almost entirely from black voters in a city in which blacks comprised slightly less than a majority, Washington needed to attract white allegiance if he were to govern effectively. Rather than simply seeking the support of business elites, as had been the solution of other black mayors, he tried also to attract the backing of white neighborhood organizations. Many of these groups had come together in a coalition called Save Our Neighborhoods/Save Our City (SON/SOC) (Bennett, 1987). SON/SOC derived its *modus operandi* from the Alinsky tradition of community mobilization, but placed a greater emphasis on coalition building than did Alinsky. Its most important goal was a linkage program in which new development would be taxed and the proceeds turned over to neighborhoods to allocate as they saw fit. Washington generally supported the principle of linkage but was never able to reach a satisfactory accommodation with SON/SOC on the components of the policy. Moreover, he could not overcome the tensions around race and generalized mistrust of government that separated his administration from his mobilized white constituents.

A black progressive mayor in New York[16] would doubtless run into even more obstacles to the enactment of his or her program than did Washington. Because New York's minority population is divided about equally between blacks and Hispanics, such a mayor would lack the solid constituency to which Harold Washington could turn. Nor does New York have any citywide grouping comparable to SON/SOC proposing a general program that would redistribute some of the benefits from downtown development to lower-income neighborhoods (Pickman and Roberts, 1985).

The separation of New York's neighborhood groups from the political arena has led them to focus on specific issues rather than on a citywide program. Hence, although no stable, broad coalition has pressed for linkage programs, community interests have attained dedicated expenditures derived from new development in certain instances. New York, in fact, is raising far more money from the proceeds of new development than is Boston, where it is estimated that linkage will generate an estimated $37 to $52 million over a ten-year period (Swanstrom, 1988). For example, when residents of Clinton, the working-class neighborhood adjacent to the 42nd Street Project Area, failed to halt redevelopment, they asked for mitigation payments from the developer. They failed to establish the principle that the developer should be responsible for the housing impacts of his project. As part of the negotiations for final project approval by the Board of Estimate, $25 million of city and state funds were pledged for neighborhood use over ten years, primarily for housing improvements (S. Fainstein, 1987b).[17]

On a much larger scale, the city and state have pledged more than $1-billion in proceeds from the development of Battery Park City in the lower Manhattan financial district to subsidize low- and moderate-income housing throughout New York. The contribution does not come from private developers, but from the Battery Park City Authority, which owns the land underlying the project and participates in the profits (Schmalz, 1987).[18] The funds are part of an announced $4.2-billion housing program. While the plan has yet to be fully specified and has already been heavily criticized by low-income housing advocates, it greatly exceeds any other U.S. city's commitment to housing development.

It is therefore possible to contend that New York's community groups, despite their symbolic and electoral failures, have achieved greater material results than their counterparts in more "progressive" cities. Such a conclusion, however, ignores the totality of development programs under the Koch administration, as well as attributing too much influence to community groups by crediting them with the impetus for the housing program. Opponents of unrestricted growth have been almost wholly unsuccessful in achieving limits on development, preventing the conversion of rental units into condos and co-ops and stopping subsidies to developers. They have not attained any kind of commitment to a more balanced growth strategy and zoning bonuses continue to be dispensed to large developers. The housing program has been pressed not just by neighborhood representatives, but also by business leaders, who fear the labor-force effects of housing shortages and share in the general desire to get the homeless off the streets. Overall, the victories that community groups have attained in affecting New York City's development policy have been piecemeal and are framed within a larger context of an intensely pro-development regime.

The Future of Community Politics

This discussion implies that New York's community activists would be more effective if they could unite behind electoral candidates and thereby have a greater impact on citywide programs. In a comparative analysis of German and American grass-roots movements, however, Clarke and Mayer (1986: 401) dispute this view: "German developments indicate that the political issues raised by economic restructuring processes cannot easily be accommodated by electoral representation processes." They argue that electoral politics is necessarily cooptative, that movement politics is cross-class while parties are class based and that the new links that have developed in both Germany and the U.S. between grass-roots groups and the state are necessarily outside party structures.

Indeed, by its very definition a social movement cannot fit within the boundaries of institutionalized party politics. At the same time, however, movements cannot achieve their goals by working only on the outside. Body-Gendrot presents the example of a successful grass-roots mobilization in Paris in which "both approaches were combined: grass-roots involvement and the use of political channels of action" (Body-Gendrot, 1987: 140). As Andre Gorz contends, politics always involves contradictions, and even while social movements cannot succeed through normal politics, neither can they achieve their aims autonomously (Gorz, 1982: 12). They must therefore work both inside and outside institutionalized politics.

At the moment, community groups in New York do not belong to either a social movement or electoral politics. Neither are they part of a production-linked coalition such as the Tri-State Conference on Steel, which has sought to prevent plant closings and to promote industrial development projects in the Pittsburgh area (Fitzgerald, 1987). Rather, they constitute a layer of interest groups that partly buffers the regime from unmediated citizen discontent and partly stimulates responses to community demands. Their character and influence has remained largely stable since 1974, through periods of both severe economic downturn and financial revival.

The reasons for the division between electoral and community politics are complex and can be discussed only briefly here. First, as indicated earlier, racial and ethnic divisions are a dominant force in New York City politics. Lower-income residents who in other cities are united in their opposition to unfettered development and supportive of neighborhood initiatives do not coalesce sufficiently around development issues to overcome their antagonisms. While Chicago and Boston also have bitter, highly politicized racial conflicts, they differ from New York in possessing potential majorities of a single racial group that supports a neighborhood strategy. In Chicago, blacks have proven able to command an electoral majority; Boston still retains sufficient numbers of working-class whites for them to elect a white mayor who is not backed by business.

Second, the size of New York City is an obvious factor. It is extremely difficult for any community leader to develop a citywide constituency.

Third, New York has had a unique institutional structure, which, until it was declared unconstitutional in 1989, made the Board of Estimate the most important policy-making body.[19] This means that city council membership, which provided the upward path for most community-based, progressive mayors, has offered little opportunity for making a name. An additional institutional factor that reinforces the separation of electoral from citizen politics is the community board system, which tends to deflect activists from more politicized modes of interest articulation.

Fourth, New York's status as a global city and the power of the business interests located within it make the pressures on the central business district extremely powerful. The advanced service industries headquartered in New York uniquely require central space, and the profits accruing to developers that provide such space are extraordinarily high. On the one hand, the city government responds to the demands of the real estate industry and the financial contributions it makes both to political campaigns and the city's treasury; on the other hand, it has difficulty identifying other opportunities for economic development during a period in which the flight of manufacturing industry from the city has seemed unstoppable.

Whether community groups can become more powerful forces within the New York scene depends on both national and local factors. The community movements of the late 1960s operated within a national context of racial self-consciousness and delegitimation of bureaucracy. A national administration that placed a priority on combating poverty also contributed to a situation conducive to community action. In the absence of national forces that give a broader meaning to local issues, New York's community groups will most likely remain pragmatic actors seeking neighborhood improvement.

Their effectiveness in determining city policy will depend on the existence of a progressive mayoral regime with broad political support. The likelihood of this occurring depends heavily on the background and alliances of mayoral candidates. The lack of integration between community and electoral politics, however, makes such a regime less likely than in some other cities. Whether Mayor Dinkens will effect a new integration remains uncertain.

Acknowledgements

This article was originally prepared for a meeting of the Dual City Working Group, Social Science Research Committee on New York City, June 1988, jointly sponsored by the Robert Wagner, Sr. Institute on Urban Public Policy, City University of New York Graduate Center. Preparation of the paper was supported by the Wagner Institute. Susana Fried, Tanya Steinberg, Laura Reed and Paul Bove provided research assistance. The comments of the anonymous referees of this journal were exceptionally helpful.

Notes

1. They often, however, oppose the interests of nonresident disadvantaged people who seek to move into their community.

2. We characterize urban regimes in these three periods as directive, concessionary and conserving, respectively (Fainstein and Fainstein, 1986).

3. We do not assume that electoral influence necessarily produces governmental inclusion; only that it is a prerequisite.

4. The argument is that the welfare state mitigates class conflict in the workplace. Worker demands for a higher standard of living fall increasingly on the state, especially the local state, which provides collective-consumption goods, rather than on employers. But, as O'Connor (1973) contends, capitalists, while welcoming the role of the state in satisfying demands that would otherwise be directed toward them, refuse to pay the bill for state services, producing a crisis.

5. Linkage programs require a commitment from developers that they will contribute housing or public services in return for permission to build a commercial project. A builder will typically put money in a housing trust fund based on the number of square feet in the building.

6. It is not the purpose of this paper to develop a general theory explaining the rise and decline of urban transformative movements; the limited nature of our empirical material at any rate precludes such pretensions. Such a theory would root episodes of uninstitutionalized social and political conflict in the shifts in social context (see Pickvance, 1984).

7. Despite its name, the term "neighborhood movement" referred to the numerous, nonmilitant neighborhood organizations that became institutionalized during the 1970s and received encouragement from the Carter Administration. While representing a collective impetus toward decentralization of power and inclusion of community interests in decision-making, they did not

constitute a social movement as defined in the beginning of this article.

8. Our characterization of post-1974 urban regimes as conserving (see Note 2 above) is based on our interpretation of them as maintaining their contacts with and responding to nonpartisan citizens' organizations, even while curtailing expenditures; thus, they are conserving rather than conservative.

9. The election of David Dinkens in November 1989 as a black mayor of New York City may eventually require a reinterpretation of New York City politics and the role of community groups in it. As of early 1990, however, Dinkens appears to be a relatively conservative mayor who functions through extant institutional structures.

10. For a more detailed discussion, see Fainstein and Fainstein (1985).

11. A recent issue of *New York* magazine had the words "Race: The Issue" emblazoned in giant letters on its cover. The feature article contended:

    > Race is an issue politicians go to great pains to avoid. It has been deemed unfit for open discussion, in all but the most platitudinous manner, for many years. The public is, oddly, complicit in this: people seem to sense that the topic is so raw, and their feelings so intense, that it is just too risky to discuss in mixed company...In private, though, race seems the *only* thing people are talking about these days...(Klein, 1989: 34, italics in original).

12. This discussion concentrates on the part of Crown Heights north of Eastern Parkway that is represented by Community Board 8. Although the district south of Eastern Parkway also has a mainly black population, its community board is dominated by Hasidic Jews. The two parts of Crown Heights were formerly treated as a single district. When the present district boundaries were established after the 1975 Charter revision, however, the city deliberately segmented off the politically influential Hasidim to allow them control of their district.

    In 1980 District 8 was 85 percent black, nine percent Hispanic and six percent white. Seventy-eight percent of its housing units were renter occupied (New York City Department of City Planning, 1983a: 60-1). The 1979 median household income of the district was $9,010, compared to the citywide median of $13,855 and the Brooklyn median of $11,919 (New York City Department of City Planning, 1983b: 2, 80).

    Although overall demographic characteristics and relative income status apparently have not changed much in the past decade, there has been a heavy influx of Haitians and other blacks from the Caribbean.

13. The authors originally studied Crown Heights in 1972 as part of the New York Neighborhood Study at the Bureau of Applied Social Research, Columbia University. Recent material, including interviews with Crown Heights community leaders, has been collected by Susan Fainstein with the principal assistance of Susana Fried.

14. Housing acquired by the municipal government for default in payment of property taxes.

15. Boston's program was modeled on San Francisco's; the latter was the first large city to adopt such an ordinance. At the time it did so, neighborhood organizations had not yet succeeded in capturing the mayor's office, but had attained considerable clout within the Board of Supervisors. The program applied to all developers of office projects adding at least 50,000 square feet of office space. Developers could satisfy their obligation by either building the housing themselves or providing a financial contribution. In Seattle, which adopted a linkage program in 1984, developers were required only to contribute to housing development in return for a density bonus (Pickman and Roberts, 1985). A slate of council candidates in Hartford won election in 1985 on a platform supporting linkage. In 1986, however, they disavowed their earlier support for the policy (Neubeck and Ratcliff, 1988).

16. As of this writing (March 1990) it is too soon to determine if David Dinkens should be characterized as a progressive mayor.

17. The money was to come from general city and state revenues rather than a tax on the project itself, and therefore the concession did not satisfy those who wanted the two linked so as to set a precedent. Ironically, while the neighborhood started receiving the funds committed to it, the project, four years after its approval by the Board of Estimate, had not yet begun. If the money had in fact been linked to the project, no return would yet have been realized.

18. In another project on city-owned land on the Lower East Side, the developer has agreed to a cross-subsidy program whereby part of the profit from market-rate condominiums will provide an estimated subsidy of $32 million for the development of rental housing (Oser, 1988a). The developer of a luxury development in Clinton agreed to rehabilitate ten buildings, to be

occupied by various lower-income groups and to be operated by a not-for-profit organization, in return for a special zoning permit (Oser, 1988b).

19. The Board of Estimate consisted of the mayor, the comptroller, the city council president and the borough presidents. The mayor cast three votes, the other citywide officials two votes each and the five borough presidents one vote. The equal representation of the borough presidents, elected from boroughs with varying populations, caused the Supreme Court to uphold a lower-court decision ruling that the body violated the principle of one person-one vote.

References

Bennett, Larry (1987) The dilemmas of building a progressive urban coalition: The linked development debate in Chicago, *Journal of Urban Affairs, 9*(3), 263-76.

Body-Gendrot, Sophie (1987) Grass-roots mobilization in the thirteenth arrondissement of Paris: A cross-national view. In Clarence N. Stone and Heywood T. Sanders (Eds.), *The Politics of Urban Development.* Lawrence: University of Kansas Press.

Browning, Rufus P., Dale Rogers Marshall, David H. Tabb (1984) *Protest Is Not Enough.* Berkeley: University of California Press.

Castells, Manuel (1977) *The Urban Question.* Cambridge: MIT Press.

Castells, Manuel (1985) Commentary on C.G. Pickvance's "The rise and fall of urban movements," *Environment and Planning D: Space and Society, 3*, 55-61.

Clark, Kenneth (1965) *Dark Ghetto.* New York: Harper and Row.

Clarke, Susan E. and Margit Mayer (1986) Responding to grassroots discontent: Germany and the United States, *International Journal of Urban and Regional Research, 10*, 401.

Cloward, Richard A. and Frances Fox Piven (1974) *The Politics of Turmoil.* New York: Pantheon.

Cox, Kevin R. (1984) Neighborhood conflict and urban social movements: Questions of historicity, class, and social change, *Urban Geography, 5*, 343-55.

Davies, James Clarence, III (1966) *Neighborhood Groups and Urban Renewal.* New York: Columbia University Press.

Fainstein, Norman I. and Susan S. Fainstein (1974) *Urban Political Movements*. Englewood Cliffs, NJ: Prentice-Hall.

Fainstein, Norman I. and Susan S. Fainstein (1976) The future of community control, *American Political Science Review, 70*, 905-23.

Fainstein, Norman I. and Susan S. Fainstein (1982) Neighborhood enfranchisement and urban redevelopment, *Journal of Planning Education and Research, 2*, 11-19.

Fainstein, Susan S., et al. (1973) *Community Leadership and the Office of Neighborhood Government in Bushwick, Crown Heights, and Wakefield-Edenwald*, Interim report, New York City Neighborhood Project, Bureau of Applied Social Research, Columbia University, mimeo.

Fainstein, Susan S. and Norman I. Fainstein (1985) Economic restructuring and the rise of urban social movements, *Urban Affairs Quarterly 21*, 187-206.

Fainstein, Susan S. and Norman I. Fainstein (1986) Regime strategies, communal resistance, and economic forces. In Susan S. Fainstein, et al., *Restructuring the City*. New York: Longman.

Fainstein, Susan S. (1987a) Local mobilization and economic discontent. In Michael Peter Smith and Joe R. Feagin (Eds.), *The Capitalist City*. Oxford: Basil Blackwell.

Fainstein, Susan S. (1987b) The politics of criteria: Planning for the redevelopment of Times Square. In Frank Fischer and John Forester (Eds.), *Confronting Values in Policy Analysis*. Beverly Hills: Sage.

Fantini, Mario, Marilyn Gittell, and R. Magat (1970) *Community Control and the Urban School*. New York: Praeger.

Fitzgerald, Joan (1987) The role of community-based social movements in promoting economic restructuring in the U.S. Paper presented at the 1987 Annual Meeting of the Association of Collegiate Schools of Planning, November.

Gorz, Andre (1982) *Farewell to the Working Class*. Boston: South End.

Jenkins, J. Craig (1983) Resource mobilization theory and the study of social movements, *Annual Review of Sociology, 9*, 527-53.

Katz, Steven and Margit Mayer (1985) Gimme shelter: Self-help housing struggles within and against the state in New York City and West Berlin, *International Journal of Urban and Regional Research, 9*, 15-46.

Key, V.O. (1963) *Public Opinion and American Democracy*. New York: Knopf.

Klein, Joe (1989) Race: The issue, *New York, 22* (May 29), 34.

Lowe, Jean (1967) *Cities in a Race with Time*. New York: Random House.

Marcuse, Peter (1987) Neighborhood policy and the distribution of power: New York City's community boards, *Policy Studies Journal, 16*, 277-89.

Marris, Peter and Martin Rein (1967) *Dilemmas of Social Reform*. New York: Atherton.

Neubeck, Kenneth J. and Richard E. Ratcliff (1988) Urban democracy and the power of corporate capital: Struggles over Downtown growth and neighborhood stagnation in Hartford, Connecticut. In Scott Cummings (Ed.), *Business Elites and Urban Development.* Albany: SUNY Press.

New York City, Dept. of City Planning (1983a) *Demographic Profile: A Portrait of New York City from the 1980 Census.* New York: Department of City Planning.

New York City, Dept. of City Planning, (1983b) *1980 Census Data, Part 1–Income, New York City Boroughs Community Districts.* New York: Department of City Planning.

New York Newsday (1987) Brooklyn: The politicians (November 5): 29.

New York Times (1985), November 3, Sec. 4.

New York Times (1986), December 28.

New York Times (1987a), January 12.

New York Times (1987b), October 7.

New York Times (1987c), December 21.

New York Times (1987d), December 22.

New York Times (1987e), December 23.

O'Connor, James (1973) *The Fiscal Crisis of the State.* New York: St. Martin's.

Oser, Alan (1988a) "Using condo sales to assist new rentals," *New York Times* (April 10), R9.

Oser, Alan (1988b) "Shaping four acres in mid-Manhattan," *New York Times* (May 22), R9.

Pecorella, Robert F. (1987) Fiscal crises and regime change: A contextual approach. In Clarence N. Stone and Heywood T. Sanders (Eds.), *The Politics of Urban Development.* Lawrence: University of Kansas Press.

Pickman, James and Benson F. Roberts (1985) Tapping real estate markets to address housing needs, *New York Affairs, 9*, 3-17.

Pickvance, C.G. (1984) The rise and fall of urban movements and the role of comparative analysis, *Environment and Planning D: Society and Space, 3*, 31-53.

Powledge, Fred (1976) New York's Bedford-Stuyvesant: A rare urban success story, *AIA Journal 65*, 45-59.

Preteceille, Edmond (1981) Collective consumption, the state, and the crisis of capitalist society. In Michael Harloe and Elizabeth Lebas (Eds.), *City, Class and Capital.* London: Edward Arnold.

Rogers, David (1968) *110 Livingston Street.* New York: Random House.

Schmalz, Jeffrey (1987) New York Reaches Accord on Housing, *New York Times* (December 27).

Schwartz, Joel (1986) Tenant power in the liberal city, 1953-1971. In Ronald

Lawson (Ed.), *The Tenant Movement in New York City, 1904-1984*. New Brunswick, N.J.: Rutgers University Press.

Shefter, Martin (1985) *Political Crisis/Fiscal Crisis*. New York: Basic.

Smith, Michael Peter and Dennis R. Judd (1984) American cities: The production of ideology. In Michael Peter Smith (Ed.), *Cities in Transformation*. Beverly Hills: Sage.

Swanstrom, Todd (1988) Urban populism, uneven development, and the space for reform. In Scott Cummings (Ed.), *Business Elites and Urban Development*. Albany: SUNY Press.

URBAN SOCIAL MOVEMENTS, INTRASTATE CONFLICTS OVER URBAN POLICY, AND POLITICAL CHANGE IN CONTEMPORARY MEXICO

Diane E. Davis
New School for Social Research

This paper charts recent political developments in contemporary Mexico through a focus on the urban domain. The main argument is that rapid and concentrated urbanization in Mexico City brings class-distributional conflicts that divide the state and lead to state incapacity, declining legitimacy and political crisis for Mexico's ruling party. This chain of events occurs because urbanization produces political dissatisfaction among urban popular and middle classes not easily addressed by Mexico's incorporated political system, which is structured primarily around appeasing the class-specific concerns of organized labor and industrial capital, and because it produces urban social demands that frequently compete with national development objectives. Accordingly, state actors often split over urban policies or priorities, depending on whether they are concerned most with the urban or the national domain and depending on their allegiances to specific classes or class-based sectors within the incorporated political system. Because these competing priorities and internal divisions limit the state's capacity to respond to accelerating urban demands, urban populations increasingly bypass formal state structures and mobilize in the form of urban social movements. As a result, the Mexican state's political hegemony weakens and opposition forces find more maneuvering room to challenge one-party rule, which can open new doors for the development of a more competitive party system in Mexico.

This paper offers a detailed account of some of the urban social pressures and intrastate conflicts over urban policy that have contributed to reduced electoral support for Mexico's ruling Partido Revolucionario Institucional (PRI). By tracing recent political changes in Mexico—up to and including the PRI's near defeat in the 1988 presidential elections—to social and political development associated with rapid urbanization in its largest and capital city, Mexico City, this paper highlights several ongoing debates over the relationships among urbanization, state power and political change. Specifically, it supports the long-held premises that urbanization increases political mobilization (Huntington and Nelson, 1976; Reyna, 1971; Ames, 1969), that industrialization-led urbanization in Mexico is associated with declining support for the ruling party (Walton and Sween, 1973) and that urban social movements play a special role in challenging state power and bringing greater prospects for democratization (Mainwaring, 1987; Henry, 1985; Ramírez, 1986; Mainwaring and Viola, 1984; Castells, 1983). It moves beyond these general propositions, though, in three critical ways.

First, by differentiating between political participation and political mobilization, and by recognizing class differences in these two patterns of political development, it suggests that rapid and concentrated urbanization in Mexico brings some groups to reduce their participation in formal politics, rather than vice-versa as is generally argued, even while others do not. Second, it traces these different ways of participating in politics among Mexico's population not to the ideological, educational, or income experiences of urban individuals, as is generally the case, but to collective urban experiences shared by particular social classes in a rapidly industrializing urban environment. Last, it identifies conflicting state actions in the urban domain, and the inability of Mexico's political structures of incorporation to channel urban demands, as determining the collective urban experiences and patterns of political mobilization as much as the changing urban environment itself.

These points bring us to a new perspective on the Mexican state by calling into question prevailing opinion about the bureaucratic, social and/or class bases of state power in Mexico. That is, we see the Mexican state not as homogeneous (Smith, 1979; Purcell and Purcell, 1977), but as divided; we see its divisions as traceable to conflicts within and over the urban domain. We also see the social bases of the Mexican state (or its legitimacy) as eroding mainly with respect to urban popular and middle classes, and not necessarily with respect to society as a whole (Newell and Rubio, 1984). Last, we see the class bases of the Mexican state's power as resting precariously on the social and political actions of its middle sectors—the urban popular and middle classes—and not necessarily on an antagonistic relationship between organized labor and capital (Cockcroft, 1983; Saldivar, 1981).

The paper begins with a general discussion of patterns of political and economic development in Mexico between 1940 and 1960; the focus throughout is on Mexico City. It continues with an analysis of the emergence of urban social movements and intrastate conflicts in Mexico City in the 1960s and early 1970s, and why they accelerated during the 1980s. To ground the discussion empirically, the focus is placed on specific urban policy debates that mobilized Mexico City's residents and divided state actors in each of the last three decades. The paper concludes with a brief discussion of the theoretical implications of the case study and a few words about the relationships between urbanization, state power and political change in contemporary Mexico. Data and evidence used in this paper are drawn from a variety of primary and secondary sources, including official documents and interviews conducted between 1980 and 1981, and again in 1987.[1]

Historical Antecedents of the Mexican Political System

Though there is little consensus within the scholarly literature on the Mexican state, particularly its cooptive nature and its relationship to dominant classes (see Cockcroft, 1983; Smith, 1979; Purcell and Purcell, 1977), there appears to be agreement on one critical issue: the institutionalized inclusion of a wide variety of social and class forces into the one-party-dominated corporatist system has facilitated the process of economic development and brought more sustained political stability to Mexico than exists in almost any other country in Latin America (Hamilton, 1982; Reyna, 1974; Córdova, 1972; González Casanova, 1970). Political stability and the PRI's hegemony have been so striking, in fact, that few scholars have looked for sources of conflict or change from within Mexico's corporatist system itself (Leal, 1986: 36). However, a closer reading of the evidence suggests otherwise: institutionalized structures of incorporation have become the source of growing tensions within the PRI, primarily because these class-based structures are ill-suited to dealing with the growing urban demands of Mexico's citizenry.

Why this is the case has a lot to do with when—and why—the incorporated political system was first introduced. To consolidate their power after the 1910 Revolution, and after close to two decades of labor unrest, peasant rebellion and political infighting, Mexico's revolutionary leadership created two national federations in the early 1930s to represent laborers and peasants within the ruling party, known respectively as the Confederación de Trabajadores (CTM) and the Confederación Nacional de Campesinos (CNC). Through these federations, organized labor and the peasantry were made principal partners in the governing coalition—not only because they played a critical role in the Revolution, but also because they held the potential to disrupt the course of rapid industrialization and economic development then favored by the ruling party (Trejo Delarbre, 1986: 187-9).[2]

Almost immediately, however, the nation's leaders faced pressure to broaden this class-based structure of political incorporation to include groups that remained outside the peasant and labor federations. Among those excluded groups making demands on the newly formed party were bureaucrats (Sirvent, 1975), small-scale urban artisans, the growing ranks of self- and underemployed urban poor (Perlo, 1981; 1982), the middle classes (Loaeza, 1986) and forces within the military (Hamilton, 1986).[3] However, even though the ruling party faced growing political problems from these critical sectors throughout the 1930s, it was not until the party lost the 1940 presidential election in Mexico City (Michaels, 1971: 81), where most of these dissatisfied populations resided, that a decision was made to incorporate social classes into the one-party-dominated corporatist system as well.

In 1941, the ruling party convened to discuss the ways in which this wide variety of occupations could be represented in the party. Because the existing corporatist system was already structured around class identities, the party leadership decided to create a third sector that would also be defined in class terms. Founded in 1943 and called the Confederación Nacional de Organizaciones Populares (CNOP), this third federation officially represented those workers and employees who were not industrial laborers, peasants or large capitalists. As a representative for the nation's intermediate classes—sometimes called "popular middle classes" in party documents—the CNOP included groups as diverse as street vendors, state bureaucrats, ex-military men, doctors, taxi drivers, teachers, squatters, shopkeepers and lawyers (Partido Revolucionario Institucional, 1984b: 45).[4] The majority of its constituents, moreover, resided in Mexico City.

With its official constitution in 1943, the CNOP rounded out the party's class-specific bases of representation and became the third principal axis of what is now known as the PRI. In the first years of its existence, the CNOP channeled demands to the party leadership about housing, rent and costs of urban services as well as employment and education (Partido Revolucionario Institucional, 1984a: 105). Given its initial concern with urban problems, though, as well as the concentration of its constituency in Mexico City, and the fact that the organization held so many different occupations with different educational requirements and workplace demands, the CNOP soon developed into a political vehicle for Mexico City residents to present urban demands (Ramírez, 1986: 40-1). The CNOP's preoccupation with mainly urban, rather than class-specific, concerns was also reinforced by the near impossibility of identifying a common class interest that this diverse collection of occupations could share. Middle classes were generally reluctant to see themselves in class terms anyway, and they rarely organized around employment or workplace demands to the same extent as the constituents in the CTM and the CNC (see Loaeza, 1988).

Institutional Origins of Urban Dissatisfaction

Fortunately for the party leaders (but not for urban populations), the heterogenous character of the CNOP's constituency weakened it organizationally. This gave the PRI-dominated state an opportunity to ignore many of the CNOP's demands about urban problems and focus greater institutional attention on smoothing capital-labor relations or keeping the peasantry under taps. Indeed, precisely because the CNOP held so many different social and class forces, it was relatively incapable of presenting a coherent position on many issues of concern to its constituents (Bassols and Delgado, 1985; Purcell, 1973). Thus, as an institutional format for making powerful demands on the party leadership, the CNOP faded into the background of Mexican politics within the first decades of its existence, and with it the urban popular and middle classes.

With rapid and concentrated urbanization in Mexico during the 1950s and 1960s, however, things began to change. Not only did urban problems accelerate, the CNOP's organizational weaknesses, and its inability to accommodate the concerns of its constituents, became the source of new political problems for the PRI. Massive rural-urban migration brought overcrowding, under-servicing, visible disorder and signs of growing urban poverty (see Garza, 1985; Unikel, 1976). As the city's growing number of new migrants faced obstacles to full employment (Muñoz, de Oliveira, and Stern, 1980), many joined the urban informal sector and the ranks of the urban poor. In response to the growing number of un- and underemployed living in central-city areas and squatting on previously uninhabited peripheral lands, moreover, longtime residents began to see the physical quality of life decline. Mexico City went from a beautiful city with parks, gardens, boulevards and numerous central-city cultural activities to a sprawling, crowded and polluted industrial metropolis with a dirty and dilapidated central city (Toledo, 1986: 40-2).

With these changes, Mexico City saw frequent land invasions by the urban poor, who established illegal settlements and made continual demands for the extension of water, electricity, roadways and other critical urban services necessary to sustain them (Schteingart and Perlo, 1984: 110-11; see also Partido Revolucionario Institucional, 1984b: 100, 106-10). More prosperous members of the middle class who worried about deteriorating urban conditions and social chaos also began to make their presence known, though they expressed a need for greater public expenditures on parks and urban beautification projects as well as for greater restrictions on street vending, squatting and other unsightly evidences of the urban poor (*El Universal*, July 7, 1965; *Siempre*, September 21, 1966). In turn, these growing antagonisms between the urban poor and middle classes, as well as the acceleration of urban problems and the CNOP's growing membership, signalled the CNOP's development into an even more vocal and active sector (Partido Revolucionario Institucional, 1984b: 92-5).

This placed the ruling party in a difficult position. If the PRI leadership openly responded to the demands of either the urban poor or the middle classes, it set itself up for criticism from within the CNOP itself, since this held the potential to call into question the logic of one large federation for popular and middle classes. But to ignore either set of demands would also challenge the CNOP's institutional efficacy and possibly delegitimize the corporatist system as a whole. Moreover, if the party leadership could overcome the CNOP's internal conflicts enough to respond to demands for more accommodating or socially sensitive urban policies, it might have to pit itself against other powerful forces within the party, such as the CTM, that favored relatively uncontrolled urbanization and that prioritized wage and infrastructure expenditures over other urban social expenditures to facilitate the nation's industrial and economic development.[5]

With these competing demands coming to the surface, by the 1960s party leaders began to feel the weight of keeping all three incorporated sectors content. As they began to quibble over how best to do so, urban policies became the source of contentious debate and growing intraparty conflict.

Urban Growth: A New Problem for the PRI

In 1970, a critical year in Mexico's political history, Luis Echeverría took over the presidency and introduced political and macroeconomic policies that broke with many of the party's past practices (Hellman, 1978; Labastida, 1977). Echeverría's policies not only generated a negative response from powerful industrial and banking interests, they also could not bring benefits quickly enough to maintain sufficient political support to counterbalance this private-sector opposition (Basañez, 1981; Saldívar, 1981). The result was the serious economic crisis of 1975-76, which in many ways heralded the debt crisis of 1981 and initiated a steady decline in the PRI's popularity (Newell and Rubio, 1984).

Many scholars of this period tend to analyze Echeverría's administration in the context of dependent development, highlighting the PRI's increasingly uneasy relationship with capitalists in a problematic and highly internationalized economy (Labastida, 1977). Others focus more on the PRI's declining legitimacy vis-a-vis civil society as a whole (Newell and Rubio, 1984; Hellman, 1978). What is generally left unexplored in studies of this critical period, though, are the ways in which growing urban conflicts, particularly the party's internal divisions and difficulties in accommodating the urban demands of popular and middle classes, contributed to the development of Echeverría's populist platform and the attendant crisis. This becomes clear with a closer look at the Echeverría Administration and the presidential administration immediately preceding his, that of Gustavo Díaz Ordaz (1964-1970).

In 1965, scarcely a year after taking the presidency, Díaz Ordaz locked heads with Mexico City Mayor Ernesto Uruchurtu and several other powerful forces within the PRI over control of urban policymaking in Mexico City. Formally at stake was Mexico City's subway, but embodied in support or opposition to the project were two competing priorities with strikingly different consequences for Mexico City's urban popular and middle classes. President Díaz Ordaz, who was backed by the CTM and other conservative forces in the party as well as the private sector (particularly real estate developers and large industrialists), saw the subway as the centerpiece for a large-scale program of rapid urban and economic modernization that would fit neatly into the nation's capital-intensive industrial-development strategies (Davis, 1986: 118-21). Three-term Mayor Ernesto Uruchurtu (1952-65) actively opposed the subway, however, and the president's efforts to use the project to foster rapid and concentrated urbanization as well. He saw the rapid urban dispersion and central-city disarray the subway was expected to produce as destroying his social and political bases of support, which were small-scale businessmen (many of whom were located in Mexico City's central areas) and the urban middle classes who felt increasingly betrayed by the CNOP and the party's rapid industrialization-led urbanization at the expense of their own demands and priorities (Davis, 1986: 174-6).

To successfully implement the project and assert control over Mexico City policy in the face of Uruchurtu's obstinacy, Díaz Ordaz forced the mayor's resignation, which he accomplished by playing on the growing internal divisions within the CNOP between the urban poor and middle classes. That is, Díaz Ordaz rallied supporters to his side by underscoring Uruchurtu's middle-class ties, his forceful razing of squatter settlements and his denial of urban services to those illegal settlements. Indeed, by mobilizing the already dissatisfied urban poor in opposition to the "bulldozer mayor" and his *petit bourgeois* allies, Díaz Ordaz made it difficult for progressive forces within the PRI who otherwise might have opposed a project that was clearly geared toward capital's interests to sustain support for Uruchurtu and his anti-urban-growth position. With both leftist and conservative representatives in the National Congress supporting Díaz Ordaz's efforts to oust Uruchurtu (Leduc, 1966: 30), the mayor was forced to resign. Three weeks later, after Díaz Ordaz appointed a new mayor, the initiation of construction works for the subway was announced to the public.

Though Díaz Ordaz was successful in implementing the subway project and his pro-urban-growth orientation, in the long run his orientations and political relationships with big business, labor and other conservatives forces in the party (Lerner and Ralsky, 1976) helped alienate large portions of Mexico City's residents, not only the middle classes but also the urban poor who had originally supported him in his struggles against Uruchurtu. For one thing, many of the urban policies introduced in Mexico City during the late 1960s, including the subway and other major urban renovations, displaced large numbers of the poor and appeared to favor the construction industry and real estate developers. For another, these policies, on top of Uruchurtu's dismissal, signalled to Mexico's urban middle classes that they had no effective political say over their urban futures and that their interests and concerns were seen as secondary to those of big capital, organized labor and powerful bureaucrats.[6] In fact, after the expensive facelift given to Mexico City by Díaz Ordaz for the 1968 Olympics, both urban poor and middle-class residents began to mobilize against the PRI and its top leadership. They began to protest their growing loss of political freedom and the general corruption in the incorporated political system, and they linked these concerns to Díaz Ordaz's efforts to favor real estate developers, financiers, large industrialists and corrupt political bosses in the organized-labor sector (Hellman, 1978: 40; Ocampo, 1967: 341).

Given the political problems created for the PRI leadership by the accelerating urban protests and Díaz Ordaz's authoritarian responses (the clearest of which were the massacres of hundreds of protesters at a middle-class housing project, Tlatelolco, in 1968) many within the party who may not have cared about urban issues, but who did care about keeping legitimacy vis-a-vis both urban popular- and middle-class sectors, called for a change of profile within the nation's top leadership.[7] They threw their support behind Luis Echeverría, who forged a populist coalition within the PRI by gearing his platform to disenfranchised urban popular and middle classes (Labastida, 1977).

To appeal to those most alienated by Díaz Ordaz's policies, Echeverría strategically interlaced an anti-urban-growth position with a nationalist and populist development strategy, and with a concern for creating greater political access and participation. Peasants left out by rapid urbanization and laborers struggling against party bosses for independent unions joined urban popular and middle classes and nationalist businessmen in repudiating Díaz Ordaz's top-down control of party structures *and* his internationalist development strategy, which appeared to support urban and national growth at all costs. In return for their political support, Echeverría increased expenditures on urban social services, devised a national plan for urban decentralization, introduced agricultural reforms, protected Mexico's economy from foreign firms and introduced several significant political reforms (Basañez, 1981; Saldívar, 1981). The political reforms, in particular, were intended to signal a democratic opening in Mexico and thus to revitalize the PRI's standing in the eyes of the urban poor, the middle classes and others who felt excluded from corporatist political structures, while the urban and economic reforms were intended to address more substantive concerns of these populations (Ramírez, 1986: 45; see also Castells, 1977).

Internal Limits to Urban Reform

By linking urban issues and national-development concerns, however, Echeverría pitted urban residents organized within the CNOP against other sectors in the party who supported rapid urban and industrial growth, particularly the CTM.[8] His efforts to actively reincorporate urban popular and middle classes into the PRI's governing franchise through a populist development strategy also generated heated opposition from large industrialists, bankers and other progrowth forces that were allied with Díaz Ordaz and still wielded power within the party. Many of these private-sector forces joined entrenched labor interests in the CTM and upwardly mobile party bureaucrats in the CNOP, who had little concern for their fellow constituents, to oppose Echeverría and his populist coalition. They actively challenged Echeverría's restrictions on urban growth, his limits on free-market trading, his public expenditures on social rather than productive services and his clear support for mobilized urban popular and middle classes (Newell and Rubio, 1984; Saldívar, 1981; Basañez, 1981).[9]

With opposition from within his own party thwarting him at every turn, Echeverría found it necessary to develop new structures and mechanisms to buttress his own power, particularly in Mexico City where he could tap support from those populations most sympathetic to his administration. Accordingly, he established a network of representative structures, known as the *delegado* system, which served as a mechanism to relay the concerns and grievances of urban popular-and middle-class forces on the neighborhood level directly to the Mexico City mayor's office, which the president was able to control through direct appointment of the mayor. The *delegado* network was independent from the CNOP, which was still riddled by intraparty conflicts. With the formation of the *delegado* system there now existed three different domains in which urban concerns could be channeled and urban populations could be mobilized for larger political purposes: the CNOP, the *delegado* structure and the mayor's office itself, which controlled funding access and urban patronage.

Contrary to Echeverría's objectives, however, these fragmented and often competing urban political structures both exacerbated intraparty conflicts over urban issues and helped set the basis for further disenfranchisement of urban populations, since there was now no single—let alone unified—organization within the party for presenting urban demands. Indeed, urban forces working within only one of the three structures now had even less strength to command party responsiveness. Moreover, with the fragmentation of mechanisms for urban participation, Echeverría's administration left a growing cynicism among urban popular and middle classes. This cynicism was furthered as Echeverría appeared to be a clear loser in his struggle with powerful and conservative forces in the party, many of whom continued to dominate the CNOP. With Mexico City's urban popular and middle classes abandoning hope that the PRI would ever meet their urban concerns, their enthusiasm for formal political participation declined and they began to see the CNOP as a controlled structure for coopting and regulating urban populations instead of a mechanism for effectively channeling grievances and facilitating political participation (Ramírez, 1986: 66).

Equally important, Echeverría's urban reform increased incentives for Mexico City populations to mobilize around urban issues. Because the *delegado* system he instituted gave residents both a reason and a formal structure for presenting urban demands, neighborhoods began organizing with greater frequency. Urban social movements in Mexico City, in fact, first gathered intense strength during the first years of the Echeverría administration (Ramírez, 1986: 46-8).[10] Accordingly, in the administration immediately following Echeverría's, that of President Jose López Portillo (1976-1982), urban residents acted on their cynicism and used local resources to create independent and autonomous urban organizations that would bypass the CNOP and represent their demands vis-a-vis the PRI-dominated state (Schteingart and Perlo, 1984: 120).

As one might expect, these urban social movements grew throughout the 1970s with the participation of populations that in previous decades had channeled demands within the CNOP, not only the urban poor, squatters and renters but also *comerciantes* and *transportistas* (Ramírez, 1986: 62-3). Yet now these same populations used urban social movements, rather than the CNOP, to pose demands about such issues as public housing, transport, roads, water and urban renewal. By the late 1970s, Mexico City had become a city of highly mobilized and well-networked urban residents with the organization and willingness to seriously challenge the PRI's urban policies and priorities. When the debt crisis hit in 1981 these mobilized residents, estimated at close to 180,000, were more organized than ever.[11]

The Dilemma of the Debt Crisis

Given the degree of mobilization in Mexico City, the debt crisis could not have come at a worse time. When the government began to cut social expenditures and raise the costs of urban services to meet austerity objectives, urban social movements sprang into action (Ramírez, 1986: 67-8). With greater frequency and greater numbers, due to the growing cadres of unemployed and underemployed, these urban movements focused their political demands on the consumption and reproduction issues that became so vital to their daily survival (Hernandez, 1987; Ziccardi, 1986: 76-7).[12] Accordingly, the PRI found it increasingly difficult to respond to the challenges and the increasing political independence of urban populations, particularly in the absence of the fiscal resources necessary to guarantee social programs and services for the city's neighborhoods (Ziccardi, 1986: 54-5).[13]

Yet debt crisis was most disastrous for the PRI because it exacerbated the nascent conflicts and tensions within the party over urban priorities. For one thing, pressures from international agencies to restore productivity and the organizational strength of the CTM pushed the government to direct political resources and scarce capital toward businesses and organized labor. This meant that the situation of social classes incorporated in the two other institutional sectors declined, both absolutely and relatively (*Unomásuno*, May 27, 1987: 14; *La Jornada*, June 19, 1987: 15); and this in turn pitted the concerns of each of the institutional sectors against each other. Not only did this force state actors to choose between restoring economic solvency and maintaining legitimacy vis-a-vis certain populations, it also exacerbated the growing divisions within the PRI and made it more difficult to come to a consensus on policy actions, particularly with respect to urban populations and their accelerating demands (*La Jornada*, June 20, 1987: 3).

We see evidence of the ways that the debt crisis and the attendant acceleration of urban social movements produced internal divisions over urban policy, and limited the PRI's capacity to act decisively, by looking more closely at debate over an urban democratic reform proposed by President Miguel de la Madrid (1982-1988) within the first several months of his administration. As a president selected through processes of internal negotiation and sectoral bargaining on the part of the PRI's various institutional bases of support, de la Madrid was well aware of growing dissatisfaction among the nation's urban popular and middle sectors. He was also aware that the new austerity plan he was under international pressure to impose called for even more drastic reductions in subsidies and public expenditures, as well as for a massive industrial restructuring (all of which suggested new profit, employment and inflationary sacrifices on the part of Mexico's citizenry) particularly in Mexico City, which had received the lion's share of federal subsidies (Connolly, 1984). Since dissatisfaction with the government was already apparent, with the acceleration of urban social movements in Mexico City in the late 1970s and early 1980s (Ramírez, 1986: 61), de la Madrid preferred to minimize additional or future protests among the urban population that might make his new economic restructuring difficult, and that might suggest an end to 70 years of one-party rule.

With these concerns in mind, President de la Madrid and several of his political allies at *Gobernacíon* (the Secretariat of the Interior) suggested the creation of a new legislative body in the Mexico City metropolitan area (de la Madrid, 1982: 26). This new body was to be governed by the principles of direct election and governance guaranteed in the constitution for all other municipal jurisdictions in Mexico except Mexico City.[14] Provisions for directly electing a governor, in all practical purposes a mayor, were equally important components of the proposed reform. Not surprisingly, President de la Madrid catered many of his statements about the new urban democratic reform to the urban middle classes, who were concerned with the absence of democratic institutions in Mexico City and who also were increasingly alarmed at the rapid deterioration in their employment prospects and overall standard of living (Comercio Exterior, December 1982: 418).[15] Even though these middle classes were not as likely to join urban social movements, they were expressing political dissatisfaction, much of which came in the form of abstentions in the 1982 presidential election (Loaeza, 1986: 232-3). At the same time, the reform was developed to appeal to the urban poor and other low-income groups that had been joining urban social movements in ever greater numbers with the advent of economic crisis (Ramírez, 1986: 67-9).

The proposed urban democratic reform was intended to create favorable conditions for structuring an efficient and decentralized administration of macroeconomic recovery plans in Mexico City.[16] Indeed, the reform was the basis for putting under popular control industrial and construction lobbies, transport and public service contractors and local patronage bosses, many of whom had supported the pro-urban-growth stance over the years. By allowing local residents more participation in the decisionmaking process, de la Madrid thought that urban democratic structures would help undermine the power of these locally entrenched construction interests who had pushed for costly and lavish urban projects in Mexico City without regard to the nation's foreign-debt obligations (see Ziccardi, 1986: 55; Iglesias, 1985: 108).

Conflicting Urban and National Priorities

The proposed reform, of course, was highly controversial. Mexico City's mayor, Ramon Aguirre, who like President de la Madrid was also a powerful party member, saw the urban democratic reform proposed by the president and his political allies as a direct threat, since it was expected to curtail power and limit functions in the mayor's own jurisdiction. He feared that by bringing direct accountability to the local citizenry, the proposed democratic reform would markedly alter the existing structure of urban decisionmaking in Mexico City as well as the types of programs and plans implemented there. This was a problem because it threatened those he relied on to manage Mexico City. Indeed, with the exception of a short period during the Echeverría presidency, most decisionmaking and urban administration in Mexico City have come under the direct influence of private-sector lobbies which have supported continued investment in construction and the infrastructure.

Why was the mayor responsive to these powerful lobbies and their efforts to fight the proposed reform? Precisely because of the leverage they already wielded over urban policy and administration in Mexico City. Their strong involvement in many projects and programs began in the 1960s when Uruchurtu was ousted from the mayorship, and over the years these local construction and engineering firms came to rank among the nation's most economically powerful conglomerates.[17] Moreover, their past experience and near monopoly over the provision of infrastructure and urban services so critical to rapid, industrialization-led development made them close to indispensable. They provided technical assistance from within and outside of the bureaucracy, and they facilitated rapid and efficient implementation of urban policy.[18] In debt-crisis conditions already seen as bringing rising dissatisfaction with the costs, extensiveness and quality of urban-service provision, the mayor, who had been in office only a few months, was understandably reluctant to alienate these technically proficient and powerful forces.[19]

In this struggle between President de la Madrid and Mayor Aguirre, then, we see several important themes, old and new. As in earlier administrations, the conflicts between the president and the mayor stemmed from their competing priorities and objectives. While this time the conflict was not over urban growth per se, but over urban control, the underlying questions were more or less the same. Were urban popular and middle-class forces going to play a role in decisions about Mexico City's development, or were powerful pro-urban-growth forces going to maintain control? Also, as in earlier periods, the conflict revolved around the nature and content of urban policy to be pursued in Mexico City, and whether it fit into the larger developmental objectives of the president. Two dimensions of this conflict were new, however. Questions of economic solvency and the fiscal implications of the reform split the mayor and the president. And, unlike in earlier mayoral-presidential conflicts, the concerns and point of view of urban popular and middle classes were actually secondary, at least if we consider that the president supported the measure as much for macroeconomic reasons as for the principled objectives of urban popular- and middle-class political participation.

Whither the Urban Popular and Middle Classes?

Precisely because the concerns of urban popular and middle classes were only indirectly represented in the conflicting positions taken by the president or the mayor, a third set of actors intervened in the debate: the party's top leadership. The third position on the reform was articulated by PRI leaders under the urging of the CNOP. They offered a compromise urban political reform, much less extreme than the president's proposal to introduce a wide-reaching democratic reform or the mayor's position that no such urban reform was necessary. Specifically, party leaders proposed to create only a new legislative body of popularly elected representatives in Mexico City and to discard any measures for direct election of the mayor. This compromise reform called for no changes in the boundaries or in the nature of the existing administrative structure in the *Distrito Federal*, and it held no provisions for overturning presidential appointment of the mayor. Party leaders proposed this compromise version because of their own specific priorities and objectives, one of which was to show responsiveness and reclaim its support among the highly mobilized, urban popular and middle classes who were slowly leaving the party and joining autonomous urban social movements.[20] Indeed, the PRI leadership reasoned that a new legislative body would not only help relegitimize the party with urban popular and middle classes, it also would absolve the party of the formal responsibility to respond to the increasingly contradictory demands posed by competing urban popular and middle class groups from within the CNOP.[21]

With the PRI leadership taking a third position on the reform, state actors now were split three ways; no compromise could be easily forged and no one set of actors wielded enough power to singularly push their position through. The debate stalled and the proposal, which still was not public, was tabled in mid-1983. However, in the wake of the 1985 election in Mexico City for representatives to the National Congress, concerns among the population that the deteriorating economic conditions were not going to brighten in the near future had surfaced boldly. The PRI gained only 42.75 percent of the local (eligible) vote, six percent lower than in 1979; and abstentions reached an unprecedented high, registering close to 50 percent in some districts of the city (*Unomásuno*, 13 July 1985; *Unomásuno*, 15 July 1985). Moreover, in the same year a city-wide organization of urban social movements, the *Coordinadora Nacional de Movimientos Urbanos Populares* (CONAMUP), reached new heights of activism and organizational strength in its challenges to the PRI, given that it united the previously disparate urban social movement organizations (Hernandez, 1986: 61).

With electoral dissatisfaction high and the organization of urban social movements at a new peak, those within the PRI and the CNOP who were most concerned about urban popular- and middle-class constituents were among the first to reintroduce the idea of urban democratic reform. Even before the issue could again work itself into a debate among the three sets of state actors, though, Mexico City was rocked by the massive earthquake of September 1985. The earthquake not only stunned the city's population and brought widespread disaster, it strengthened urban social movements and highlighted the government's inadequacy.[22] Neighborhood associations flourished in the quake's aftermath, even as the government continued to show little resolve in dealing with the injured and the thousands of homeless, and urban populations began to see themselves as functioning effectively *without* the PRI (Presidencia de la República, 1986). This was particularly the case with the city's middle classes, since two relatively affluent areas had been among those most destroyed by the quake. In coming to these conclusions, then, urban residents directly challenged the PRI's legitimate claim to authority, at least in Mexico City where the party appeared to lose its monopoly on the capacity to deliver the goods (Massolo, 1986: 196-8).

Overcoming Internal Conflict

With the elections and the earthquake occurring back to back, almost all forces within the government felt that something must be done to immediately restore public confidence, and that any prolonged debate over what type of political reform was most appropriate would not be expedient given the urgency of the situation (*Unomásuno*, 1 October 1985; *Excelsior*, 1 February 1986).[23] Given that it seemed closest to a compromise position, the PRI's initial stance gained sufficient support within the government to carry it through.[24]

To keep from losing momentum and to rapidly restore some image of political responsiveness, the PRI held public hearings on the initiative, during which it openly committed itself to the urban legislative reform.[25] Precisely because the debt crisis made political and social conditions so volatile, though, internal conflicts and governmental indecision emerged once again before the proposal for a new legislative body in Mexico City could be submitted to the National Congress and approved. As before, urban protests and growing political dissatisfaction from urban populations produced the indecision. But now protests in other regions lent greater urgency to the PRI's new-found concerns about opposition in Mexico City. The catalyst was the July 1986 election for state governors in several key states, including Chihuahua, a stronghold of conservative opposition. Although the PRI claimed victory, most doubted the results. In the ensuing cries of election fraud, the right-wing PAN organized a serious of protests and marches that garnered international attention and at times broke into violence.

This delicate situation with respect to PAN, which was increasingly becoming identified as the party of middle classes (Loaeza, 1988), coupled with the accelerated social protests that continued in Mexico City after the earthquake and the 1985 election, brought more opposition to than support for the urban democratic reform within the PRI-dominated state. The party leadership, which earlier had been so confident about its political skills and its capacity to maintain popular support, now feared that urban popular and middle classes might have greater cause to support opposition parties, who were gaining a national presence and broader political appeal as a result of the debt crisis. If introducing a local legislative body would result in the PRI losing its majority to either the PAN or some temporary coalition of right and left opposition parties, such a result could be devastating, particularly given Mexico City's centrality in national politics.

Just as important, even those allies of the president who had intransigently supported the idea of reform from the beginning also changed their position, primarily because it now appeared that their macroeconomic objectives might not be well served by such a reform. For one thing, urban social movements were starting to link their urban demands to demands about national development policies; that is, urban residents began to see their daily problems as a product of development strategies pursued by the PRI at the behest of international monetary authorities (Ziccardi, 1986: 78-80; see also Walton and Ragin, 1989). This meant that introducing these democratic mechanisms might easily guarantee national authorities less, rather than more, maneuvering room, since it would give local residents an institutional format to repudiate national austerity policies. For another, President de la Madrid and his allies now had reason to be concerned about the financial costs of successfully maintaining political power once the urban democratic structure was in place. One spokesman noted that what really dampened the original proponents' enthusiasm—in addition to concerns about popular demands for debt repudiation and other calls for major changes in macroeconomic policy that were beginning to accompany the urban social protests—was the massive amount of money the PRI had to spend just to hold its own in 1986 elections.[26] Maintaining the PRI's electoral monopoly in a more institutionally open political system, they now concluded, might require even greater amounts of money. This realization hit the de la Madrid team of proponents where it most mattered: it directly jeopardized their austerity programs and macroeconomic recovery plans.

Failed Urban Democratic Reform: The Beginning of the End

Just as rapidly as it had risen to prominence, then, the compromise proposal for a democratically elected legislature was no longer seen as beneficial or expedient, but as a risky measure that might be too radical in such volatile conditions. With diminishing support for urban democratic reform from almost all quarters within the government, the question now was what to do. Because public audiences had been held and expectations raised in Mexico City about a substantive political change, the idea could not be dropped entirely. Doing so would be political suicide, giving a clear indication that the ruling party was opposed to democratic participation in Mexico City after all. This thought was already widely held by many urban residents and right- and left-wing opposition parties who criticized the limited nature of the publicly-offered compromise and argued for direct mayoral election as the principal route toward democratic change (SIPRO, 1987: 55). Yet internal divisiveness was so great that no consensus on the three proposals could be reached either, even the moderate compromise first offered by the PRI leadership.

Caught in the midst of social pressures from outside the state and growing conflicts within, state actors muddled through to an entirely new stance: a proposed local assembly to be called the *Asamblea del Distrito Federal*. The representatives to the new *asamblea* were to be directly elected, but the assembly was to hold no legislative power. Indeed, its activities were limited to channeling recommendations and nonbinding initiatives concerning programs and policies administered in Mexico City. The assembly, in fact, was only a slightly more sophisticated version of the current *delegado* system in Mexico City.

This proposal was quickly approved by the National Congress in April 1987 with relatively little debate. Given the high expectations and the seriousness of the political crisis in Mexico City at the time, however, this *asamblea* turned out to be more of an embarrassment for the PRI than anything else. One national subsecretary called it "the reform that nobody wanted," and in very uncharacteristic fashion, once the bill was passed it received little party fanfare or press attention. Government spokesmen all but ignored it, and several prominent PRI leaders actually criticized the plan in public. One esteemed senator even labeled it "insufficient" in a public statement covered by all the major newspapers (SIPRO, 1987: 55). Social movement organizations and opposition leaders, who might have responded more favorably to a more substantive democratic reform, openly called it a joke and made clear their recognition that it would make no substantive changes in urban governance in Mexico City (SIPRO, 1987: 55). In short, introducing this emasculated version of the original proposal for urban democratic reform did little to address the growing legitimation crisis facing the PRI vis-a-vis its urban popular- and middle-class constituents in Mexico City. On the contrary, its limited scope underscored the image of a political system that was unwilling—or unable—to respond to allow urban residents direct political participation.

As a result, political dissatisfaction and cynicism among urban popular and middle classes in Mexico City reached new heights in 1987, and scarcely a year later the PRI saw the results. Opposition candidate Cuauhtémoc Cárdenas swept Mexico City in the July 1988 presidential elections, defeating PRI candidate Carlos Salinas. Nationally, Cárdenas also fared relatively well; he received 39 percent of the official vote, compared to 51 percent for Salinas. For the first time in close to half a century, opposition parties, combined, gained more national electoral support (59 percent) than did the PRI's candidate (51 percent).

City, State and Politics in Mexico: Some Concluding Remarks

Institutional and political divisions within the Mexican state, generated by ongoing conflicts over urban policies, have contributed to growing political dissatisfaction of urban popular and middle classes and thus to the PRI's steadily declining electoral support. The 1988 presidential election results attest to this in two specific ways. First, opposition candidate Cuauhtémoc Cárdenas relied on urban popular sectors, many of whom were urban social-movement participants, for much of his grass-roots support (Gilly, 1990). Second, observers also note that significant portions of the middle class, particularly those concerned with austerity and deteriorating living conditions, supported Cárdenas as well, much to the surprise of the right-wing PAN, which polled the same degree of support as it had in the last presidential election. That urban popular and middle classes were among those most likely to support Cárdenas is also made clear by the fact that Cárdenas overwhelmingly defeated PRI candidate Salinas in Mexico City, the only place besides his home state of Michoacan where the opposition leader received such uniform and overwhelming support. Of course, Cárdenas also received electoral support from workers who were increasingly disenfranchised from the party. Yet given the importance of demands for democratic participation in Cárdenas's campaign, the PRI's failure to implement a veritable urban democratic reform in Mexico City undoubtedly contributed to the groundswell of support for Cárdenas from urban popular and middle classes, who had clamored most for this democratic reform.

Cárdenas, however, was successful in rallying the support of urban popular and middle classes not only because of their political dissatisfaction; he also was aided by previously-loyal party leaders with past institutional linkages to these populations, who themselves were abandoning the PRI. Many of Cárdenas' strategists and strongest political allies, such as Porfirio Muñoz Ledo, also were ex-party leaders who had been active within the CNOP. Until he formally left the party in late 1987, in fact, Cárdenas himself was an active PRI member who geared much of his reformism to the disenfranchised urban popular and middle classes. And Cárdenas clearly maintained connections with the CNOP and its constituents even when he began to distance himself from the PRI leadership. This is evidenced by the fact that the CNOP publicly supported Cárdenas when other party leaders first demanded his expulsion in spring 1987 (*La Jornada*, 30 June 1987: 4). Accordingly, while the organized-labor sector stayed publicly loyal to Salinas throughout the presidential campaign, many observers note that the CNOP played a much smaller role than in the past.

That the CNOP and its previously loyal members lent even a limited amount of support, most of it covert, to the Cárdenas campaign underscores the importance of conflicts within the state itself in the recent electoral outcomes and the near demise of the PRI. Indeed, the disloyalty of this cadre of party activists would have been almost unthinkable in the past. Yet it is not so now that internal conflicts have destroyed the party's cohesion and consensus, particularly with respect to the social and political demands of the urban popular and middle classes: the failed urban democratic reform is perhaps the most striking example of this. Accordingly, it is not surprising that many previously loyal leaders and followers of the CNOP have lost faith in the party leadership's capacity and legitimacy to rule and have thrown their support to an opposition candidate who spoke more directly to their concerns.

On a more theoretical level, these findings suggest several important things about the origins of political change, the nature of the state and the future of one-party rule in Mexico. For one, the fact that rapid and concentrated urbanization played a central role in bringing organized political opposition and intrastate conflicts suggests a new twist on prevailing arguments about the relationship between urbanization and political change in developing countries like Mexico (see Huntington and Nelson, 1976). Of course, many already have noted that it is not changing values or higher education levels, or even the more ready access to information accompanying the growth of cities, that link urbanization to political change. Rather, rapid urbanization negatively affects people's everyday lives, which in turn inspires urban residents to organize and make political demands about their local needs and living conditions (see Walton and Sween, 1973). While our case supports these findings, we have also seen that it is much more complex than that, at least in Mexico: urbanization brings competing urban priorities and divisions within the state, which make state actors unwilling or incapable of responding to urban demands. Thus, the mobilization of urban populations and their growing support for opposition candidates can also be traced to the inadequacies of the incorporated political system, which over the years has offered fewer and fewer formal mechanisms for urban populations to successfully present their grievances or truly participate in decisionmaking.

This conclusion suggests that we might look more carefully at claims about democratization coming from the most recent urban social movement literature. Clearly, this literature takes us far by underscoring the importance of urban social movements in mobilizing political opposition and creating legitimization problems for state actors (see Henry, 1985; Mainwaring and Viola, 1984). Its weakness, nonetheless, comes from what it ignores: the critical role played by state actors and the sources of their incapacity to respond to growing urban social pressures. Most important, perhaps, is that those arguing that urban social movements contribute to greater democratization by creating a grass-roots democratic culture (see Mainwaring, 1987) are surprisingly silent on how or why urban mobilizations, in particular, are influential in this regard. Our findings suggest, though, that the urban context in which mobilizations arise is a critical element; it helps us understand the nature and historical origins of the pressures from below, why they are not channeled into formal politics, how they are interpreted by state actors and the extent to which state actors can respond to these pressures.

Our discussion, however, also shows that why the urban domain is so critical has as much to do with the incorporated political system and the ways it structures political participation and political consciousness as with the nature of urban problems per se. The implications for understanding the nature and future of state power in Mexico are striking, since it suggests that growing intrastate conflicts, the rise of urban social movements and declining political support for Mexico's PRI rests on the obsolescence of its class-based system of incorporation. While this system sustained political stability for many decades, with rapid urbanization its internal contradictions and external weaknesses emerged, leading to the current crisis and an uncertain political future.

To note the obsolescence of the class-based political system, however, is not to say that recent changes in Mexican politics cannot be understood with a view to class relationships or class identities. On the contrary, it may be that the class-based structures of the corporatist system have produced a common "class" consciousness among urban popular and middle classes, at least if we see class identity as influenced by common urban experiences and common patterns of political and economic exclusion (see Katznelson, 1981), if we identify urban popular and middle sectors as "intermediate classes" caught somewhere between large capital and organized labor and if we see class identity as much a defensive as an offensive posture. Accordingly, to the extent that popular and middle classes in Mexico have defined urban demands as among the most pressing in their daily lives, or they have started to see their own interests as politically and economically distinct from those of capital and labor (who in contrast have monopolized political privileges within the incorporated political system) then it may well be a common intermediate class identity that has driven them to repudiate the ruling party and the incorporated political system and to support opposition candidates.

Of course, those occupations falling into this intermediate class category are quite diverse with respect to lifestyle, ideology and income. This might ultimately prevent them from staying unified as a powerful political force to challenge the PRI's political hegemony, particularly if the incorporated political structures that group them together as a collectivity disappear and are replaced by democratic structures that drive them to participate in politics as individuals. More important, the very real differences between them may make some urban popular and middle classes support right-wing opposition parties while others support the left, something that also increases the PRI's capacity to hold a monopoly on political power. But this is not always the case: Cárdenas's recent electoral challenge to the PRI was unprecedented precisely because it united urban popular and middle sectors that had been divided, and divided state actors who once had been united. Urban problems plaguing Mexico City helped set the stage for this fateful and historic turn of events. Whether they will continue to keep the PRI weak and a diverse opposition movement strong remains to be seen.

Notes

1. Interviews were conducted with individuals from the following: Government agencies: Secretaría de Programación y Presupuesto, Secretaría de Gobernación, Gobierno del Distrito Federal, Secretaría de Desarrollo Urbano y Ecología, Renovación Popular, Comisión de Vialidad y Transporte and the Comisión Nacional de Salubridad Popular. Political parties: Partido Revolucionario Institucional (PRI) (including special interviews in the Confederación Nacional de Organizaciones Populares), Partido de Acción Nacional (PAN) and Partido Socialista Unido de Mexico (PSUM). Urban social movements: Confederacíon Nacional de Movimientos Urbanos Populares (CONAMUP), Asamblea de Barrios and Mujeres Para el Diálogo. In the interests of protecting sources, no names and few direct quotes are used in this article. However, all statements about party involvement in urban policy conflicts have been corroborated by at least two sources.

2. Still, the political participation of these class-specific organizations was always mediated by the party's centralized leadership, which also worked closely with the businessmen's federations, which were also relatively well organized, albeit outside the formal confines of the party (see Bravo Ahuja and Michel, 1976). At that historical moment, then, it made sense to build a political system around the institutionalized inclusion of laborers and peasants.

3. Although both the military and bureaucrats were active participants in the PRM, in those first years they did not have their own institutional sectors for channeling this participation, like peasants and organized labor.

4. There is some controversy about the inclusion of teachers in the CNOP, which is worth noting because it sheds light on the problematic nature of the CNOP's identity as a sector for "popular middle classes." Because the teachers' union was highly organized, and in fact had participated within the labor federation before the formation of the CNOP, some scholars suggest that the formation of the CNOP, or at least the inclusion of teachers within it, was dictated by the party's concerns with dividing opposition within the organized working class. A closer historical reading of the evidence, however, shows that even before the formation of the CTM, teachers (who may indeed be "workers," but under very different productive conditions than factory workers, say) had been organized with other artisans and middle-class professions in the Confederación Regional de Obreros Mexicanos (CROM). Moreover, over the late teens and twenties the CROM had distanced itself from another organization (the Confederación General de Trabajadores) representing factory laborers and other more proletarianized professions that would come to form the basic constituency of the CTM, thereby suggesting the class logic of dividing the CTM from the CNOP (see Davis, forthcoming).

5. Because their jobs were often at stake, the organized-labor sector represented by the CTM tended to ally with the spokesmen for business in the party, who tended to promote rapid industrialization, and thus rapid urbanization, at any cost (see Barkin and Esteva, 1986: 138; Carr, 1986: 209-10). Of course, this is not to say that organized labor never acted independently of capital. Rather, it suggests that labor's concerns as producers tended to outflank its concerns as urban consumers, at least as represented by the CTM. For a more thorough discussion of the labor movement and its uneasy relationships with the CTM and the PRI leadership, see Carr, 1986 and Trejo Delarbre, 1986.

   I do not want to imply that urban demands of popular or middle classes were never met. The urban services were extended to squatter areas on certain occasions and Mexico City was beautified. But these policies were generally implemented only when they were compatible with larger development objectives or also promoted by capitalists (see Perlo, 1982: 41) or real estate developers (see Ramírez, 1986: 38-9; Schteingart and Perlo, 1984: 110-12).

6. This is not to say that Mexico's urban middle classes were politically inconsequential. In a study of Mexico's middle classes from the Revolution through the mid-1960s, Soledad Loaeza (1988) carefully documents the important role they played in legitimizing the PRI and in forcing certain accommodations from the leadership. She also notes, however, that it was not until the 1960s that middle-class activism generated party responsiveness, and this came as much from general social pressure as through their representative organization, the CNOP. In fact, Loaeza suggests that middle classes actually mediate between the political and social systems in Mexico (Loaeza, 1986: 229), a view that suggests their exclusion from the party's corporatist structures.

7. While of course the protests at Tlatelolco were directed to much more substantive concerns than simply urban issues or demands, concerns were expressed about conspicuous consumption on nonessential urban redevelopment. Moreover, the ways the government responded brought a loss of legitimacy vis-a-vis middle classes that the PRI had not yet faced (see Hellman, 1978: 30-48).

8. Castells (1977: 1189-91), in fact, argues that Echeverría used urban policies to empower independent forces within the organized labor movement, thereby challenging the efficacy of the CTM as run by its leader, Fidel Velazquez.

9. Indeed, conflicts within the party surfaced over Echeverría's urban orientation several months after he took office. As a result, Echeverría was challenged by forces tied to Díaz Ordaz and other progrowth forces who used the CNOP and the Mexico City mayorship to launch an attack on the president and his urban-oriented, populist agenda (Davis, 1986: 278; Hellman, 1978: 163, 170). Echeverría was successful in forcing the resignation of then-Mayor Alfonso Martínez Domínguez, who was linked to ex-President Díaz Ordaz and other pro-urban-growth forces in the party; and after appointing a new mayor who served as his political ally, Echeverría was able to effectively control urban policy in the capital. However, the conflicts over urban policy and Echeverría's urban popular- and middle-class constituency continued throughout his term.

10. It is noteworthy that while these movements tended to blossom in *barrios populares*, or so-called popular neighborhoods, all over the city some of the first originated in the oldest neighborhoods (Moctezuma and Navarro, 1980, c.f. Ramírez, 1986: 43), which also held concentrations of artisans, street vendors, small shopkeepers and others who at one time were considered critical constituents of the CNOP.

11. Figures on the strength of urban social movements are hard to come by. Most scholars of urban social movements in Mexico, in fact, do not give numbers in their accounts. Part of this has to do with the large number of local organizations, which began to organize themselves in a larger network only in the late 1970s. In a case study of one such organization, the Unión de Colonias Populares del Valle de México, however, Ramírez (1986: 141) identifies its membership at approximately 2,000 by 1981. If we take into account that Ramírez names and identifies 87 different urban movements as active in the Mexico City metropolitan area (1986: 81-3), we can estimate that participation hovered around 180,000.

12. These general conclusions about the relationship between the debt crisis and urban mobilization in Mexico are consistent with recent research findings from several eminent Latin American urbanists. In a comparative research project on social protests in 13 Latin American countries, urbanization was found to be highly correlated with social protests during debt crises (Walton and Ragin, 1989: 226; see also Walton, 1989). And a recently published study of urbanization patterns in Latin America during the debt crisis shows that formal-sector employment declines and informal sector employment rises with debt crises, which further concentrates dissatisfaction and protest at the neighborhood and community level as much as in the workplace (Portes, 1989: 26-32; Portes and Johns, 1989: 118-19).

13. According to Peter Ward (1986: 9), "(a)s a proportion of total expenditure, (government investment in) social development has declined from an average of almost 23 percent under Echeverría (1970-76) to around 18 percent during the following six years, with a particularly sharp fall from 1980 onwards."

14. In fact, in prerevolutionary periods and up through the first two decades of revolutionary rule, Mexico City was organized around a municipal structure that provided such rights. In 1928, though, after much debate about establishing Mexico City as a Federal District (*Distrito Federal*) much along the same principles governing other national capitals such as Washington, D.C., the municipal system was eliminated and replaced by the current system

with no direct electoral representation. Since that time, Mexico City's mayor has been appointed by the president, and any deliberations over local concerns have been undertaken in the national legislature along with other national issues.

15. For example, reduced subsidies, removal of protective measures, rapid inflation and higher costs of imports for domestic businesses, principal components of stabilization and austerity policies demanded by the IMF, are disadvantaging small and medium-sized firms (Estrategia, 1983: 56; Comercio Exterior, December 1982: 418), and thus they create concern among this vocal and well-organized sector of Mexico's urban middle classes, most of whom technically fall under the organization of the CNOP. With reduced government expenditures mandated by stabilization policies as well, middle-class employees in the government, such as doctors, teachers and lower-level bureaucrats, are now directly threatened, since layoffs in the public sector are a common cost-cutting measure. Moreover, an increase in the value-added tax, inflation and the rising costs of luxury and other foreign imports bring higher costs for non-essential commodities. They also contribute to a reduction of single-family housing construction and higher interest rates for housing mortgages, and they have produced up to 100 percent increases in the cost of private education (Comercio Exterior, June 1982: 205).

16. Clearly, the urban democratic reform proposed by President de la Madrid concerned more than "home rule," or the struggle for local representation in a capital city, a common problem recently seen in such cities as Washington, D.C. and Paris. Given the potential national repercussions of growing political dissatisfaction among Mexico City's residents, as well as the fact that the proposed reform also grew out of a concern for facilitating national recovery, maintaining international credit-worthiness and creating an efficient and productive economic environment for the nation's largest and most promising industries, it must be seen as much a national as a local issue.

17. One of the best known is Ingenieros Civiles Asociados (ICA), Mexico's largest construction firm, also involved in industry and real estate development, which essentially has controlled urban infrastructural policy in Mexico since the 1960s (see Davis, 1986). This, in fact, helps explain the limited power of urban popular and middle classes to affect urban policy programs and decisions in Mexico City in subsequent periods.

18. Another set of forces in Mexico City that strengthened Mayor Aguirre's decision to oppose the proposed urban reform were the planners, technicians and career bureaucrats in Mexico City's government, many of whom constituted Aguirre's political team and thus buttressed his political power within the PRI. Though of course there were exceptions, by and large local technocrats also tended to oppose the urban political reform proposed by Gobernacion because they feared it would infringe upon their professional autonomy and responsibility. With greater citizen access to and participation in programming and policymaking, planners and bureaucrats would be limited in their actions. Many of the technocrats employed in the local bureaucracy, moreover, were directly networked with powerful private sector firms, since a common pattern in Mexico is for planners and other technicians (generally engineers and architects) to move back and forth between public and private sector jobs, relying on contacts and expertise accumulated in each domain to grease the wheels of policy implementation and contracting.

19. We must also recognize that Mayor Aguirre may have had his own reasons for opposing the reform. It was widely known that Aguirre had strong presidential aspirations, and because of this he wanted to leave unblemished his image as one with full control over Mexico City. Since the reform would make him a lame duck, so to speak, and thus prevent him from fostering political linkages, wielding power and maintaining a good administrative reputation, he opposed the reform for personal reasons as well. Moreover, from the point of view of legitimizing the political system through popular participation and absorbing future urban grievances, the mayor's office also felt the *delegado* system itself might sufficiently serve such a purpose. With a system of limited participation already in place, one which was complementary rather than threatening to the existing power structure (see Gilbert and Ward, 1985), the mayor saw little need for supporting the president's proposed urban reform.

20. Of course, because the PRI represents labor and the peasantry as well as urban popular and middle classes, there were substantial differences in opinion within the PRI over the urban democratic reform (*La Jornada*, July 25, 1986). While the CNOP tended to support the idea of the compromise reform, the PRI's strongest sector, the CTM, actively opposed it (Sánchez Vázquez, 1986). Moreover, even within the CNOP there was not necessarily consensus, which is not unusual since it is such a large and heterogeneous organization. Nonetheless, according to a wide range of informants, the balance of support within the PRI was for the compromise reform, given the growing crisis of legitimacy vis-a-vis urban popular and middle classes.

21. According to high-level PRI members whom I interviewed, the compromise proposal for a new legislative body was seen to be one that served two important objectives: 1) bringing middle classes back into direct engagement with the political system; and 2) providing a format in which urban groups would recognize that their conflicts and problems are among themselves, not between them and the government.

22. For more detailed discussion of this see the April 1986 issue of the *Revista Mexicana de Sociología*, entitled "Sismo: Desastre y Sociedad en la Ciudad de Mexico."

23. In fact, in December 1985 the CNOP held a national convention to discuss its growing political problems. Two of the main topics addressed by the delegates were the extent to which the CNOP had a unifying purpose, given that "the members of each its (affiliated) groups had different interests," and the growing perception that "there was a conflict or rivalry between the three sectors of the PRI" (*Unomásuno*, Dec. 18, 1985: 4).

24. While some of the president's political allies still actively supported the more wide-reaching reform, even they were beginning to recognize that the economic situation was not going to markedly improve between that point (1985) and 1988, when national elections were to be held. Since the urban protests and disastrous local governmental response to the earthquake had all but eliminated Mayor Aguirre's independent political influence, for the first time the PRI leadership faced relatively little opposition over the compromise reform.

25. Two factors weighed heavily in the decision to hold public hearings. First, remnants of controversy and disagreement between the different sets of state actors still existed (*La Jornada*, 25 July 1986). Clearly, to legitimize forceful pursuit of the centrist path in the midst of internal conflict, it was important for the PRI leadership to tap, if not generate, widespread public support for the initiative. With the public forum, then, the PRI took advantage of external forces and conditions to justify and politically reinforce its own intermediate alternative. Indeed, one journalist noted that the public hearings "only constituted the formalization of an already 'cooked' process" (*El Diá*, 22 July 1986). Second, the social and economic conditions following the 1985 elections and earthquake were highly volatile, marked by regular marches to the city's central plaza, or Zocalo, and by a growing visibility of the city's urban social movements. In such conditions the PRI thought the public hearings themselves would serve as a format for offering an immediate and notable degree of citizen participation, giving clear kudos to

the PRI by evidencing its responsiveness to social demands and the idea of democratic participation.

26. One informant noted that the PRI's coffers were practically empty after spending inordinate sums of money on campaigning in the northern states in the 1986 elections. Even with such expenditures their claims to victory were widely challenged.

References

Ames, B. (1969) Bases de Apoyo del Partido Dominante en México, *Foro Internacional, 41*(1): 32-49.

Barkin, D. and G. Esteva (1986) Social conflict and inflation in Mexico. In N. Hamilton and T.F. Harding (Eds.), *Modern Mexico: State, Economy, and Social Conflict.* Beverly Hills and London: Sage: 128-48.

Basañez, M. (1981) *La Lucha por Hegemonía en México, 1968-1980.* México, D.F.: Siglo Veintiuno.

Bassols, M. and A. Delgado (1985) "La CNOP y las Organizaciones de Colonos." Paper presented at the Seminar on the State and Urban Social Movements, Universidad Nacional Autonoma de México, August.

Bravo Ahuja, V. and M.A. Michel (1976) Alianza de clases y dominación: México, 1930-1946, *Historia y Sociedad, 9*: 49-78.

Carr, B. (1986) The Mexican economic debacle and the labor movement: A new era or more of the same?" In N. Hamilton and T. F. Harding (Eds.), *Modern Mexico: State, Economy, and Social Conflict.* Beverly Hills and London: Sage: 205-33.

Castells, M. (1983) *The City and the Grassroots: A Cross-cultural Theory of Urban Social Movements.* Los Angeles and Berkeley: University of California Press.

Castells, M. (1977) Apuntes para un análisis de clase de la política urbana del Estado Méxicano, *Revista Méxicana de Sociologiá*, 1161-91.

Cockcroft, J. (1983) *Mexico: Class Formation, Capital Accumulation, and the State*. New York: Monthly Review Press.

Comercio Exterior, December 1982: 418.

Comercio Exterior, June 1982: 205.

Connolly, P. (1984) Finanzas públicas y estado local: El caso del departamento del distrito federal, *Revista Azcapotzalco, 5*(11): 57-91.

Córdova, A. (1972) *La Formación del Poder Político en México.* Mexico, D.F.: Ediciones Era.

Cornelius, W. (1975) *Politics and the Migrant Poor in Mexico.* Stanford, CA: Stanford University Press.

Davis, D.E. (1986) The rise and fall of Mexico City's subway (METRO) policy, 1964-1976: Urban policy, national development strategies, and the state in contemporary Mexico. Unpublished Ph.D. thesis, University of California at Los Angeles.

Davis, D.E. (forthcoming) *Rapid Transit to Ruin: State, Class, and Urban Conflict in the Transformation of Contemporary Mexico, 1910-1988.*

de la Madrid, M. (1982) *Nacionalismo Revolucionario: Siete Tesis Fundamentales de Campaña.* Mexico, D.F: Partido Revolucionario Institucional.

(El) Diá (1986) "Voz Popular: Municipios Sí, Delegaciones No," 22 July: 3.

Estrategia (1983) "Las Capas Medias Entre la Espada y la Pared," vol. 51: 56.

Excélsior (1986) "El Pueblo se Inquietará si los Recursos Para la Reconstruccion no son Empleados Ahora," 1 February: 4a.

Garza, G. (1985) *El Proceso de Industrializacion en la Ciudad de México, 1821-1970.* Mexico, D.F.: El Colegio de México.

Gilbert, A. and P. Ward (1985) *Housing, the State, and the Urban Poor.* London: Cambridge University Press.

Gilly, A. (1990) Opposition politics in Mexico, *Journal of International Affairs, 43*(2), in press.

González Casanova, P. (1970) *Democracy in Mexico.* New York: Oxford University Press.

Hamilton, N. (1986) Mexico: The limits of state autonomy. In N. Hamilton and T.F. Harding, *Modern Mexico: State, Economy, and Social Conflict.* Beverly Hills and London: Sage: 67-106.

Hellman, J.A. (1978) *Mexico in Crisis.* New York: Holmes and Meyer.

Henry, E. (1985) Urban social movements in Latin America: Towards a critical understanding. In D. Slater (Ed.), *New Social Movements and the State in Latin America.* Netherlands: CEDLA: 127-47.

Hernandez, R. (1987) *La Coordinadora Nacional del Movimiento Urbano Popular (CONAMUP): Su Historia 1980-1986.* Mexico, D.F.: Equipo Pueblo.

Huntington, S. and J. Nelson (1976) *No Easy Choice: Political Participation in Developing Countries.* Cambridge: Harvard University Press.

Iglesias, P. (1985) La política financiera pública del D.F., 1970-1983, *Revista Azcapotzalco, 6*(15): 107-23.

Katznelson, I. (1981) *City Trenches: Urban Politics and the Patterning of Class in America.* New York: Pantheon.

(La) Jornada (1987) "La CNOP No Pidio La Expulsion De La Corriente Democrática, Aseguro Guillermo Fonseca Alvarez," 30 June: 4.

(La) Jornada (1987) "La Crisis Ha Representado Un Riesgo Para La Estabilidad Social: MMH," 20 June: 3.

(La) Jornada (1987) "Cierre De Pequenas Empresas Por La Apertura Comercial," 19 June: 15.

(La) Jornada (1986) "El Partido Contra El Presidente?" 25 July: 2.

Labastida, J. (1977) Proceso político y dependencia en México: 1970-1976, *Revista Méxicana de Sociologiá, 39*(1): 193-227.

Leal, J.F. (1986) The Mexican state: 1915-1973: A historical interpretation. In

N. Hamilton and T.F. Harding (Eds.), *Modern Mexico: State, Economy, and Social Conflict.* Beverly Hills and London: Sage: 21-43.

Leduc, R. (1966) Bulldozers y Diputados, *Siempre*, September 21: 18.

Lerner, B. and S. Ralsky (1976) *El Poder de los Presidentes: Alcances y Perspectivas (1910-1973).* Mexico, D.F.: Instituto Méxicano de Estudios Políticos, A.C.

Loaeza, S. (1988) *Clases Medias y Politica en México.* Mexico, D.F.: El Colegio de México.

Loaeza, S. (1986) Las Clases Medias Méxicanos y la Coyuntura Económica Actual. In P. González Casanova (Ed.), *México Ante la Crisis: El Impacto Social y Cultural/Las Alternativas.* Mexico, D.F.: Siglo Veintiuno: 221-38.

Mainwaring, S. (1987) Urban popular movements, identity, and democratization in Brazil, *Comparative Political Studies, 20*(2): 131-59.

Mainwaring, S. and E. Viola (1984) New social movements, political culture, and democracy: Brazil and Argentina in the 1980's, *Telos, 61*: 17-47.

Massolo, A. (1986) Que el Gobierno Entienda, lo Primero es la vivienda! *Revista Méxicana de Sociologia, 48*(2): 195-239.

Michaels, A.L. (1971) Las elecciones de 1940, *Historia Méxicana, 21*(1): 80-134.

Moctezuma, P. and B. Navarro (1980) Las luchas urbanos populares en la coyuntura actual, *Teoría y Política* (5): 101-24.

Muñoz, H., O. de Oliveira, and C. Stern (1980) Migración y marginalidad ocupacional en la ciudad de México. In *El Perfil de México, 3.* Mexico, D.F.: Siglo Veintiuno: 327-59.

Newell, R. and L. Rubio. (1984) *Mexico's Dilemma: The Political Origins of Economic Crisis.* Boulder and London: Westview Press.

Ocampo, T. (1967) *México: Huelga de la UNAM, Marzo-Mayo, 1966.* Cuernavaca, Mexico: Centro Intercultural de Documentación.

Partido Revolucionario Institucional (1984a) *Historia Documental de la CNOP*, vol. I. Mexico, D.F.: Edicap.

Partido Revolucionario Institucional (1984b) *Historia Documental de la CNOP*, vol. II. Mexico, D.F.: Edicap.

Perlo, M. (1982) *Política y Vivienda en México, 1910-1952.* Mexico, D.F: Instituto de Investigaciones Sociales, UNAM.

Perlo, M. (1981) Apuntes para una interpretacion en torno al proceso de acumulación capitalista y las políticas urbanas del D.F., 1920-1980, unpublished manuscript, Instituto de Investagaciones Sociales, Universidad Nacional Autonoma de México (UNAM).

Portes, A. (1989) Latin American urbanization during the years of the crisis, *Latin American Research Review, 24*(4): 7-44.

Portes, A. and M. Johns (1989) The polarization of class and space in the contemporary Latin American City." In W. Canak (Ed.), *Lost Promises: Debt, Austerity, and Development in Latin America.* Boulder: Westview

Press: 111-38.
Presidencia de la República (1986) *Terremotos de Septiembre: Sobretiro de las Razones y las Obras.* Mexico, D.F.: Fondo de Cultura Economica.
Purcell, S.K. (1973) Decision-making in an authoritarian regime: Theoretical implications for a Mexican case study, *World Politics, 26*(1): 28-53.
Purcell, S.K. and J. Purcell (1977) Mexican business and public policy. In J. Malloy (Ed.), *Authoritarianism and Corporatism in Latin America.* Pittsburgh: University of Pittsburgh Press.
Ramírez, J. (1986) *El Movimiento Urbano Popular en México.* Mexico, D.F.: Siglo Veintiuno.
Reyna, J.L. (1971) *An Empirical Analysis of Political Mobilization: The Case of Mexico.* Ithaca, N.Y.: Cornell University Press.
Reyna, J.L. (1974) *Control Político, Estabilidad, y Desarrollo.* Mexico, D.F.: El Colegio de México, Cuadernos del CES #3.
Saldívar, A. (1981) *Ideología y Práctica del Estado Méxicano: El Conflicto Estado-Inciativa Privada, 1970-1976.* Mexico, D.F.: Universidad Nacional Autonoma de México.
Sánchez Vázquez, S. (1986) "La CTM y la Renovación Electoral en el D.F." *El Diá*, 2 August.
Schteingart, M. and M. Perlo (1984) Movimientos sociales urbanos en México, *Revista Méxicana de Sociologia, 46*(4): 105-27.
Siempre (1966) "Uruchurtu hizo un milagro," 21 September: 5.
SIPRO (1987) Cronologías e indicaciones internacionales y nacionales, *Síntesis de Prensa de Diciembre, 3*(30).
Sirvent, C. (1975) La burocracia política central en el sistema de dominación Mexicano, Doctoral Dissertation, Universidad Nacional Autonoma de Mexico.
Smith, P. (1979) *Labyrinths of Power: Political Recruitment in Twentieth Century Mexico.* Princeton: Princeton University Press.
Stevens, E. (1977) *Protest and Response in Mexico.* Cambridge: MIT Press.
Toledo, M. (1986) La crisis ecológica. In P. González Casanova, *México Ante la Crisis.* Mexico, D.F.: Siglo Veintiuno.
Trejo Delarbre, R. (1986) The Mexican labor movement: 1917-1975. In N. Hamilton and T.F. Harding (Eds.), *Modern Mexico: State, Economy, and Social Conflict.* Beverly Hills and London: Sage: 177-205.
Unikel, L. (1976) *El Desarrollo Urbano de México.* Mexico, D.F.: El Colegio de México.
(El) Universal (1965) "Servicio Camionero," 7 July: 11.
Unomásuno (1985) "Reconoce El PSUM Su Derrota En Los 40 Distritos del D.F.," 13 July: 1.
Unomásuno (1985) "D.F.: 50% de Abstención y 40 Triunfos Del PRI," 15 July: 1.

Unomásuno (1985) "Proponen Diputados Priistas Crear un Plan Nacional de Participación Ciudadana En Casos De Destastres," 1 October: 11.

Unomásuno (1985) "El PRI Afronta Problemas Y Pierde Elecciones Cuando Selecciona A Malos Candidatos: CNOP," 18 December: 4.

Unomásuno (1987) "Las Medidas Económicas De México, Basadas En El FMI, Son El Camino Adecuado: Mendoza Fernández," 27 May: 14.

Walton, J. (1989) Debt, protest, and the state in Latin America. In S. Eckstein (Ed.), *Power and Popular Protest: Latin American Social Movements.* Berkeley: University of California Press.

Walton, J. and C. Ragin (1989) Austerity and dissent: Social bases of popular struggle in Latin America. In W. Canak (Ed.), *Debt, Austerity, and Development in Latin America.* Boulder: Westview Press.

Walton, J. and J. Sween (1973) Urbanization, industrialization, and voting in Mexico: A longitudinal analysis of official and opposition party support, *Social Science Quarterly, 52*(3).

Ward, P. (1986) *Welfare Politics in Mexico: Papering Over the Cracks.* Boston: Allen and Unwin.

Ziccardi, A. (1986) Problemas urbanos: Proyectos y alternativas ante la crisis. In P. González Casanova, *México Ante la Crisis.* Mexico, D.F.: Siglo Veintiuno.

MOVING TOWARD DEMOCRACY?
SOUTH KOREAN POLITICAL CHANGE IN THE 1980s

David A. Smith
University of California, Irvine

Su-Hoon Lee
Institute for Far Eastern Studies, Seoul

The 1980s were widely heralded as a decade of democratization throughout the world. Scholarly arguments about the affinity between "bureaucratic-authoritarian regimes" and rapid economic development gave way to analysis of the "transitions to democracy." This paper examines the movement toward political liberalization in South Korea during this past decade. It begins by examining how the Republic of Korea's (ROK) pattern of "dependent development" and semiperipheral status in the world constrains its internal politics and class structures. Understanding the international political-economic context also illuminates the structural openings that can be used by the proponents of democracy. The main focus of this paper is on the societal forces within *South Korea that affect its politics. The key role of the ROK state in directing the "economic miracle," and the relationship that developed among the state, capital and labor during the past 30 years, is highlighted. We isolate crucial collective political actors–industrial workers, students and intellectuals, business groups, technocrats, the military, the urban semiproletariat–and discuss their current and/or potential role in the struggle for democratization. The conclusion traces political changes through mid-1989, emphasizing the incomplete nature of the accomplished reforms and the potential complications that the reunification issue raises for further democratization. We conclude that the political reform movement faces a number of structural constraints generated by issues of international competitiveness and the configuration of interests in the domestic political economy. This suggests that, at best, South Korea is likely to end up with a "restricted" or "controlled" form of democracy.*

In the late spring and early summer of 1989, the world's attention was riveted on China, where students and workers galvanized a movement demanding democratization, only to be met, ultimately, by machine guns and armored personnel carriers on the bloody streets of Beijing. While the events unfolded on Tiananmen Square, a longer-running struggle for political liberalization continued in Seoul. In this paper we will examine this contest for democracy in South Korea and the social forces and movements on both sides.

The South Korean battle for democratization has attracted far less media attention in the West than recent events in China. On the surface one is tempted to attribute this to less violence and loss of life. Korean protests in the last two or three years have become highly ritualized affairs: heaved Molotov cocktails and police beatings have led to many injuries but few deaths. "The Kwangju incident" in 1979, however, in which the South Korean military massacred hundreds and perhaps thousands of demonstrators, has an almost eerie resemblance to the bloodshed in Beijing, right down to government efforts to deny and cover up the magnitude of the repression. (Geo-politics probably has more to do with the attention being focused on Beijing rather than Seoul.) Demonstrators in China are battling against a communist regime; in South Korea, the government is stridently anticommunist and a staunch U.S. ally. Opinion leaders and citizens in the West find it much easier to sympathize with protestors battling political injustice imposed by leaders whose ideology and allegiances are supposedly antithetical to their own. While Chinese students are now seen as courageous fighters for basic freedoms and human rights, Korean demonstrators were often cast in a less-than-heroic light as potential disruptors of the 1988 Olympic Games. The focus on China and lack of interest in Korea is all the more ironic since there is little doubt that officials of the Peoples' Republic consider South Korea a potential development model and the Chinese students undoubtedly emulated the political activism of Seoul students in their own protests.

In both the scholarly world and the popular press, the 1980s have been heralded as the decade of democratization. Earlier arguments about the affinity between "bureaucratic-authoritarian" regimes and rapid economic development (O'Donnell, 1973) have given way to analysis of transitions to democracy (O'Donnell, Schmitter and Whitehead, 1986). The demise of dictatorial regimes in Spain and Latin America in the late 1970s and early 1980s spread to Asia in the 1986 "People Power" revolt in the Philippines. Burgeoning movements pressing for political liberalization have emerged in several newly industrializing countries (NICS), including Taiwan and South Korea. More recently, the pressure for democratization has grown in Eastern bloc nations such as Poland, China and the Soviet Union. While the specific contexts of these changes and challenges varies enormously, the simultaneous rise of many national movements pressing for political pluralism suggests that some global forces may be at work.

This paper focuses on the South Korean case. At the outset it is necessary to contextualize political change in that nation in terms of Korea's dynamic role in the international system. Therefore, we begin by examining how the Republic of Korea's (ROK) pattern of "dependent development" and semiperipheral status bear on its internal political economy and class alignments (for a fuller development of this argument see Smith and Lee, forthcoming). A world-system perspective helps to illuminate the social forces and structural openings that can be used by proponents of democracy, as well as map some of the constraints and difficulties they face. This idea of relating Korean mobilization for political change to its global context is consistent with an emerging body of research linking popular social movements to the dynamics of the world economy (Smith and Tardanico, 1987; Walton, 1987; Burke, 1988).

The main topic of this paper, however, is not world economic forces. Instead, the intersocietal forces and structures within South Korea that affect its politics will be discussed. Which classes and interest groups are the major players in the current political struggles? Which have the most to gain or lose from democratization? How will the state respond to competing demands? How might the structure and balance of forces of the political economy of the ROK set limits on how far the process of political liberalization will proceed? These are some of the questions this paper addresses and for which it provides preliminary answers.

Korea in the World-System: Dependent Development in the Semiperiphery

The political economy of the world-system approach has become widely accepted in comparative research in recent years. Among the key concepts of this framework are the ideas of a "semiperipheral" strata of intermediate nations in the global economy and the possibility of upward mobility in the international hierarchy through "dependent development" (for an excellent discussion, see Evans, 1979). The idea of an economically and politically distinct semiperiphery is particularly important. Within this "level" economic production is a mixture of "corelike" technologically sophisticated industrial production and labor-intensive "peripherylike" activities (Chase-Dunn, 1980; 1988). Arrighi and Drangel (1986) point out that the precise nature of activities and products which are either "corelike" or "peripherylike" is historically bounded and related to current technology and product-cycles (Schumpeter, 1964; see Cumings, 1984 relating this to contemporary northeast Asia).

Core activities embody the latest technical and organizational innovations and are extremely profitable (Arrighi and Drangel, 1986). Whereas in the eighteenthth century this might be epitomized by wooden ship building (Chase-Dunn, 1980), in the late twentieth century automobiles or computers fit (Cumings, 1984). Semiperipheral countries, with a growing mix of activities that includes some "corelike" production, are much more likely to attract foreign and/or local capital to manufacturing industries than peripheral economies. Technology, whether "homegrown" or (more likely) imported, becomes increasingly important in rapidly developing, semiperipheral societies. Development remains "dependent," though, in that it remains severely constrained by outside forces in the international economy, which is dominated in the most advanced sectors by the superior technological, financial and commercial resources of core nations. In the late twentieth century this semiperipheral dependence is all the more evident in the majority of those countries in which development efforts have been financed by enormous foreign debt, and the engine of economic growth has been export-led industrialization. Industrial production in leading industries in the semiperiphery is often inserted at intermediate links of global commodity chains, with factories in these countries providing components and parts for final assembly in core countries.

Politically, the semiperiphery is quite different from either the periphery or the core. The more even mix of core-periphery activities changes the nature of the dominant class coalitions, and means that semiperipheral state policies often have more direct influence on local capital accumulation. In fact, Wallerstein (1985: 35) claims that "semiperipherality is important because it points to a concentration of state-oriented political activity by major internal (and external) actors." Chase-Dunn and Rubinson (1977: 472) argue that semiperipheral countries "tend to employ more state-directed and state-mobilizing development policies than do core countries."

This emphasis on "dependent development" in the semiperiphery in world-system analysis clearly moves the state into central focus. While early critiques of Wallerstein decried his lack of attention to political and class forces (Brenner, 1977; Skocpol, 1977), recent research in this tradition has made every effort to "bring the state back in" (Evans, Rueschemeyer and Skocpol, 1985). The concerns of this paper are solidly within the "new comparative political economy" which is dedicated to historical-structural analysis of classes, elites, coalition-building, regime breakdown and politics (Evans and Stephens, 1988).

While this shift toward greater attention on "internal" factors and the articulation between national and local political economies is one key theoretical shift, an equally important change has occurred in the conceptualization of the world system itself. Increasingly, international political economists insist that a thorough understanding of the global system requires that both the world economy and the international state system be taken into account. These twin aspects of the world-system are intertwined, but neither is reducible to the other (Chase-Dunn, 1981; Evans and Stephens, 1988). Growing research interest in northeast Asia has directly contributed to theoretical advance; studies of this world region have increased the awareness that geopolitics and military strategies are sometimes critical elements in development and social change (Cumings, 1984; Lim, 1985; Nemeth and Smith, 1985; Koo, 1987).

Indeed, recent research on South Korea and other east Asian NICs has provided crucial refinements to the international political-economy approach (Deyo, 1987a). These nations initially appear to be "deviant cases" that "disprove" simplistic formulations of the world-system arguments that associated dependency with stagnationist underdevelopment (Barrett and Whyte, 1982; Gold, 1986; Barrett and Chin, 1987). Upon closer examination, however, a more nuanced variant of the world-system perspective clearly does help one understand these cases, particularly if these countries are conceptualized as semiperipheral states undergoing the process of dependent development (Cumings, 1984; 1989; Evans, 1987; Koo, 1987).

World-system explanations of the trajectories of the East Asian NICs begin with the historical analysis of the area's relationship to the international system. Detailed arguments, relating the developmental distinctiveness of Korea and Taiwan to their similar experience of late incorporation into the modern world-economy through Japanese colonialism, have been developed elsewhere (Cumings, 1984; Lim, 1985; Nemeth and Smith, 1985). After World War II, the absence of a strong, indigenous, landed class, rule by the Allied Military Government and the infusion of massive U.S. aid created a situation in South Korea which eventually led to a strong development-oriented state. What Cumings calls a "bureaucratic authoritarian industrializing regime" (BAIR) ultimately emerged; it directed the export-led manufacturing that emerged in the 1970s and has been heralded as "the Korean economic miracle" (Cumings, 1984; Lim, 1985; Nemeth and Smith, 1985; Koo, 1987). The state continues to play a crucial role in contemporary South Korea as the intermediary between the nation and the world-system. Deyo (1987c: 237) emphasizes this with his argument that "state mediation of dependency involves the institutional channeling of most external linkages through bureaucratic agencies that are thereby enabled to introduce strategic criteria into the construction of foreign market, technology and capital relationships." South Korea, like other semiperipheral nations, has a state with the capacity to "negotiate dependency" (Evans, 1979).

Probably the most obvious way the ROK state has done this is by controlling the extent and nature of foreign-capital penetration. Peter Evans (1987) perceptively notes that the correlation between relatively low foreign direct investment and the rapid economic growth of the east Asian NICs is a resounding confirmation of a basic tenet of the world-system argument. State policy has, perhaps implicitly, followed what *dependistas* would have prescribed. While strictly limiting the entrance of multinational firms (Evans and Tigre, 1989 illustrate this in the computer sector), South Korea has relied heavily on external capital flows. In the immediate postwar period, the main sources were huge grants from the U.S. (Nemeth and Smith, 1985; Haggard and Cheng, 1987), but from the 1960s onward the government turned increasingly toward international loans to foster industrialization (Lim, 1985; Haggard and Cheng, 1987; Evans, 1987). Some observers suggest that this high level of debt dependence may eventually cause the ROK serious economic difficulties (Cumings, 1984; Lim, 1985).

Undoubtedly, however, this borrowing and the way the Park Chung Hee government managed it enhanced the pivotal role that the state played: positioned between foreign lenders and local capitalists. Central financial institutions that allowed the state to control and channel the flow of capital to Korean business-people and companies were set up. The management of this debt became a potent tool for state-directed economic planning (as well as a potential focus for corruption and payoffs). Evans summarizes the effects:

> (R)eliance on loan capital has not meant simply a shift from dependence on industrial transnational to dependence on transnational bankers. From the beginning, reliance on loan capital has strengthened the hand of the Korean state in relation to the local bourgeoisie...Because access to low-cost, foreign-loan capital was crucial for competitive advantage, the Korean state became a principal arbiter of which local groups could expand and in which areas they could expand (1987: 216).

E. Kim (1988) argues that the absolute power and autonomy of the South Korean state has eroded in the 1980s as the giant conglomerate companies (*chaebol*) have become increasingly influential. This does not indicate that the economy is more genuinely competitive; instead, Kim's analysis documents the continuing monopolization of economic planning by an alliance of leading firms and the state.

An equally important way in which the South Korean state has intervened in the economy to maintain or bolster its international market position (and mitigate the effects of dependency) involves the control and repression of labor. There is little doubt that the government's relations with labor have been as integral to the Korean "economic miracle" as the state's mediation between international and local capital. Deyo flatly asserts that the tremendous success of "export-oriented industrialization" (EOI) throughout East Asia is directly attributable to "disciplined and low-cost labor" (1987b: 183). Political demobilization and exclusion keep wages low and labor-intensive manufacturing globally competitive. In fact, South Korean labor laws and policies were even more repressive than those of the other East Asian NICs, and, at least until recently, were "becoming ever more repressive" (Koo, Haggard and Deyo, 1986). Cumings' (1984) discussion of the BAIR strikes the same theme. Drawing inspiration from Latin American research on "bureaucratic-authoritarian states" (O'Donnell, 1973; Collier, 1979), he argues that the BAIR in South Korea provided the political conditions (repressed labor and deferred consumption) necessary for the success of the export-led manufacturing strategy. Anti-union activities (often in the guise of "anti-Communism") and political demobilization have contributed to the country's competitiveness in the international market by reducing the cost of Korean exports.

Despite (or, perhaps, because of) its success, the contradictions of this development strategy were becoming clear as early as the 1970s. During that decade South Korean planners targeted steel, petrochemicals and shipbuilding for investment; by 1980 "two-thirds of government industrial loans were directed to heavy and chemical industries" (Deyo, 1989: 26). In the late 1980s, planners and policymakers in South Korea recognized that low-wage EOI was no longer viable.

There is a growing awareness of the limited developmental opportunities afforded by an economy stuck on the lower rungs of the industrial product cycle (see Cumings, 1984) and heavily dependent on "reverse engineering" (Smith and Lee, forthcoming). The ROK is caught in the "sandwich effect," unable to compete in highly sophisticated, core-type production but rapidly losing its ability to provide very low-wage, industrial labor in comparison to the peripheral countries (in, for instance, Southeast Asia) (Gereffi, 1988). Planners see "the Korean economy at the crossroads" (Cho, 1989) facing a number of choices, perhaps moving toward more capital-intensive technologically innovative production. These changes, however, will be conditioned both politically and economically by the constellation of social and class forces which the BAIR and EOI have created. Any change in economic development strategy will also affect the future of democratization, and vice versa.

Images of the State: Domination and Class Dynamics

While an understanding of Korea's role in the global system is an important beginning, political change cannot be adequately addressed using reductionist approaches, which focus only on the nation's international status or are overly economistic. Instead, the relationship between the world-system context and national political economy must be seen as complex, contingent and recursive. The historical subtleties of classes, states and the world economy must be interwoven to fully capture a process as complicated as the dynamics of political democratization. Obviously, it is not possible to completely untangle this complex weave of theoretical threads in this paper. Our focus, instead, will be on two major theoretical angles on the South Korean state and the push for political liberalization. One stresses the dual (sometimes contradictory) function of the capitalist state–to promote economic accumulation while maintaining political legitimacy. The other emphasizes the state as a "relatively autonomous" actor and an organization staffed by people who develop their own distinct interests in perpetuating the political-economic status quo.

The image of the state fulfilling dual imperatives was initially developed with advanced capitalist states in mind (O'Connor, 1973; Wolfe, 1977). Wolfe analyzes the history of Western parliamentary government in terms of "the tension between capitalism as an economic system and democracy as a political one." Although the overriding goal of the state is the reproduction of capitalism, Wolf and O'Connor remind us that both business profitability and the confidence of the electorate must be maintained in a liberal, democratic polity. While accumulation and legitimation often clash, attention to both is necessary for those who would retain state power.

Not surprisingly, work on transitions from authoritarianism to democracy also emphasizes the accumulation/legitimation tension. It is a recurrent theme in the case studies and theoretical chapters in the recent volume edited by O'Donnell, Schmitter and Whitehead (1986). Authoritarian regimes often are much better at promoting profitability and economic growth than in engendering political legitimation. Often military/bureaucratic authoritarian rulers came to power as the "solution" to perceived economic mismanagement and sluggish growth. In the short run, attainment of rapid "economic development" itself provides a measure of popular legitimacy (this seems to have been the explicit strategy of Park Chung Hee in South Korea). In the longer term, however, the success of the program for economic growth may lead to a serious "legitimation problem," as "those sectors of the population which are excluded and victimized" demand "the removal of the authoritarian regime and its replacement by a democratic one" (O'Donnell and Schmitter, 1986: 15). In the case of South Korea, this type of pressure from below built up throughout the Chun regime–leading ultimately to a full-fledged "legitimation crisis" in early 1987 and a sudden "loosening up" in June of that year. This does not imply an immediate political transformation; the transition to democracy is filled with uncertainty and contingencies involving various "accumulation and legitimation options" (Kaufman, 1986: 100-7) and "negotiating (and renegotiating) pacts" among key class and interest groups (O'Donnell and Schmitter, 1986: Chapter 4). Empirically, though, it does appear that the South Korean state under Roh has lost a substantial amount of both "state capacity" (the ability to get its policies implemented) and legitimation (the degree to which it can mobilize national consensus around its goals).

Deyo (1987c: 231-3) argues that the ability of contemporary East Asian authoritarian regimes to deal with "the effectiveness-legitimacy dilemma" has been enhanced by the weak and disorganized nature of "the popular sector" (i.e., peasants and workers). This distinguishes the East Asian NICs from bureaucratic, authoritarian regimes elsewhere (for example, Latin America's "southern cone") where popular mobilization has been higher, but Deyo points out that South Korea is a little different from Taiwan or Singapore. In the ROK he cites "more repressive regimes...imposed in response to sometimes violent opposition from middle-class intellectuals, students and workers" that have made the tension between accumulation and legitimacy more palpable than in other semiperipheral East Asian states (1987c: 241).

To understand the dynamics of this process it is necessary to move to the second theoretical issue: the nature of the state as both an actor and an organization made up of various interests. Again, the literature that reformulated theories of the state initially grappled with power in the advanced-core countries. Fred Block's 1977 article presents a concise, nonreductionist, structural, neo-Marxist argument. He moves decisively away from the "instrumentalist" view of the state toward one stressing "relative autonomy," in the tradition of Poulantzas (1969) and others. He claims that in a capitalist society the state is neither run directly by the capitalists nor does it simply reflect the interests of that dominant class. In fact, various capitalists will have distinct economic interests, making a unitary dominant class consciousness nearly impossible. Block's structural theory of the state explains "the tendency of state managers to pursue policies that are in the general interest of capital" in terms of their own interests which "are dependent on the maintenance of some reasonable level of economic activity" (1977: 15). To maintain steady flows of productive investment, state policies must maintain overall "business confidence," which may not be consistent with the economic interest of each individual business or business-person. Retaining "business confidence" also involves dealing with "class struggle" and granting concessions to workers. It is in the interest of state managers to respond to this political pressure by rationalizing production and expanding the role of the state. Ironically, "class struggle" becomes the motor propelling "economic dynamism." The state's motivation to maintain "business confidence," and the role of "class struggle" in forcing societies to adopt more sophisticated production technology and organization, may offer particularly useful insights into recent developments in South Korea (although the limits of "dependent development" may limit the degree of "rationalization" possible in this case).

Skocpol (1979) further develops the idea that the state has its own distinct material interests by pointing to a multiplicity of state personnel–bureaucrats, police, military, politicians–who share the broad goal of maintaining social order, political peace and business confidence, but who have specific interests in that conflict. These competing interests become particularly transparent in times of crisis and can play a critical role in the demise of a regime. This emphasis on the role of strategic, "state-based" interests in political change is crucial to understanding the Korean case as well. The fissures among interests within the ROK state have become clearly visible in the past two years of crisis and uncertainty. This has led to an increasing lack of internal coordination among different government agencies and ministries across a gamut of issues and policies, further weakening state capacity vis-a-vis a civil society that is continually gaining political strength and losing confidence in the government. The result is a degree of stalemate within the state that makes popular demands difficult to resist. Nevertheless, still lurking in the background is the general imperative to maintain "business confidence." The crucial issue in this period of flux is, at what point are interests in the South Korean state likely to coalesce and reimpose a more repressive solution?

In an attempt to directly wrestle with "politics in the semiperiphery," Mouzelis (1986) also formulates a nonreductionist approach to the state. He, too, uses the "relative autonomy" argument as a springboard to develop an alternative to O'Donnell's BA state approach–which is partially correct but overly economistic. While not abandoning "the tradition of Marxist-oriented approaches" entirely, Mouzelis urges "new concepts which give serious attention to the specificity of political structures" (1986: 203). He suggests an expanded terminology, including "the mode of political domination" (similar to the "mode of production"). The semiperipheral mode of domination is generally characterized by "incorporative relations of production" (p. 205) that exclude the masses from meaningful political participation and often promote the "praetorian tendency" (toward military domination) in "late-late industrializing societies" (p. 184). Echoing arguments made earlier by Evans (1979), Mouzelis highlights the power of the state in the semiperiphery to guide economic development and to shape class interests/configurations (rather than to act as an "instrument" of the dominant classes). Like Block and Skocpol, Mouzelis is arguing for the key role of "a non-economistic conceptualization of political institutions and actors," but one which still operates under the broad rubric of the Marxist political theory:

> As will have become clear by now, what I am advocating is a rapprochement between Marx's political-economy approach and Weber's political sociology (especially his insights on types of domination, on the crucial importance of not only the means of production, but also the means of administration, coercion, and so on) (Mouzelis, 1986: 217-18).

In a similar vein, Skocpol summarizes her synthetic approach:

> The state, in short, is fundamentally Janus-faced, with an intrinsically dual anchorage in class-divided socioeconomic structures and an international system of states. If our aim is to understand the breakdown and building-up of state organizations...(w)e must...focus upon the points of intersection between international conditions and pressures, on the one hand, and class-structured economies and politically organized interests, on the other hand. State executives and their followers will be found maneuvering to extract resources and build administrative and coercive organizations precisely at this intersection (1979: 32).

The tumultuous changes of the late 1980s are occurring at the vortex of international and domestic pressures. In terms of the global market, the South Korean economy is at a critical crossroads. Crucial choices that will determine the nation's developmental trajectory well into the twenty-first century must be made. At the same time, domestic pressure for more political and economic inclusion has built to the boiling point, prompting students and workers to launch violent strikes and street protests. The growing realization of the importance of technology and "research and development" in maintaining global competitiveness, coupled with an appreciation that the "social costs" of low-wage, export manufacturing has become politically intolerable, have converged to create a growing consensus among planners and policymakers that the country must embark on a new development path (Smith and Lee, forthcoming). The ROK's need to wriggle free of the "sandwich effect," as well as a political climate in which working-class acquiescence to "labor discipline," subsistence wages and restricted consumption can no longer be taken for granted, combine to compel a search for new political-economic strategies.

Of course, if Block is correct, this situation of heightened working class consciousness is potentially a motor for the further development of the "productive forces" of the South Korean economy: "*Class struggle is the economic dynamism of capitalism*" (1977: 21, italics in original). This proposition, though, may work best in advanced capitalist societies with a tradition of political pluralism and a capacity to sustain indigenous technological change. The constraints of "dependent development" in the ROK case suggest more tension between "rationalization" (and continued democratization) and repression (and an attempt to carry on with export manufacturing dependent on wage restraint/ political demobilization). At any rate, this underlying dynamic of class struggle reminds us of the political struggles among classes/interest groups in South Korean society that affect the fate of democratization much more directly than shifts in economic development strategy do.

Struggle for Democracy: The Collective Actors

A variety of classes and interest groups have played a role in political change in South Korea in the 1980s. Other segments of the population have been less active, but may become less quiescent in the future. An overview of some of the potentially most important collective actors and suggestions on the role they may play in the struggle for a more democratic society follows.

The most basic conflict is between the basic capitalist classes: workers and those who own/control business. To understand these dynamics, we must recall the history of Korean "dependent development" and incorporation into the world system on the semiperiphery. One legacy of Japanese colonialism and post-World War II American occupation was "a highly fluid class structure without an old agrarian upper class or a comprador bourgeoisie" (Koo, 1987: 171; see also Cumings, 1981; Nemeth and Smith, 1985). The American-sponsored government played a central role in the process of economic development. Unlike in many other Third World societies, the military and bureaucrats did not have to face an entrenched elite wary of development policies promoting industrialization; on the contrary, creating and fostering an indigenious capitalist class became an important goal of the state. Only with the success of export-oriented manufacturing and the institutionalization of the giant *chaebol* as major economic forces in the 1970s and early 1980s did this capitalist class become a major political force no longer dominated by the state (Koo, 1987; E. Kim, 1988). Today, as business becomes more powerful, some members of the capitalist class are calling for decreased intervention in the economy by technocrats and favor limiting the political prerogatives of the military. Thus, many members of this emerging capitalist class are advocating economic liberalization, and some favor limited forms of political liberalization–although they are also aware of the potential problems that unions, strikes, increased demands for a social wage and higher labor costs might bring if democracy proceeds too fast or too far.

On the other side, the working class, obviously, is also a key component in the current political balance. Again it is necessary to adopt a historical perspective. At least from the time of the U.S. occupation there has been a major effort to marginalize the political left and disorganize and exclude urban working-class groups from political participation (Cumings, 1981; Haggard and Cheng, 1987). As previously mentioned, Deyo (1987b) identifies "disciplined low-cost labor" as the basic element of export-oriented industrialization and points to increasing levels of labor repression under Park Chung Hee. He points out that after Park seized power in 1961 strikes declined from an average of 79 per year (1955-60) to 15 per year (1963-71) (Deyo, 1987b: 186). After Park's narrow presidential victory in 1971 (and "the Yushin Constitution" in 1972), even more controls were placed on workers and unions. Still, labor repression actually intensified in the early 1980s (Deyo, 1987b) as President Chun Doo Hwan "suspended all collective bargaining and banned organized labor protests and the formation of independent labor unions" (Fineman, 1987).

In the face of this repression and political exclusion, the latent power of the South Korean working class was gradually growing as the success of export oriented industrialization was dramatically transforming the occupational structure. The result of this economic transformation is a proletarianized and urbanized South Korea. When "political cracks" began to appear in the mid-1980s (created by a legitimation crisis in the Chun dictatorship), the pent-up demands of the working class rapidly coalesced. In a *Los Angeles Times* article in July 1987 a foreign missionary noted "a tremendous surge in labor activity" and said "the explosion is understandable when you consider the labor sector is the most suppressed of any in society today" (Fineman, 1987). Workers unleashed a wave of strikes demanding wage increases, collective bargaining rights and guarantees and better working conditions (in 1986, 1,718 ROK workers were killed and 141,809 disabled by on-the-job injuries [Fineman, 1987]). This appears to reflect a feeling among workers that they have deferred consumption long enough. Beyond acting for their own narrow self-interest in work stoppages, though, workers have also joined in numerous demonstrations to support students' calls for more democratic reforms and Korean reunification. The developing class consciousness of Korean workers seems to transcend the narrow economism which appears to characterize the core proletariat.

As interesting and important as growing working-class demands is the response from the ruling elites. While some businesspeople and government officials insist that worker demands for wage increases, increased workplace safety and institutionalization of collective bargaining are no threat to overall profitability (examples in Fineman, 1987), others are not so sure. A Hyundai manager complained in an August 1988 story in the *Korea Herald*, "Our workers used to be highly disciplined and do whatever the company wanted them to do but since the government announced democratic reforms in June last year, the workers' attitude changed completely" (Moon, 1988). In October 1988, Kim Woo Chong, the chairman of Daewoo, told a *Los Angeles Times* reporter, "If it hadn't been for labor trouble the GNP would have grown 20 percent last year instead of 12 percent" (Jameson, 1988). More recently, President Roh Tae Woo said "strikes have cost $2.4 billion in lost production and $600 million in reduced exports this year (1989)" (Associated Press, 1989). Clearly, business and government leaders are acutely aware of the economic costs of democratic and labor reforms, although they may also feel that it is not feasible to "roll back" the reforms. As argued above, one of the imperatives that the state must fulfill is maintaining "business confidence"–at some point further reforms may come into sharp conflict with this function.

Throughout this paper, the critical role of the state in South Korea has been emphasized. Concretely, the state-based interests are represented by middle-class technocrats and the military.[1] Both groups are potentially important, and both could lose power and privilege if the momentum of democratic reform increases. South Korea's technocrats have been the pilots of the "developmentalist state" (Deyo, 1989). Since the 1960s, the major source of capital has been foreign loans channelled through government-controlled banks en route to private companies. Thus, bureaucrats in key "gatekeeping" positions in the Economic Planning Board and the Bank of Korea have wielded tremendous power. Asserting that these state functionaries enjoyed "relative autonomy" during the Park regime, was, if anything, an understatement. It is more accurate to see the capitalist class as "a bourgeoisie that has been nurtured, developed and controlled by the state" (Barone, 1983: 61, cited by Deyo, 1989: 46). It is this core of technocrats, mindful of the need to balance accumulation and legitimacy, and eager to upgrade South Korea's ability to compete internationally, that has consistently pushed for "rationalization" of the economy. In the 1970s they targeted heavy industries and petrochemicals; in the late 1980s they championed the need for autonomous technological innovation and research and development. Their successes of the last decade, however, have created a new capitalist class with vested interests that sometimes conflict with the goals of the developmentalist state. They are also confronted by another powerful force within the state: the armed forces. It is the entrenched military that appears to have the most to lose if democratic reforms succeed.

Koo (1987) refers to South Korea as "hypermilitarized." The impetus for a military-dominated society began, again, under U.S. occupation in the late 1940s, and has continuously been justified through reference to the presence of a hostile, Communist North Korea (Cumings, 1981; Koo, 1987). The legitimate need for a defensive capability against a belligerent neighbor has also served as "a permanent excuse for violence and repression" directed at civil society (Koo, 1987: 172). The military dominance of the state has been continuous over the past 30 years–Presidents Park, Chun and Roh were all high-ranking military men whose links to the armed forces were extremely tight. Both the power and the legitimacy of the ROK military has been bolstered by its links to the U.S. armed forces, which maintains a legal status as an occupying force in Korea. This means that particularly bloody repression–such as the Kwangju massacre in 1981 –must have had at least tacit American support (which contributes to the virulent anti-American feelings of many young South Koreans). While Daewoo executive Kim seems to express a majority sentiment when he says, "We are now in a transition from an army government to civilian rule...the army has no choice," there is considerable doubt among the citizenry that the military would be willing to allow "certain people" (e.g., Kim Dae Jung) to become president. A political advisor to one of the opposition parties ascribed the difficulty of moving from a military-dominated regime to "patronage," in which many connected people who have benefitted from the old system will lose under a new more democratic one. This raises serious questions about how acquiescent the military ultimately will be if changes begin to threaten their basic prerogatives.

Traditionally, intellectuals were accorded great respect and social prestige in Korean society. Academics and their work continue to be taken seriously today and education is seen as extremely important for young people–to the extent that superior schools and/or colleges are frequently cited as the key component in family decisions to migrate to Seoul. Given the central role of scholarship in Korean life, it is not surprising that students and student movements play a critical role in the social and political dynamics of the nation. Since the "student uprising" of 19 April 1960 (which was instrumental in the fall of the government of Syngman Rhee) students have consistently led challenges against the legitimacy of nondemocratic elements in the state. In 1979 their mass protests forced Park Chung Hee's 19-year dictatorship to collapse. During the 1980s, student dissidents formed the vanguard of the mobilization against the Chun regime. Their unprecedented sacrifices–staging thousands of protest demonstrations, enduring relentless tear gas barrages and torture and beating at the hands of the police (culminating in the widely publicized torture killing of Seoul National University student Jong Chul Park in 1987)–won them the respect of the nation and the world and the moral high ground in their battle against Chun's autocratic regime. Clearly, this struggle was an integral part of Roh Tae Woo's decision (as leader of the ruling party) to support calls for direct presidential elections. That basic concession created an atmosphere that led to a variety of other steps toward political liberalization in late 1987 and 1988.

Clearly, the students would have only marginal power without support from other groups. They garnered this both nationally and internationally. Particularly prior to the Olympic Games in 1988, the students (with cooperation from the international media) succeeded in gaining a great deal of global attention and support. Within the ROK, students needed support and sympathy from the middle and working classes. Establishing linkages with these groups was one of the keys to the increased success of the student movement of the 1980s. Before the Chun period, demonstrations and action had largely been confined to campuses, with few ties to other social groups. But in the 1980s, an "organic linkage" between defiant students and increasingly class-conscious industrial workers was established. Labor in the relatively new heavy industries was particularly likely to become radicalized and ally with the student movement (Deyo, 1989).

Large numbers of students within the movement have "disguised" themselves and taken factory jobs in an effort to merge with the urban proletariat. As Cumings (1989) notes, in the past few years the labor movement has become increasingly intertwined with the radical student movement. Today in South Korea the expression "labor-student linked struggle" appears in newspapers, on campuses and in factories, as well as in academic writing.

Other social groups may also be important in determining the future trajectory of political change in South Korea. One group that has received relatively little attention is the mass of urban poor eking out a subsistence in the "urban informal sector." Recent evidence suggests that this group makes up a significant percentage of the population of Seoul and other major cities, and that its numbers are growing. Up to now it has not become a major political force; the pressing concerns of day-to-day living leave these people little time and energy even to protest their plight. During the summer of 1988, however, the substandard conditions in urban shantytowns and "moon villages" were becoming a political issue for the opposition parties (*Korea Herald*, 1988; and *Washington Post*, 1988). "Informalization" might offer one "solution" to the rising wage pressure that capitalist enterprises face (for a discussion, see Portes and Sassen-Koob, 1987). If the size of this sector of the population continues to rise (particularly in the capital city), it is hard to imagine that it won't eventually become a potentially volatile political force. The demands of the urban poor may become a pressing issue in South Korean politics as the nation moves into the twenty-first century.

Struggle for Democracy: Successes and Failures in the Late 1980s

Since early 1987, the battle for political liberalization in South Korea has intensified and led to genuine democratic reforms. Continued progress toward political pluralism is hardly unproblematic, though, as the forces pressing for change struggle against those who favor the status quo, as well as more reactionary forces pushing for the rollback of reforms already granted. While there is no doubt that South Korean society is much more open and free than it was in 1986, the trajectory of further political change is unclear. The current national situation resembles many Seoul street protests, matching students against police. Despite occasional ebbs and flows favoring one side or the other, there was an uneasy stalemate in the ROK polity in 1989.

An interview with Lee Shin Boom in August 1988 illustrates the extent and limits of the reforms. (Lee himself is a symbol of political liberalization. In the early 1970s he narrowly escaped a death sentence as a "communist sympathizer"; today he is a lawyer and an influential political advisor to one of the opposition parties, Kim Young Sam's Reunification Democratic Party.) Electorally, Lee pointed to the direct election of the President as the most crucial change, but other electoral reforms which have allowed the opposition to capture the majority in the legislature are significant as well. This legislative power shift has permitted the opposition to change some laws governing the KCIA, the Bank of Korea and government control of the media. While these legal and electoral changes are intrinsically important, Lee argues that the struggle for them has created a growing political consciousness among the Korean people, who are proud of their newly expanded democracy. At the same time, however, he conceded that a "rollback" of political rights and freedoms is quite possible, with the power of the military the most likely impetus. He also expressed frustration that laws governing assembly and demonstrations, as well as many labor laws and regulations, on the books under the Chun regime remained unchanged. Nine months later, in March 1989, Lee told a journalist from the *New York Times* that many repressive laws had still not been amended, and that legal safeguards against the repetition of past human rights abuses had yet to be put in place (Chira, 1989).

Proponents of further South Korean democratization found 1989 to be a sobering year. On 20 March, President Roh announced the cancellation of a scheduled referendum on his first year in office for fear of electoral "confusion and violence" (*New York Times*, 1989a; *Los Angeles Times*, 1989a). Three days later, Roh ordered a crackdown on "leftist forces trying to overthrow the government," authorizing police to use deadly force against violent protesters (*New York Times*, 1989b). While student demonstrations and labor strikes continued throughout the country, the Roh government's response became increasingly repressive. Perhaps the most dramatic confrontation occurred at the Hyundai shipyards in Ulsan. Thousands of riot police were sent into the compound, and a pitched battle between workers with rocks and firebombs and police with tear gas ensued. The police also battled about 1,000 students from Ulsan University who were attempting to join the strikers at the shipyard. More than 700 strikers were arrested and a number were injured, according to reports in the Western media (*International Herald Tribune*, 1989; *Los Angeles Times*, 1989b). The *Los Angeles Times* (1989c) subsequently reported that "Labor activists say Hyundai's reliance on the police to quell the worker unrest in Ulsan, coming just two weeks after 6,000 riot police crushed a subway strike in Seoul, is a throwback to the way managers handled labor relations" prior to democratic reforms (Schoenberger, 1989: 2). In early May, after six riot police were killed in a fire at a Pusan university, President Roh announced that he was considering invoking "emergency powers" to quell future unrest (*Los Angeles Times*, 1989d). The death of a student in Kwangju a few days later, apparently at the hands of the security forces, set off another national wave of demonstrations, countered by police repression. In late May, a landmark attempt to organize a national schoolteachers' union was met with a wave of repression: about 1,500 primary and secondary teachers were dismissed from their jobs and leaders of the new union were prosecuted.

The escalating cycle of violence, sometimes initiated by radical students and workers but usually heightened by the massive retaliation of the authorities, does not bode well for continued political reform. By October the deteriorating situation was being noted in the U.S. press, as the *Washington Post* noted reports of "a resurgence of human rights violations in South Korea" and opposition discontent. "In the past six months, hundreds of politicians, students, journalists, dissidents, artists, unionists, teachers and priests have been thrown in jail for breaking the security law or a related one that limits rallies" (*Washington Post*, 1989).

Many of the most serious charges have been levelled at dissidents who have attempted to travel to or make contact with North Korea. The link between democratization and reunification issues is increasingly clear. The attention that students and the opposition parties are paying to reunification taps a deeply felt Korean nationalism. There is a real yearning for an end to North-South hostility and division, which in many cases has left families separated for 40 years (see C. Kim, 1988). In some ways, the reunification issue dovetails neatly with the push for political liberalization. Reducing hostility with communist North Korea would also remove the main "bogeyman" of the political right wing. Without the imminent danger of an overtly aggressive neighbor, internal vigilance against any activity that can conceivably be labeled "communist" would be unnecessary. This might make suppression of the legitimate demands of workers and students more difficult to justify. On the other hand, shifting the focus from political liberalization to reunification may allow the Roh government to consolidate its power and maintain many elements of authoritarian rule. The government could claim that dissent must be squelched in the interests of negotiating with the North Koreans with one "unified voice." Thus, pressing the issue of reunification may present a two-edged sword for proponents of democratic reform.

Structural Constraints and the Democratization Movement

The political reform movement in South Korea faces a number of potential obstacles, some of which are world-systemic. Internationally, the country faces a number of pressures that combine to threaten its international economic competitiveness. The continuously changing, global industrial division of labor has created a situation in which Korea can no longer provide labor as cheaply as impoverished peripheral societies. Ironically, wage costs have risen as a direct result of the success of the developmentalist state; the rise of a new, more organized urban industrial working class makes the old low-wage strategy politically untenable. From the advanced core nations, which are the main markets for EOI, comes the threat of protectionism and pressure to inflate the *won*. While the move toward innovative capital-intensive production seems to provide a path to restored world competitiveness, the difficulty of overcoming technological dependency and developing state-of-the-art research and development facilities and personnel is enormous (Smith and Lee, forthcoming). Fears of declining global competitiveness redound through the political arena as established capitalists connect democratic reforms with increases in wages and rises in the general cost of doing business in South Korea.

These issues are not idiosyncratic to the Korean case. Rather, they are characteristic of contradictory forces operating in semiperipheral societies in general. On the one hand, the "deepening" of industrialization leads to genuine national economic growth and engenders a new class equation in which both the national bourgeoisie and the industrial working class become increasingly important. These changes provide growing constituencies for incipient movements to democratize previously bureaucratic, authoritarian states. New and demographically larger segments of "civil society" are present; their interests may diverge from that of even a developmentally minded state. On the other hand, countervailing forces within the semiperipheral state and its "external" relations with the global system tend to subvert popular movements for political change. Internally, entrenched bureaucrats and military men, who are accustomed to wielding tremendous power, may feel personally and/or collectively threatened by the direction of reform. Historical or contemporary patterns of uneven development and regional disparities, which are likely to be particularly prevalent in semi-perhiperhal societies, may inhibit the degree to which various popular forces of students, workers, the middle class, the political opposition, etc. are able to unite into a movement for progressive political change. Globally, the established international division of labor may present a formidable obstacle. Patterns such as technological and debt dependency or rising core protectionism are particularly intractable problems facing all newly industrializing, semi-peripheral states.

All of these counterpoised pressures make the semiperiphery politically volatile (see Wallerstein, 1979). This suggests that, while it is in precisely these countries that the forces of change are likely to produce the class-state configurations conducive to popular movements, it is by no means clear that these democratization movements will always succeed. This analysis further suggests that international and domestic structural conditions may make those semi-peripheral nations that have "democratized" vulnerable to reimposition of more repressive regimes in the future. Will the "redemocratization" of the 1980s give way to the "reauthoritarianization" of the 1990s? This is a possibility that those who see Western-style bourgeois democracy as "the end of history" have failed to consider. Attempting to map out a "generic" pattern of social movements for democratization in the semiperiphery may be of limited value, since most sophisticated world-system analysis uses such concepts as semiperipherality as a referential context for locating specific historical cases (see Duvall, 1978, on dependence). What are some of the conjunctural aspects of the South Korean case that are particularly relevant? One involves internal class structure: The emergence of a large, politically active, industrial working class with the savvy to seek coalitions with other opposition movements seems to bode well for genuine, lasting political change and democratization. In terms of global linkages, the Roh government's sensitivity to the need to maintain national and international legitimacy may also deter attempts to move back toward repression.

Nevertheless, the economic and political constraints on the pace and extent of political reform are formidable. Peter Evans (1987) suggests that South Korea might follow Japan's lead politically as well as economically. If so, rather than ending up with the "tumultuous democracy" of Latin American semiperipheral societies, the ROK might end up with a Japanese-style "controlled parliamentary system" characterized by "restricted" electoral competition "with a minimum of repression" (p. 223). This seems plausible, although recent repression against labor and the political left suggests that more pessimism may be prudent. The military remains firmly entrenched and could reassert its rule in a societal crisis. Depending on the country's success in overcoming technological dependence, there is the possibility that the economy's relatively precarious competitive position in the global division of labor could worsen significantly. In a situation of slow growth or economic stagnation even a return to Rhee-like corrupt politics is conceivable. What seems most unlikely is the blossoming of full-blown, Western-style democracy in South Korea in the near future.

Of course, predicting social change is always a perilous task. In the past, the people of South Korea have taken on major challenges against very long odds and succeeded. The democratization movement in the 1980s brought together a formidable coalition of students, workers, intellectuals and middle-class people. They may be able to push their society toward a distinctly Korean form of democracy, overcoming some of the constraints suggested in the paper. One of the purposes of this paper is to contribute to that effort by outlining some of the obstacles. These constraints will be more readily overcome if they are acknowledged, understood and confronted head-on.

Note

1. A reviewer of an earlier draft of this manuscript asked, "What about the parties and political leaderships?" Because of the autocratic nature of successive ROK regimes in the post-World War II era, political parties have been marginally important. Even in the 1980s, opposition parties' support and leadership is drawn from an elite/middle class social base similar to that of the ruling Democratic Justice Party (DJP). The most important distinctions among parties represent regional cleavages rather than distinct class or ideological allegiances. The 1987 presidential elections demonstrated the opposition's weakness and division, as Roh won a small plurality in a three-way race. The two major opposition parties (led by Kim Dae Jung and Kim Young Sam) are committed to maintaining and enlarging the recent political opening. Both are narrowly "reformist" and not likely to move to the forefront of struggles for basic political changes (Hart-Landsberg, 1988). While political parties could eventually become important components in the democratization movement (particularly if a truly popular progressive party arises), they have not been major players thus far.

References

Arrighi, Giovanni and Jessica Drangel (1986) The stratification of the world-economy: An exploration of the semiperipheral zone, *Review (Fernand Braudel Center) 10*(1): 9-74.

Associated Press (1989) S. Korean police arrest strikers in factory raids, *Los Angeles Times*, 19 April.

Barone, Charles (1983) Dependency, Marxist theory, and salvaging the idea of capitalism in South Korea, *Review of Radical Political Economics, 15*(1): 43-67.

Barrett, Richard, and Martin Whyte (1982) Dependency theory and Taiwan: Analysis of a deviant case, *American Journal of Sociology, 87*: 1064-89.

Barrett, Richard and Soomi Chin (1987) Export-oriented industrializing states in the capitalist world system: Similarities and differences. In F. Deyo (Ed.), *The Political Economy of the New Asian Industrialism.* Ithaca, N.Y.: Cornell University Press: 23-43.

Block, Fred (1977) The ruling class does not rule: Notes on the Marxist theory of the state, *Socialist Revolution, 33*: 6-28.

Brenner, Robert (1977) The origins of capitalist development theory: A critique of neo-Smithian Marxism, *New Left Review, 104*: 24-92.

Burke, Edmund, III (Ed.) (1988) *Global Crises and Social Movements: Artisans, Peasants, Populists and the World Economy.* Boulder: Westview.

Chase-Dunn, Christopher and Richard Rubinson (1977) Toward a structural perpsective on the world system, *Politics and Society, 7*(4): 453-76.

Chase-Dunn, Christopher (1980) The development of core capitalism in the United States: Tariff policies and class struggle in an upwardly mobile semiperiphery. In Albert Bergesen (Ed.), *Studies of the Modern World System.* New York: Academic Press: 189-230.

Chase-Dunn, Christopher (1981) Interstate system and capitalist world economy: One logic or two? *International Studies Quarterly, 25*(1): 19-42.

Chase-Dunn, Christopher (1988) *Global Formation: Structures of the World Economy.* New York: Basil Blackwell.

Chira, Susan (1989) Korea's Road to Democracy: Paved with Contrary Legacy. *New York Times*, 13 March: A1.

Cho, Soon (1989) "Korean economy at a crossroads: Blueprint for internationalization." Speech to Foreign Correspondents Club, Seoul, 18 January (reprinted in *For Your Information* bulletin, Korea Economic Institute, January 27).

Collier, David (Ed.) (1979) *The New Authoritarianism in Latin America.* Princeton: Princeton University Press.

Cumings, Bruce (1981) *The Origins of the Korean War.* Princeton: Princeton

University Press.

Cumings, Bruce (1984) The origins and development of the northeast asian political economy: Industrial sectors, product cycles, and political consequences, *International Organization, 38*: 1-40.

Cumings, Bruce (1989) The abortive apertura: South Korea in the light of Latin American experience, *New Left Review, 173*: 5-32.

Deyo, Frederic C. (Ed.) (1987a) *The Political Economy of the New Asian Industrialism.* Ithaca, N.Y.: Cornell University.

Deyo, Frederic C. (1987b) State and labor: Modes of political exclusion in East Asian development. In F. Deyo (Ed.), *The Political Economy of the New Asian Industrialism.* Ithaca, N.Y.: Cornell University Press: 182-202.

Deyo, Frederic C. (1987c) Coalitions, institutions, and linkage sequencing: Toward a strategic capacity model of East Asian development. In F. Deyo (Ed.), *The Political Economy of the New Asian Industrialism.* Ithaca, N.Y.: Cornell University Press: 227-47.

Deyo, Frederic (1989) *Beneath the Miracle: Labor Subordination in the New Asian Industrialism.* Berkeley: University of California Press.

Duvall, Raymond (1978) Dependence and dependency theory: Notes toward precision of concepts and argument, *International Organization, 22*(1): 51-78.

Evans, Peter (1979) *Dependent Development.* Princeton: Princeton University Press.

Evans, Peter (1987) Class, state and dependence in East Asia: Lessons for Latin Americanists. In F. Deyo (Ed.), *The Political Economy of the New Asian Industrialism.* Ithaca, N.Y.: Cornell University Press: 203-26.

Evans, Peter, Dietrich Rueschemeyer, and Theda Skocpol (1985) *Bringing the State Back In.* Cambridge: Cambridge University Press.

Evans, Peter and John Stephens (1988) Studying development since the sixties: The emergence of the new comparative political economy. In N. Smelser (Ed.), *The Handbook of Sociology.* Beverly Hills: Sage.

Evans, Peter and Paula B. Tigre (1989) Paths to participation in "hi tech" industry: A comparative analysis of computers in Brazil and Korea, *Asian Perspective, 13*(1) 5-35.

Fineman, Mark (1987) Labor Movement puts S. Korea Democratic Reforms to Test. *Los Angeles Times*, 27 July: Business Section.

Gereffi, Gary (1988) "Industrial restructuring in Latin America and East Asia." Paper presented at the Annual Meeting of the American Sociological Association, August, Atlanta.

Gold, Thomas (1986) *State and Society in the Taiwan Miracle.* Armonk, N.Y.: M.E. Sharpe.

Haggard, Steven and Tun-jen Cheng (1987) State and foreign capital in the East

Asian NICs. In F. Deyo (Ed.), *The Political Economy of the New Asian Industrialism*. Ithaca, N.Y.: Cornell University Press: 84-135.

Hart-Landsberg, Martin (1988) South Korea: The "miracle" rejected, *Critical Sociology, 15*(3): 29-51.

International Herald Tribune (1989) "Seoul Crushes a Strike: Riot Police Arrest Hundreds in Raid at Hyundai Yard," 31 March: 1.

Jameson, Sam (1988) "Daewoo Chief Worries Over Labor Strife but Bullish on South Korea." *Los Angeles Times*, 6 November: Business Section.

Kaufman, Robert (1986) Liberalization and the institutonalization of military-dominated polities in Latin America. In G. O'Donnell, P. Schmitter, and L. Whitehead (Eds.), *Transitions from Authoritarian Rule: Prospects for Democracy*, Part III. Baltimore: Johns Hopkins University Press: 85-107.

Kim, Eun Mee (1988) From dominance to symbiosis: State and chaebol in Korea, *Pacific Focus, 3*(2) 105-21.

Kim, Choong S. (1988) *Faithful Endurance: An Ethnography of Korean Family Dispersal*. Tucson: University of Arizona Press.

Koo, Hagen (1987) The interplay of state, social class, and world system in East Asian development: The cases of South Korea and Taiwan. In F. Deyo (Ed.), *The Political Economy of the New Asian Industrialism*. Ithaca, N.Y.: Cornell University: 165-81.

Koo, Hagen, Steven Haggard, and Frederic Deyo (1986) Labor and development strategy in the East Asian NICs, *Items* (Social Science Research Council Bulletin), 40.

Korea Herald (1988) 16 July.

Lim, Hyun-Chin (1985) *Dependent Development in Korea: 1963-1979*. Seoul: Seoul National University.

Los Anqeles Times (1989a) "South Korean Leader Calls Off Referendum on his Record, March 20.

Los Angeles Times (1989b) "Police Storm Hyundai Yard," 30 and 31 March.

Los Angeles Times (1989c) "Violence Grows as S. Korean Labor Unrest Intensifies," 10 April.

Los Angeles Times (1989d) "Flames in Pusan Reflect New Mood in S. Korea," 6 May.

Moon, Ihl-wan (1988) Hyundai Aims at U.S. Car Market with 'Sonata,' *Korea Herald*, 6 August.

Mouzelis, Nicos (1986) *Politics in the Semi-Periphery*. London: MacMillan.

Nemeth, Roger and David Smith (1985) The political economy of contrasting urban hierarchies in South Korea and the Philippines. In M. Timberlake (Ed.), *Urbanization in the World-Economy*. New York: Academic Press: 183-206.

New York Times (1989a) "South Korea Chief Reneges on Pledge for a

Referendum," 20 March.

New York Times (1989b) "Korean Leader Turns to Compromise," 25 March.

O'Connor, James (1973) *The Fiscal Crisis of the State.* New York: St. Martin's.

O'Donnell, Guillermo (1973) *Modernization and Bureaucratic-Authoritarianism.* Berkeley: University of California Press.

O'Donnell, Guillermo and Philippe Schmitter (1986) Tentative conclusions about uncertain democracies. In G. O'Donnell, P. Schmitter, and L. Whitehead (Eds.), *Transitions from Authoritarian Rule: Prospects for Democracy* (part IV). Baltimore: Johns Hopkins University Press.

O'Donnell, Guillermo, Philippe Schmitter, and Laurence Whitehead (1986) *Transitions From Authoritarian Rule: Prospects for Democracy.* Baltimore: Johns Hopkins University Press.

Portes, Alejandro and Saskia Sassen-Koob (1987) Making it underground: Comparative material on the informal sector in western market economies, *American Journal of Sociology, 93*(1): 30-61.

Poulantzas, Nicos (1969) Problems of the Capitalist State, *New Left Review*: 58.

Schoenberger, Karl (1989) "Violence Grows as S. Korean Labor Unrest Intensifies." *Los Angeles Times*, 10 April.

Schumpeter, Joseph (1964) *Business Cycles: A Theoretical, Historical, and Statistical Analysis of Capitalist Process.* New York: McGraw-Hill.

Skocpol, Theda (1977) Wallerstein's world capitalist system: A theoretical and historical critique, *American Journal of Sociology, 82*: 1075-90.

Skocpol, Theda (1979) *States and Social Revolutions.* Cambridge: Cambridge University Press.

Smith, David A. and Su-Hoon Lee (forthcoming) Limits on a semiperipheral success story: State dependent development and the prospects for South Korean democratization. In William Martin (Ed.), *Semiperipheral States in the World-Economy.* Westport, Conn.: Greenwood.

Smith, Michael P. and Richard Tardanico (1987) Urban theory reconsidered: Production, reproduction and collective action. In Michael P. Smith and Joe R. Feagin (Eds.), *The Capitalist City.* New York: Basil Blackwell: 87-110.

Wallerstein, Immanuel (1985) The relevance of the concept of semiperiphery to Southern Europe. In G. Arrighi (Ed.), *Semiperipheral Development.* Beverly Hills: Sage: 31-54.

Walton, John (1987) Urban protest and global political economy: The IMF riots. In Michael P. Smith and Joe R. Feagin (Eds.), *The Capitalist City.* New York: Basil Blackwell: 364-86.

Washington Post (1989) "Roh Arrives in U.S. Amid Criticism," 16 October.

Wolfe, Alan (1977) *The Limits of Legitimacy.* New York: Free Press.

DEINDUSTRIALIZATION, ECONOMIC DEMOCRACY, AND EQUAL OPPORTUNITY: THE CHANGING CONTEXT OF RACE RELATIONS IN URBAN AMERICA

Gregory D. Squires
University of Wisconsin-Milwaukee

Despite many victories in the civil rights arena, increasing numbers of black elected officials and more tolerant attitudes on the part of whites in recent decades, racial disparities persist in many critical economic indicators, particularly in urban areas. Structural changes in the U.S. economy and the response on the part of private capital to declining profits have dramatically altered the context in which racial disparities are generated. A critical analysis of traditional explanations for racially based, labor-market inequalities and empirical evidence from selected employee-owned businesses demonstrate the importance of more democratically organized economic institutions in reducing racial inequality, and suggest important policy implications for achieving greater racial inequality during an age of deindustrialization of the American economy and the nation's cities. For an urban policy to effectively address the problem of racial inequality in cities, it must confront the changing political economy of the postwar years by complementing traditional liberal civil rights remedies with tactics that will inject more democratic participation in economic institutions.

In its annual report, *The State of Black America 1988*, the National Urban League concluded that "more blacks have lost jobs through industrial decline than through job discrimination" (Dewar, 1988: 155). Hardly insensitive to the realities of racism, the Urban League is attuned to the increasingly complex dynamics that shape the objective conditions of black life, particularly at the core of urban America today.

The persistence of racial disparities in many critical socio-economic indicators over the past two decades suggests that racism may indeed be as American as apple pie. Yet there have been many legal victories in the civil rights arena, the number of black elected officials has multiplied and available evidence suggests increasing acceptance of equal opportunity among all groups in American society. At the same time, there have been dramatic changes in the structure of the U.S. economy and its labor market that have adversely affected both U.S. cities and the nation's minority population. If many of these changes have been inextricably connected with evolving patterns of race relations in America, it is also true that many of the forces shaping urban communities, and adversely affecting minorities, cannot be explained primarily, if at all, in terms of race.

There has been much debate in recent years over the relative significance of race and class in determining the objective life-chances of minorities (Wilson, 1978, 1987; Willie, 1979; Landry, 1987). Most partisans to this debate have contributed to a fuller understanding of the changing realities of urban communities and the nation as a whole. Unfortunately, the debate has occasionally been polarized into unproductive, either/or terms. That important racial disparities persist in American life is simply a matter of documented fact. Equally true is the continuing reality of racial prejudice. The context of race relations, however, has changed in the past 20 years.

Central to understanding the frustration encountered by policymakers trying to reduce racial inequality are the ideological blinders that shape most analyses of race relations and urban development. Such work has been rooted in an individualistic framework that is most explicit in human-capital explanations of racial inequality. Emerging neoconservative analyses of the so-called "underclass," the nature of urban poverty and the role of race build upon the individualistic assumptions that have long informed the neoclassical tradition in general, particularly its human-capital proponents (Gilder, 1981; Murray 1984). Ignored by this perspective are the structural determinants of racial inequality and uneven development, determinants that have assumed increasing importance in the postwar globalization of the U.S. economy. Disjunction between the structural causes and individualistic explanations of uneven development and racial inequality gave rise to growing disenchantment with the potential of liberal reforms and opened the door to neoconservative contentions that little could be done in the policy arena, particularly in terms of government intervention, to mitigate these problems (Wilson, 1987).

To effectively address the seemingly immutable facts of racial inequality and uneven urban development, structural responses to structural problems are needed. The phenomenon of employee ownership, particularly in its more democratic formulations, illustrates how structural economic change can give rise to greater racial equality and ameliorate uneven development.

Deindustrialization of the nation's urban core and the flight of capital to the suburbs, the Sunbelt and beyond are the central structural forces that have devastated many urban communities and contributed directly to the persistence of racial inequality in those communities. Such unchecked, uncontrolled and uneven development can be addressed through more democratic intervention into what have traditionally been viewed as the prerogatives of the ownership and management of private businesses. More democratic economic structures in general, particularly of many of the organizational characteristics frequently associated with employee ownership, offer potentially powerful tools for addressing the changing dynamics of race relations in urban America. None of this suggests any curtailment in equal-employment-opportunity law enforcement, voluntary affirmative action programs or other civil rights initiatives. For an urban policy to effectively address the issue of racial inequality, though, it must complement traditional, liberal civil rights remedies with other tactics that will inject a strong dose of democracy into the nation's economic institutions. This paper examines the changing context of race relations over the past two decades and explores critical policy implications.

The next section briefly documents continuing racial inequalities despite positive developments in the civil rights arena in recent decades. Key structural changes in the U.S. economy during the postwar era and corporate response to those changes are traced, along with the adverse racial effects of these developments. Alternatives to the corporate agenda for economic recovery are identified, including calls for more democratic control over economic activity and increased employee ownership. Implications of such an approach for addressing racial inequality are noted. The two sections that follow examine the growth of employee ownership in the U.S. economy and recent developments in our theoretical understanding of racial inequality, along with the question of why such developments reveal the potential of employee ownership as a civil rights strategy. In light of these emerging theoretical understandings, the next section offers empirical evidence that further suggests the utility of employee ownership as an effective tool in efforts to reduce racial inequality. The concluding section discusses critical policy implications, focusing on the issue of why an effective urban policy could not only strengthen traditional civil rights organizing and law enforcement efforts, but also incorporate broader economic concerns, including employee ownership and economic democracy.

The Continuing Significance of Race

Employment and income may be the two most critical indicators of objective life conditions and relative status of individuals and groups in American society. According to these two indicators, racial disparities in the nation and its cities have remained the same or increased for at least the past 20 years since the landmark Kerner Commission report (*Report of the National Advisory Commission on Civil Disorders*, 1968) was released. Nonwhite unemployment in 1968 was 6.7 percent nationwide, compared to 3.2 percent for whites, a nonwhite/white ratio of 2.19. In 1986, nonwhite unemployment rose to 13.1 percent and white unemployment reached 6 percent for a ratio of 2.18. Within the nation's metropolitan areas, the nonwhite/white unemployment ratio rose from 1.9 percent in 1973 to 2.2 percent in 1986. Labor-force participation rates reflect similar racial disparities. The nonwhite, nationwide labor-force participation rate (62.2 percent) was actually higher than the white rate (59.3 percent) in 1973, but by 1986 the white rate (65.5 percent) had surpassed the nonwhite rate (63.7 percent). In the nation's central cities, whites had a slight advantage over nonwhites in 1973 (60.3 percent vs. 59.9 percent), which increased by 1986 to 64.7 percent vs. 62.2 percent (Hamal, 1988).

Family-income figures in the U.S. reveal a similar story. The median black family income, as a percentage of the median white family income, dropped from 60 percent in 1968 to 57.1 percent in 1986 (U.S. Bureau of the Census, 1987 a, b); in metropolitan areas the decline was from 63.7 percent to 57.4 percent. For metropolitan areas with a population more than one million, the decline among central-city families was steeper, from 69.7 percent to 59 percent (U.S. Bureau of the Census, 1969, 1987b).

These disparities persisted despite several positive developments in civil rights and race relations. Federal civil rights laws have been strengthened and the number of equal opportunity laws and programs at the state and local levels has grown. Despite efforts by the Reagan administration to turn back the clock on civil rights (Chambers, 1987), the U.S. Supreme Court issued several decisions in 1986 and 1987 that rejected Reagan's interpretation of federal equal-employment-opportunity laws and advanced affirmative action efforts. Contrary to the Reagan administration's claim that Title VII of the Civil Rights Act of 1964 (the principal federal statute outlawing employment discrimination) applies only to individual, identifiable victims of discrimination and allows only for "make-whole" relief for actual victims of an employer's illegal discrimination, the Supreme Court has interpreted that act much more broadly. In *Wygant vs. Jackson Board of Education*, the Court ruled that governments may be allowed to use hiring preferences for minorities to redress past discrimination. In *Firefighters vs. City of Cleveland*, the Court found constitutional a plan to hire one black or Hispanic for each white person hired, claiming that voluntary plans "may include reasonable race-conscious relief that benefits individuals who were not actual victims of discrimination." In *Local 28 Sheetmetal Workers vs. EEOC* the Court upheld a 29-percent hiring quota arguing, in part, that "the purpose of affirmative action is not to make identified victims whole, but rather to dismantle prior patterns of employment discrimination." Last, in *Johnson vs. Santa Clara County Transportation Agency*, the Court confirmed that race or sex could be taken into consideration in hiring or promotion decisions even in the absence of a prior finding of discrimination on the part of the employer. In a series of decisions handed down in 1989 (*Richmond vs. Croson, Wards Cove Packing Co. vs. Atonio, Martin vs. Wilks, Lorance vs. AT&T, Patterson vs. McLean Credit Union, and Jett vs. the Dallas Independent School District*) the Court placed additional burdens on minority plaintiffs' and others' efforts to implement affirmative action plans. While it is likely that legislation will be introduced in Congress in efforts to remove these impediments, the outcome of such efforts is by no means certain, so the impact of these decisions remains to be determined. At least through 1988, however, the Supreme Court consistently supported affirmative action initiatives.

In addition to these legal victories, black political participation has grown substantially in the past two decades. Prior to passage of the Voting Rights Act in 1965 there were fewer than 200 black elected officials in the U.S. In 1986 there were more than 6,500 (Persons, 1987: 167).

White Americans appear to have more tolerant attitudes toward blacks on most issues, particularly on the question of equal employment opportunity. If discrimination was taken for granted by most white Americans as recently as the 1940s, the dominant expressed belief today is that blacks deserve the same treatment as whites in the labor market. While debate persists on methods of implementation, the question of whether or not blacks deserve equal treatment appears to be resolved in the affirmative (Schuman, Steeh, and Bobo, 1985; Firebaugh and Davis, 1988).

The racial gap appears to be closing in other, more concrete, ways. Educational-attainment differences are smaller today than just a few years ago. Among those working full time, the occupational status and individual wages of blacks is closer to that of whites today than was the case 20 years ago (Farley, 1984).

Despite areas in which gains have been made, disparities persist in most critical areas. As indicated above, the proportion of blacks and whites working full time remains as far apart today as it was 20 years ago. For most individuals, family income determines their objective life conditions, and the gap between blacks and whites in this area has increased. If there have been important legal, political and attitudinal advances, critical economic disparities remain.

The perpetuation of these racial disparities reflects, in part, fundamental structural changes in the American economy that evolved primarily in response to considerations other than race. The declining position of the U.S. in the international economy (the U.S. share of world economic output declined from 35 percent in 1960 to 22 percent in 1980 [Reich, 1987: 44]), and the declining rate of profit in the post-World War II years, stimulated several responses on the part of corporate America to reverse that decline. A central objective of that strategy has been to solidify managerial control over production and surplus wealth generated by the economy. Technological advances in communication, transportation and production enabled U.S. manufacturers to expand their operations overseas, particularly in low-wage countries, and facilitated their efforts to shift investment and production around the globe. A range of antilabor tactics at home have been employed, and corporations have been able to pit capital-starved communities against each other in efforts to secure the most favorable terms of operation, from the corporate perspective (Bluestone and Harrison, 1982, 1988; Bowles, Gordon, and Weisskopf, 1983; Shaiken, 1984).

Encouraged by supply-side tax cuts and an antiregulation climate at the federal level, corporate America demanded and received further incentives from state and local governments (e.g., tax abatements, industrial revenue bonds, land cost write-downs) which felt the only available response was to "meet the competition" (Goodman, 1979). In the 1980s, urban policy virtually disappeared in the name of "reindustrialization." *Business Week* (1980) argued that the "aspirations of the poor, the minorities, [and other] special-interest groups must recognize that their own unique goals cannot be satisfied if the U.S. cannot compete in world markets." President Carter's Commission for a National Agenda for the Eighties, in prescient anticipation of his successor, argued that the "economic health of our nation's communities ultimately depends on the health of our nation's economy," which in turn depends on the creation of "an attractive investment climate." Claiming that "cities are not permanent," the Commission argued, in the spirit of Joseph Schumpeter's concept of "creative destruction," that federal policy should be directed toward moving people to where the jobs are and to letting cities go through their natural "transformation" (President's Commission for a National Agenda for the Eighties, 1980: 64-72, 165-9).

Such a definition of the situation expedited the flight of capital from central cities to their suburban rings, from the Northeast to the Sunbelt, and from the U.S. to foreign shores. Urban-to-suburban shifts were well documented in the 1960s, triggering perhaps the most famous observation of the Kerner Commission report:

> To continue present policies is to make permanent the division of our country into two societies; one, largely Negro and poor, located in the central cities; the other, predominantly white and affluent, located in the suburbs and in outlying areas *(Report of the National Advisory Commission on Civil Disorders*, 1968: 22).

Unclear at that time was that such shifts constituted just one part of a much larger pattern of uneven development, and that impending economic crises would exacerbate such uneven development, with racial minorities again enduring a disproportionate share of the burden.

Racial minorities are concentrated precisely in those geographic locations, industries and occupations that have been hardest hit by deindustrialization. Fifty-five percent of all blacks live in central cities, compared to just 23 percent of whites. While minorities constitute approximately 12 percent of the U.S. work force, they represent more than 14 percent of auto and steel workers, two of the hardest-hit industries. Managerial and professional positions, in which unemployment rates have generally remained below five percent even when total unemployment reached double digits, appear to be better protected from the vicissitudes of uneven development. Blacks, though, are half as likely as whites to be employed in these occupational classifications (Hearings before the Subcommittee on Economic Stabilization, 1984: 43). Mismatches noted by Kain (1968) 20 years ago, between the skills possessed by minorities and available jobs, have been exacerbated by contraction of manufacturing jobs and expansion of financial, administrative and related professional service jobs in the nation's cities in recent years (Lichter, 1988).

Two local case studies are illustrative. In Illinois, among a sample of firms that shut down between 1975 and 1978, 20 percent of the former employees of these firms were nonwhite even though racial minorities constituted only 14 percent of the statewide labor force at that time. Among firms relocating from central cities to their respective suburban rings during these years; minority employment dropped by almost 25 percent, compared to less than 10 percent for whites (Illinois Advisory Committee, 1981: 32-43). Since 1975, the city of Milwaukee has lost approximately 30,000 industrial jobs paying an average annual wage of $23,600 in 1984 dollars. The highest concentration of black employment, more than 35 percent of all black workers, is in precisely these relatively higher-paid industrial jobs that the city is losing most rapidly (McNeely and Kinlow, 1987: 21, 57).

Capital mobility adversely affects minorities in many additional ways. Holding a disproportionately small share of equity in American businesses, minorities receive a disproportionately small share of profits from plant closings, openings and relocations. (The typical white household has 12 times the net worth and almost four times the equity in a business or profession of the typical black household [Tidwell, 1987: 195, 202]). Particularly when a plant moves from a central city to a suburban location, minorities face greater difficulties in finding transportation to the jobs or housing in the new location. Consequently, minorities are more likely not to move with the firm (assuming they have that option) or to quit after a short time because of the logistical problems created by the move. When new jobs are created in the suburbs, minorities are less likely to hear about, and therefore apply for, those positions. In many ways, some of which have little if anything to do with an explicit consideration of race, uneven development has adversely effected racial minorities in the U.S (Illinois Advisory Committee, 1981).

In recent years, several economists and public officials have called for industrial policies that expressly acknowledge the conflicts that give rise to, and the social costs (including urban disinvestment and exacerbation of racial inequalities) that result from, capital mobility and uneven development. Specific ingredients of such proposals often include more effective targeting of resources to distressed areas, requirements of performance standards to be met in exchange for public subsidies (including affirmative action and contract-compliance requirements), plant closing prenotification and other tactics to protect public needs while serving private interests. A central focus of these proposals is the incorporation of workers, residents and other members of the community who are affected by investment decisions into those decisionmaking processes that have traditionally been the sole prerogative of private capital. Recognizing the growing public costs of private enterprise, at least some observers have rejected supply-side incentives predicated on trickle-down assumptions in favor of a bargained or linkage approach to economic development and urban redevelopment, based on a more democratic approach to economic decisionmaking that seeks balanced growth as a direct outcome (Bluestone and Harrison, 1982; Bowles, Gordon, and Weisskopf, 1983; City of Chicago, 1984; Mier, Moe, and Sherr, 1986; Thurow, 1981; Squires, et al., 1987).

A central component of many such plans is advocacy (frequently coupled with commitment of financial and other concrete resources) for the creation of new business organizations, or restructuring of existing firms, to permit employees to participate in investment, production and other management decisionmaking and, in turn, allow employees to share equitably in the rewards as well as the responsibilities, of managing the business. Employee ownership, particularly in its more democratic configurations, embodies critical civil rights implications that have long been ignored. The following section examines the concept of employee ownership to illustrate the potentially advantageous implications of more democratic work organizations and economic planning for the civil rights issues facing the nation today.

Employee Ownership: An Emerging Economic Phenomenon

Employee ownership has become an increasingly popular tool for economic development in recent years. Though the concept is certainly not without its critics, many benefits are attributed to employee ownership. Virtually no systematic attention has been paid, however, to the experiences of racial minorities in employee-owned firms or the civil rights implications of this type of business organization. There are, however, theoretically plausible reasons and scattered empirical evidence to suggest that employee ownership ameliorates employment disparities associated with race.

An employee-owned Washington, D.C. insurance company, for example, pays its black employees an average salary of $21,200, compared to $30,100 for whites, a black/white ratio of .71 (Mariam, 1985). For the insurance industry as a whole in Washington, D.C., however, the black/white ratio is just .54 (U.S. Bureau of the Census, 1981). Racial minorities clearly are doing far better relative to whites in this employee-owned company than they are industrywide in the nation's capital.

After reviewing the growing interest in employee ownership in this section and prevailing theoretical perspectives on racial inequality in the U.S. labor market in the following section, it will be argued that in light of the structural forces shaping those inequalities and the organizational characteristics frequently associated with employee ownership, racial inequalities will be smaller in democratically structured, employee-owned firms than in traditionally organized business entities. The section which follows will then offer empirical support for this conclusion. This egalitarian effect suggests several important policy implications, discussed in the final section, in the areas of economic development and civil rights, particularly in light of the widespread public support and proliferation of employee ownership in recent years and the likelihood of continued support in the near future.

A perusal of the popular press, academic journals and the behavior of government agencies and other community organizations reveals a striking increase in the interest being paid to the concept and practice of employee ownership. Though not a new concept, the nation's recent economic troubles have led many observers to conclude that the time for employee ownership has come. Rosen, Klein, and Young (1986) of the National Center for Employee Ownership conclude that this form of ownership provides the solution for what are often viewed as contradictory ends: equity and growth. In their introduction, entitled "Mr. Smith, Meet Mr. Marx," they argue, "By making employees owners, programs that enhance capital investment automatically enrich workers" (1986: 5).

The idea of employee ownership in the U.S. is as old as the nation itself. The Founding Fathers frequently noted the utility of widespread property ownership, including business ownership, primarily as a device to assure the commitment of as many citizens as possible to the value of private property (Russell, 1985: 8-11). Today it is an idea that appeals to all ends of the political spectrum, from Ronald Reagan, Russell Long and the Pope to Ted Kennedy, Tom Hayden and the Teamsters. Similarly, it is criticized by proponents of diverse political perspectives, including many representatives of the business community and organized labor. Today, though, there are more than 8,000 firms, representing more than seven percent of the work force, in which employees share in the ownership. In most cases employees own between 15 and 40 percent, with employees owning a majority of stock in 10 to 15 percent (Rosen, Klein, and Young, 1986: 1, 2, 16; Rosen and Quarry, 1987). In recent years there has been increasing debate over the concept of employee ownership, along with more substantial public and private support of efforts to encourage the practice.

The motivations for turning employees into owners are diverse. A major attraction is the utility of employee ownership in raising capital for reinvestment (including leveraged buyouts to prevent hostile takeovers) or to facilitate the acquisition or divestiture of subsidiaries. This is particularly true for employee stock-ownership plans (ESOPs) which have grown from approximately 300 in 1974 to more than 7,000 today because of various federal tax breaks associated with this financing vehicle (Rosen, Klein, and Young, 1986: 14-31; Russell, 1985: 196-219). Another incentive is provided by evidence that employee-owned firms, compared to conventionally structured firms, are often more productive and more profitable, with one of the reasons for such performance being better labor relations and employee morale in such settings (Frieden, 1980; Conte and Tannenbaum, 1980; Blumberg, 1973; Select Committee on Small Business, 1979). The most recent evidence also suggests that employee-owned firms grow more rapidly, in terms of sales and total employment, and such effects are greater where ownership and meaningful participation are combined (Rosen and Quarry, 1987).

A related motivation is the desire to save a business that might otherwise be shut down through conversion to employee ownership (Midwest Center for Labor Research, 1985; Rosen, Klein, and Young, 1986: 27-9; Russell, 1985: 193-219). Such initiatives can help strengthen ties between workers and their local community, enhance labor solidarity and save many jobs in the process (Swinney, 1985). As indicated above, the stagnation of the U.S. economy in recent years has convinced many within business, labor and government to view employee ownership as part of the solution to economic ills in general, and to act on that belief (Russell, 1985: 196-212). Many industrial-policy and urban-redevelopment proposals have incorporated elements of employee ownership (Bradley and Gelb, 1983; Bluestone and Harrison, 1982: 257-62; Bowles, Gordon, and Weisskopf, 1983: 261-390). For some, the desire for a more democratic workplace provides a major attraction to employee ownership, particularly when coupled with worker control. In some instances, the more democratic structure is viewed as a means to more productive ends, while for others the appeal is for democracy as a value itself, regardless of any effect on productivity (Zwerdling, 1978; Cohen and Rogers, 1983).

At the same time, strong objections to employee ownership have been raised. In addition to the philosophy of some business leaders that "management's job is to manage," there are many within the labor movement who view employee ownership as antithetical to the interests of the majority of workers.

At a time when more militant tactics are required to confront capital, according to some (Slott, 1985; Zwerdling, 1978: 165-80), employee ownership results in complicity with management by labor leaders and redirection of union members' energy to helping their employers survive in the marketplace. A related contention is that employee ownership is simply the successor to bureaucratic control (Edwards, 1979) as a mechanism for management to assure the loyalty of, and manipulate and control, their workers (Russell, 1985: 197-202). Without additional structural changes that provide for control as well as ownership, an employee-owned firm, particularly in the form of an ESOP, may constitute "second-class ownership" for the workers, without any of the advantages traditionally associated with ownership (Ellerman, 1985; Blasi, 1988).

More concrete costs have been asserted. Employee ownership can be used as a vehicle for securing substantial wage cuts (Rothschild-Witt, 1985; Lynd, 1985). In some cases, workers assume extreme risks when their jobs, investments and retirement funds become dependent on the profitability of one business, particularly if it is a financially troubled firm to begin with (Russell, 1985: 205-7).

Despite these criticisms, employee ownership has grown, in no small part as a result of public support for turning employees into owners. Since 1973, there have been at least 15 federal laws, along with legislation in more than 14 states, to provide such aid as technical assistance in conducting feasibility studies, loans, tax breaks and other financial support for the creation of employee-owned businesses (Rosen, Klein, and Young, 1986: 251-5).

Amid this flurry of activity, no attention has been paid to the civil rights implications of employee ownership. It has been argued that self-management can provide an effective structure for black economic development (Williams, 1976) and that ESOPs constitute an effective vehicle for black capital accumulation (Whittaker, 1977). No effort has been made, however, to systematically assess the effect of employee ownership on racial inequality, yet there are plausible arguments and scattered empirical evidence to suggest that at least some forms of employee ownership ameliorate racial disparities in the labor market.

Theoretical Perspectives on Racial Income Inequality

The potential of employee ownership as part of an urban policy geared toward the amelioration of racial inequality is demonstrated by recent developments in our theoretical understanding of race relations. This section reviews the development of social theory in this area. Additional empirical support for this finding is reviewed in the following section and the policy implications are then discussed in the concluding section. For any policy to be effective, though, it must be premised on a sound theoretical understanding of the issue at hand. Important progress toward this end has been made in the area of race relations in recent years.

Human-capital theory and the neoclassical paradigm in which it is rooted have long been the dominant conceptual tools used to explain the distribution of wages as well as inequalities associated with race. This perspective, as Donald Schwab recently told the U.S. Commission on Civil Rights, "has remained the principal economic explanation of micro wage-setting behavior for over 100 years" (U.S. Commission on Civil Rights, 1985: 26). According to this perspective, wages and salaries are determined primarily by the demand for and supply of particular skills and services in a free, unitary labor market. Individual buyers (i.e., employers) and sellers (i.e., employees) meet in the marketplace to negotiate the price at which people will go to work, that is, the wage level at which the market will clear. The more skills, education and experience desired by employers that an employee can bring to the market–the greater his or her human capital–the higher the price will be that the employer will have to pay for that employee. A free labor market, like the free market for any product or service, provides for maximum societal efficiency in the utilization of labor resources. In general, whites have accumulated more human capital than nonwhites. Consequently, whites have been able to command higher wages (Friedman, 1984).

While whites as a group possess more human capital, on average, than nonwhites, a central assumption of human-capital theory and the neoclassical paradigm is that levels of education, experience and career trajectory are functions of individual choice. A key question that each person confronts is whether to maximize current consumption (to be achieved in part by getting a job now) or to spend current time obtaining more education and training to maximize future consumption. Such preparation enhances future earnings because the individual would be qualified at a later time for jobs requiring higher levels of skill (and consequently paying higher wages) and the individual would be able to compete for a broader range of jobs, thus enhancing his or her opportunities to secure better-paying positions. The critical assumption, again, is that the job one holds or the career one chooses to pursue is the result of voluntary, individual choice, presumably unaffected by race, sex or any other social or cultural factors.

By explaining labor-market and related economic inequalities among racial groups in these voluntaristic and individualistic terms, human capital theory provides a relatively simple and seemingly plausible solution to racial inequality that benefits not only those at the lower end of the economic spectrum, but the entire community. The basic solution resides in increased education and training. Consequently, not only will the individuals receiving these services benefit by accumulating more human capital and becoming more competitive in the labor market, society will benefit as well by the increasing productivity that results from a more highly-skilled work force. To the extent that lower-income people obtain their fair share of education and training opportunities, economic equality will be enhanced, again because of market forces that operate in an open, competitive economy. As Lester Thurow (1972) has noted, there are three basic reasons, according to the human-capital perspective, why this is the case. First, increased education and training will help poor (and previously untrained) people obtain better jobs. Second, as the supply of unskilled workers diminishes, the growing scarcity of such workers will bid up the price of unskilled labor. Third, as the supply of highly skilled people increases, particularly where it exceeds demand, the price for such labor will decline.

Any discrepancies between the wages of whites and nonwhites that are not predicated on different levels of human capital cannot long prevail, according to the assumptions of the neoclassical paradigm. If a given employer were to pay whites higher wages than nonwhites who possess equivalent human capital, the workings of the free market will soon punish that employer. By exercising his or her taste for discrimination, that employer will be paying a higher wage for a given level of human capital than will the competition, ultimately forcing that employer out of business. The basic solutions to problems of discrimination, therefore, are the preservation of a free labor market and more effective training programs to enhance the human capital of those entering that market (Becker, 1957, 1964; Friedman, 1962; Sowell, 1981 and 1984; Williams, 1982).

This perspective has been challenged in recent years by many who reject the neo-classical paradigm in general and human-capital theory in particular. The fundamental points of contention are the assumption of a unitary labor market, reliance on characteristics of individuals to explain wage patterns and the voluntary nature in which career choices are presumably made. While not denying that positive returns are associated with education, skills and related attributes, the dominant perspective ignores a range of structural characteristics of the economy and society generally that shape the overall distribution of wages as well as those associated with race. In efforts to overcome these deficiencies, alternative models have been offered.

Several economists and sociologists have advanced a number of dual-economy and segmentation conceptualizations. The dual economy, constituted by core and periphery firms (Averitt, 1968; Tolbert, Horan, and Beck, 1980) and a dual labor market consisting of primary- and secondary-sector jobs (Baron and Hymer, 1971; Gordon, Edwards, and Reich, 1982; Edwards, Reich, and Gordon, 1975) have been identified in which wages are shaped by the characteristics of the sector, industry and job of the individual, independent of the human capital he or she has accumulated. Such factors as industry and company size, concentration (monopoly vs. competitive), capital intensity, unionization rates and degree of government regulation define various sectors of the economy and influence wages paid within them. Wages are also frequently a function of the characteristics of jobs as well as of job holders. Primary sector jobs have been identified that are characterized by job security, opportunities for promotion, good working conditions, fair administration of work rules and higher earnings. Secondary jobs, on the other hand, offer little security, little chance for promotion, poor working conditions, arbitrary administration of work rules and low earnings. Not only are human-capital theory's individualistic assumptions challenged by such segmentation, but to the extent that these sectors operate independently of each other (that is, workers compete within industrial sectors or job markets) unitary assumptions about the job market are undermined as well. Racial minorities are "crowded" (Bergmann, 1971) into the less desirable jobs in such "split-labor markets" (Bonacich, 1972), thus reducing their wages relative to whites and seriously challenging voluntary assumptions about career choice. Given these conditions, race ceases being just an individual characteristic, since wages are downgraded in those positions because they have a high concentration of racial minorities (Friedman, 1984; U.S. Commission on Civil Rights, 1985: 18).

Human-capital theory's reliance on the external labor market as the major wage-setting force is challenged by researchers who have demonstrated that characteristics of internal labor markets frequently shape wage levels (Doeringer and Piore, 1971). In efforts to reduce recruitment and training costs, and to stabilize the work force and reduce production costs generally, employers often offer higher wages and other benefits than they could receive in the external labor market to current employees. For example, an employer may rely on word-of-mouth advertising to fill new jobs, thus enabling employees to help their family and friends and reducing their own recruitment costs. When the current work force is predominantly white, one likely, though perhaps unintentional, result is to perpetuate the racial composition of the work force.

Other structural characteristics of organizations that deny opportunities to racial minorities have also been identified. Rigid hierarchical bureaucracies in which decisionmaking is highly centralized, narrowly defined job responsibilities and a "corporate culture" that reinforces conformity to conventional stereotypes tend to restrict the opportunity, power and informal support for employees at the lower rungs, particularly for racial minorities (Kanter, 1977).

A variety of personnel practices shape the distribution of wages independently of the human capital of workers, mitigate the free play of the market and adversely affect nonwhites. These include screening devices that use averages among diverse groups to draw conclusions about individual members that, intentionally or unintentionally, adversely affect racial minorities. Educational credentials unrelated to job requirements are often used as a convenience for the employer and to reduce recruiting costs, but at the expense of black applicants. Such "statistical discrimination" (Arrow, 1972) has been declared illegal under certain circumstances, but this has not eliminated these practices nor ended their impact on racial inequality (U.S. Commission on Civil Rights, 1981).

Another factor that mitigates the operation of a truly free labor market is the unequal availability of information about job opportunities. A critical assumption of the neoclassical theory of free markets is universal availability of information among buyers and sellers. The absence of such universality means that those with information that others lack have an advantage, one which undermines the operation of a free market. A free labor market would require that all participants be aware of all employment opportunities, and therefore be able to compete on the basis of the marginal productivities they bring to the market. Knowledge of job openings, though, is not universally available. Those who are part of, or have access to, the "right" networks have an obvious advantage. Where informal or subjective criteria are used in employment decisions, knowledge of opportunities may be limited strictly to those on the inside. Nonwhites are less likely to be part of such networks, particularly those involving the allocation of more prestigious and higher-paid positions.

Inequality in the training and education that people receive and in the economic resources held by themselves or their families prior to entering the labor market further undermines human-capital-theory assumptions regarding the individual and voluntary nature of job and career choices. Unequal resources devoted to the education of whites and nonwhites, and racial steering by teachers, guidance counselors and other school administrators, as well as other discriminatory practices within the nation's educational institutions, result in greater opportunity for whites to exercise free choice as they prepare for and enter their chosen careers. Since white families on average have more economic resources than nonwhites, white children are also more free to decide whether they want to take a job now and maximize current consumption or delay entry into the job market by getting more education, thereby maximizing future consumption. Obviously, when a family is poor and cannot afford either the cost of higher education or the foregone income resulting from fulltime school attendance, the voluntary nature of such choices is restricted (Rist, 1970; Rehberg and Hotchkiss, 1972; Carnoy and Levin, 1985).

More radical formulations have focused on the failure of the neoclassical paradigm to account for the significance of class, conflict and power relations in shaping wage levels. Human-capital theory has been effectively criticized for treating economic behavior as if it occurs independently of politics and other social relations and institutions (Friedman, 1984). It is the unequal relation between capital and labor, however, that most fundamentally determines aggregate wage levels and the distribution among diverse populations (Reich, 1981; Boggs and Boggs, 1970; Geschwender, 1977; Lieberson, 1980). The concept of a reserve army of labor, in which a steady pool of unemployed people provides employers with substantial leverage in negotiating wages along with other terms of employment, perhaps most explicitly illustrates this relationship. One's position in the class structure, as determined by the extent of control over the production process, consequently affects wages, independent of human capital considerations (Wright, 1979). The reemergence of the phrase "political economy" symbolizes the thrust of this perspective.

Evidence of the political dimensions of wage allocations and other personnel practices includes the fact that such decisions are often shaped by the desire of capital to control labor and rationalize the production process as well as by supply-and-demand conditions in the external labor market (Braverman, 1974; Edwards, 1979). The ability of labor to resist such initiatives and to secure higher wages is, at least in part, a function of the power of unions, again independent of the human capital of individual union members.

Though widespread discrimination has long characterized the practices of organized labor (Hill, 1977, 1982) minorities have also benefitted from the equalizing effect that unions have had on the distribution of wealth between capital and labor (Freeman and Medoff, 1984). Contrary to the assertion of human capital theory that discrimination hurts employers, a recent study found that employer profits were larger in those cities where unions were weaker, inequality among all workers was more extensive and racial inequality was more pronounced. Workers, particularly black workers, benefit–at the expense of employers–where unions are strongest (Reich, 1981). Two key conclusions emerge from this study. Racial inequality and inequality among all workers go hand in hand, and power is critical in determining wage levels generally and racial disparities in particular. These findings are particularly important given the deindustrialization of America that has occurred since the late 1960s.

The role of the state in determining wage levels is another important factor that the neoclassical paradigm ignores. Relations among capital, labor and government influence the level and distribution of the costs and benefits of tax expenditures, government contracts and guaranteed loans, tariffs, inheritance laws, minimum wage, labor-law and civil rights enforcement and other factors that dramatically alter the context within which labor markets presumably clear. In efforts to assure private-capital accumulation while providing legitimacy for the resulting inequalities–and to preserve their own positions–public officials *do* shape wage levels in ways that are responsive to a range of messages, in addition to the signals of the market (O'Conner, 1973; Lindblom, 1977). Recent debates over industrial policy and the competitiveness of the American economy are simply more visible manifestations of what has long been a central role of politics in shaping the U.S. economy, urban-redevelopment initiatives and the opportunity structure for various participants (Judd, 1984; Reich, 1983).

The political-economy perspective offers perhaps the most sweeping critique of the neoclassical paradigm, particularly human-capital theory. There are important commonalities, though, in the various challenges to what still remains the dominant perspective. Where neoclassical economists see individuals competing in an efficiency-maximizing, unitary market on the basis of particular skills developed as a result of voluntary career choices, ultimately for the benefit of society generally, their critics see groups of people and institutions operating in a segmented and often exploitative environment using collective tactics to further what are frequently conflicting interests. The former perspective sees a free market with appropriate education and training as the key to ending racial discrimination; the latter calls for changes in those structural characteristics of the economy and society generally that perpetuate such discrimination.

Employee Ownership, Equality and Equal Opportunity

In light of what has been learned about the structural determinants of racial inequality, the organizational characteristics of many employee-owned firms may suggest approaches that can be taken to better understand the dynamics of racial inequalities and to ameliorate them. These empirical realities, coupled with the theoretical developments discussed above, suggest important urban-policy implications that will be discussed in the conclusion.

The principal characteristic of many employee-owned firms that is conducive to smaller racial inequalities than in conventionally structured firms is the existence of a conscious effort to provide for a more equal distribution of resources, responsibility and revenues among all employees. This is accomplished through a variety of policies and practices.

Management perquisites, such as executive parking lots and lunchrooms, are frequently eliminated (Rosen, Klein, and Young, 1986: 10). Employees often participate in what have traditionally been considered management responsibilities, including sitting on boards of directors. In some cases, employees own and control all phases of the operation. Special training programs are sometimes implemented to prepare workers for tasks they have not previously performed. Job-rotation programs may be implemented to give workers experience in various operations. New job ladders may be created to facilitate upward mobility. The responsibilities of individual jobs may be changed so that each position will entail more diverse responsibilities, thus reducing the rigidity of the division of labor and providing for a more egalitarian job structure. In some firms, a cap is set on the maximum allowable difference between the salaries given to the highest- and lowest-paid employees. Profits are often distributed equally among all employees. When business is slow, employee-owned firms are less likely to lay off workers and are more likely to temporarily reduce wages of all employees or accept lower profits (Russell, 1985: 61-4). In the insurance company referred to above, no employee can earn more than five times the salary of the lowest paid worker compared to a 17-fold average difference industry-wide, temporary salary reductions among all are accepted as an alternative to layoffs, workers have management responsibilities, training is available to prepare workers for those responsibilities, and several other policies have been implemented to provide for what the company refers to as "its own participatory democracy" (Mariam, 1985). Many of these practices do upgrade the human capital of employees, but it is the structural changes that permit such upgrading and, more importantly, which account for the egalitarian effects. These kinds of policies are not unique to employee-owned businesses, of course, but they are more prevalent in such settings.

To the extent that employee ownership and the associated personnel practices change the structural characteristics that have blocked opportunities for racial minorities (e.g., expand responsibilities and rewards for lower-level jobs to increase the number of primary sector jobs and reduce the number of secondary jobs, create job ladders linking lower and higher level positions, or enhance the position of labor relative to management) and alter the power relationships that have denied opportunities to these groups (e.g., provide employee representation –if not control–on boards of directors or redistribute management responsibility among workers), the concept of employee ownership can be a valuable tool for ameliorating racial inequalities in the U.S. labor market. None of this suggests that education, training and human capital are unimportant, particularly in a postindustrial society in which "high-tech" will be a vital avenue of upward mobility for many. The opportunity for racial minorities to obtain the necessary human capital, however, will itself depend on structural changes in the political economy of the U.S. To focus on human-capital variables, at the exclusion of the various structural characteristics of the labor market that shape racial inequalities, would ignore much of what is now known theoretically and empirically about the causes of those inequalities, and therefore would lead to ineffective public policy.

Employee ownership and the types of egalitarian personnel policies cited above are not implemented primarily, if at all, for the purposes of ameliorating racial inequality, although many employee-owned firms have implemented affirmative action plans. Given the concentration of racial minorities among the lower rungs of the American occupational structure, though, any efforts to reduce inequality generally will favorably alter the relative position of minorities.

In addition to the case of the insurance company cited above, preliminary analysis of one set of employee-owned companies further suggests the egalitarian effects of democratically structured work organizations. In examining 37 ESOPs for which data were available, racial income disparities were found to be smaller in those firms that had created formal worker-participation groups (i.e., groups designed to involve nonmanagerial employees in selected management decision-making areas pertaining to production) than in those firms which had not created such groups. In addition, where workers had input into pay, hiring and firing decisions, wage disparities between whites and nonwhites were smaller (Squires and Lyson, forthcoming). These findings may represent little more than further anecdotal evidence, but they are in the hypothesized direction and indicate the need for further research on these issues.

Policy Implications

If an urban policy is to address the issue of racial inequality in the nation's cities effectively, traditional civil rights struggles must be complemented with efforts that will democratize the nation's economic institutions. Enactment of a series of laws prohibiting employment discrimination, an increase in black elected officials and expression of more tolerant racial attitudes by whites do not mean that "the battle for civil rights was fought and won," as some suggest (Sowell, 1984: 109). If the federal government has led the way to significant civil rights victories in recent years, it must be recalled that, historically, the federal government, has been a fickle friend of black freedom struggles. The institution of slavery was sanctioned by the federal government with the Supreme Court confirming its constitutionality in the Dred Scott decision. A decade of reconstruction was followed by withdrawal of federal troops (and with them the protections granted by the Civil War amendments) and the onset of the infamous "black codes." Not until Franklin D. Roosevelt issued a series of Executive Orders banning discrimination in the nation's defense industries did the federal government again act positively on civil rights concerns.

If the 1960s constituted a decade of progressive action by two presidents and their administrations, the retreat of the 1980s showed how fragile that posture can be. The favorable affirmative action decisions by the Supreme Court in 1986 and 1987, followed by the setbacks in 1989, are additional reminders of that fragility. Vital political victories of the civil rights movement over the past three decades do remain intact, but they provide tools to build with, not laurels to rest upon. Proliferation of employee ownership may constitute one direction toward which to work.

If the implementation of employee ownership and the egalitarian personnel policies frequently associated with this form of ownership enhance the relative earnings of racial minorities, one obvious conclusion is that the proliferation of such policies will enable more minorities to assume greater responsibilities, earn more money and contribute more to the development of their families and communities. In turn, these conclusions suggest tactics that would enable organizations to take better advantage of the talents that racial minorities can bring to the workplace. Society would gain from the enhanced productivity of these individuals and organizations.

If employee ownership reduces wage disparities associated with race, the particular policies that appear most responsible for that outcome would suggest tactics that employers could use voluntarily or that civil rights officials might use in their enforcement efforts. Redesigning job responsibilities, rotating jobs, creating new job ladders, providing additional training, decentralizing authority, sharing burdens of unemployment (thus mitigating the "last hired, first fired" syndrome), capping wage differentials, sharing profits and flattening employment hierarchies generally are, in fact, already advocated by many equal-employment-opportunity consultants and utilized in some affirmative action plans (Kanter, 1977: 265-303; U.S. Commission on Civil Rights, 1981: 43-56). One critical advantage of these approaches is that they do not necessarily involve the kinds of numerical goals, timetables, or quotas that have been the subject of such heated controversy for more than 20 years (Glazer, 1975; Ryan, 1982; Leadership Conference on Civil Rights, 1985).

Employee ownership is viewed as an increasingly attractive approach to economic development by a broad spectrum of the U.S. population. Equal opportunity is a firmly established value in American culture, though disputes rage over how to achieve it. Proliferation of employee ownership, at least certain forms, may provide paths for addressing two of the nation's most pressing, divisive and increasingly interdependent problems–economic stagnation and discrimination–but in a manner that builds on sources of consensus that prevail in American society while minimizing points of contention and conflict.

The form and location of ownership, however, is critical. As indicated above, in the absence of meaningful democratic control, employee ownership can lead to lower wages, more subtle yet more effective manipulation and control of workers and increasing economic risk as all eggs are concentrated in one basket, and a possibly leaking one at that. If employee ownership is perceived simply as a potential bailout for failing businesses, few benefits are likely to be realized. Feasibility studies, market analyses and sound business planning generally are as essential for these kinds of entrepreneurial ventures as for any other investment. Such technical assistance is increasingly available through organizations like the New York Center for Employee Ownership, the Midwest Center for Labor Research in Chicago, the Midwest Employee Ownership Center in Detroit and the National Center for Employee Ownership in Oakland. Experiences in more democratic formulations of employee ownership, though, suggest the potential of the establishment of more egalitarian workplace organizations as one tactic for ameliorating racial inequality and enhancing the productivity of the local economy. Commitment to preserving jobs and local communities, characteristics of many employee-owned businesses (and many locally owned firms), make such businesses important contributors to local economic-development efforts, which should translate into increasing opportunities for the racial minorities concentrated in the nation's major urban communities.

None of this suggests that employee ownership, in and of itself, can resolve the serious economic problems that plague the U.S. economy, its cities, and particularly its minority population. Nor does this suggest any reduction in voluntary affirmative action planning or civil rights enforcement. What this does suggest is that, as part of a much broader effort to confront changing economic realities and develop appropriate democratic responses, there may be some additional tools, or new twists on some old tools, that might be considered in the urban-redevelopment and civil rights arenas.

The racial disparities found by the Kerner Commission in 1968 in such critical economic areas as income, unemployment and labor-force participation persist today. This hardly suggests, however, that the U.S. labor market has remained unaltered. The American economy, its cities and the structure of opportunity confronting blacks have changed dramatically since 1968. It is no longer sufficient, if it ever was, to simply address the allocation of various groups across the occupational distributions of American employers or the human capital accumulated by the U.S. work force. The public costs of private enterprise for far too many American families and communities have become too great to abdicate fundamental investment and economic structural decisionmaking to private authorities alone. Macrolevel economic policy decisions and the internal structural characteristics of individual economic organizations must become the focus of public policy in civil rights as well as economic-development arenas. As the Joint Center for Political Studies recently concluded:

> We believe policies that do not take into account the changing characteristics of the national economy–including its rate of growth and demand for labor, including factors that affect industrial employment such as investment and technology, and including demographic changes that accompany industrial transformations–cannot possibly respond effectively to the economic and social dislocations of low-income blacks (Joint Center, 1983: 5).

Injecting a strong dose of democracy into the nation's economic institutions is essential to remedying the diverse problems confronting those most vulnerable to the vagaries of uneven development. Just more of what was demanded in the 1960s will not be adequate for the nation's cities and their minority populations during the remainder of this century and beyond.

References

Arrow, Kenneth (1972) Some mathematical models of race discrimination in the labor market. In Anthony Pascal (Ed.), *Racial Discrimination in Economic*

Life. Lexington, Mass.: D.C. Heath.

Averitt, Robert T. (1968) *The Dual Economy: The Dynamics of American Industry Structure*. New York: Horton.

Baron, Harold M. and Bennett Hymer (1971) The dynamics of the dual labor market. In David M. Gordon (Ed.), *Problems in Political Economy: An Urban Perspective*. Lexington, Mass.: D.C. Heath.

Becker, Gary S. (1957) *The Economics of Discrimination*. Chicago: University of Chicago Press.

Becker, Gary S. (1964) *Human Capital: A Theoretical and Empirical Analysis With Special Reference to Education*. New York: Columbia University Press.

Bergmann, Barbara (1971) The effect on white incomes of discrimination in employment, *Journal of Political Economy, 79*: 294-313.

Blasi, Joseph R. (1988) *Employee Ownership: Revolution or Ripoff?* Cambridge, Mass.: Ballinger.

Bluestone, Barry and Bennett Harrison (1982) *The Deindustrialization of America: Plant Closings, Community Abandonment, and the Dismantling of Basic Industry*. New York: Basic Books.

Bluestone, Barry and Bennett Harrison (1988) *The Great U-Turn: Corporate Restructuring and the Polarizing of America*. New York: Basic Books.

Blumberg, Paul (1973) *Industrial Democracy: The Sociology of Participation*. New York: Schocken Books.

Boggs, James and Grace Boggs (1970) *Racism and the Class Struggle*. New York: Monthly Review Press.

Bonacich, Edna (1972) A theory of ethnic antagonism: The split labor market, *American Sociological Review, 37*: 547-59.

Bowles, Samuel, David M. Gordon, and Thomas E. Weisskopf (1983) *Beyond the Wasteland: A Democratic Alternative to Economic Decline*. New York: Anchor Press/Doubleday.

Bradley, Keith and Alan Gelb (1983) *Worker Capitalism: The New Industrial Relations*. Cambridge, Mass.: MIT Press.

Braverman, Harry (1974) *Labor and Monopoly Capital: The Degradation of Work in the Twentieth Century*. New York: Monthly Review Press.

Business Week (1980) "The Reindustrialization of America," special issue (30 June).

Carnoy, Martin, and Henry M. Levin (1985) *Schooling and Work in the Democratic State*. Stanford: Stanford University Press.

Chambers, Julius L. (1987) The law and black Americans: Retreat from civil rights. In Janet Dewart (Ed.), *The State of Black America 1987*. New York:

National Urban League.
City of Chicago (1984) *Chicago Works Together: Chicago Development Plan.* Chicago: Office of the Mayor.
Cohen, Joshua, and Joel Rogers (1983) *On Democracy: Toward a Transformation of American Society.* New York: Penguin.
Conte, Michael and Arnold Tannenbaum (1980) *Employee Ownership.* Ann Arbor: Survey Research Center, University of Michigan.
Dewart, Janet (Ed.) (1988) *The State of Black America 1988.* New York: National Urban League.
Doeringer, Peter B. and Michael Piore (1971) *Internal Labor Markets and Manpower Analysis.* Lexington, Mass.: D.C. Heath.
Edwards, Richard C. (1979) *Contested Terrain: The Transformation of Work in the Twentieth Century.* New York: Basic Books.
Edwards, Richard C., Michael Reich, and David Gordon (Eds.) (1975) *Labor Market Segmentation.* Lexington, Mass.: D.C. Heath.
Ellerman, David P. (1985) ESOPs and co-ops: Worker capitalism and worker democracy, *Labor Research Review, 6*: 55-69.
Farley, Reynolds (1984) *Blacks and Whites: Narrowing the Gap?* Cambridge: Harvard University Press.
Freeman, Richard B. and James L. Medoff (1984) *What Do Unions Do?* New York: Basic.
Frieden, Karl (1980) *Workplace Democracy and Productivity.* Washington, D.C.: National Center for Economic Alternatives.
Friedman, Milton (1962) *Capitalism and Freedom.* Chicago: University of Chicago Press.
Friedman, Samuel R. (1984) Structure, process, and the labor market. In William Darity, Jr. (Ed.), *Labor Economics: Modern Views.* Boston: Kluwer-Nijhoff.
Geschwender, James A. (1977) *Race and Worker Insurgency.* New York: Cambridge University Press.
Gilder, George (1981) *Wealth and Poverty.* New York: Basic.
Glazer, Nathan (1975) *Affirmative Discrimination: Ethnic Inequality and Public Policy.* New York: Basic.
Goodman, Robert (1979) *The Last Entrepreneurs: America's Regional Wars for Jobs and Dollars.* New York: Simon and Schuster.
Gordon, David M., Richard C. Edwards, and Michael Reich (1982) *Segmented Work, Divided Workers: The Historical Transformation of Labor in the United States.* New York: Cambridge University Press.
Hamal, Harvey R., Economist, Bureau of Labor Statistics (1988) Letter to

Gregory D. Squires, (1 February).

Hearings before the Subcommittee on Economic Stabilization of the Committee on Banking, Finance and Urban Affairs, House of Representatives (1984) *Industrial Policy.* Washington, D.C.: U.S. Government Printing Office.

Hill, Herbert (1977) *Black Labor and the American Legal System: Race, Work and the Law.* Washington, D.C.: Bureau of National Affairs.

Hill, Herbert (1982) Race and labor: The AFL-CIO and the black worker: Twenty-five years after the merger, *The Journal of Intergroup Relations, X*: 5-49.

Illinois Advisory Committee to the U.S. Commission on Civil Rights (1981) *Shutdown: Economic Dislocation and Equal Opportunity.* Washington, D.C.: U.S. Government Printing Office.

Joint Center for Political Studies (1983) *A Policy Framework for Racial Justice.* Washington, D.C.: Joint Center for Political Studies.

Judd, Dennis R. (1984) *The Politics of American Cities: Private Power and Public Policy.* Boston: Little, Brown.

Kain, John F. (1968) Housing segregation, Negro employment, and metropolitan decentralization, *Quarterly Journal of Economics, 82*: 175-97.

Kanter, Rosabeth Moss (1977) *Men and Women of the Corporation.* New York: Basic Books.

Landry, Bart (1987) *The New Black Middle Class.* Berkeley: University of California Press.

Leadership Conference on Civil Rights, Information package on Executive Order 11246 (1985) Washington, D.C.: Leadership Conference on Civil Rights.

Lichter, Daniel T. (1988) Racial differences in underemployment in American cities, *American Journal of Sociology, 93*: 771-92.

Lieberson, Stanley (1980) *A Piece of the Pie: Black and White Immigrants Since 1880.* Berkeley: University of California Press.

Lindblom, Charles E. (1977) *Politics and Markets: The World's Political-Economic Systems.* New York: Basic.

Lynd, Staughton (1985) Why we opposed the buy-out at Weirton Steel, *Labor Research Review, 6*: 41-53.

Mariam, Aster H. (1985) letter to Gregory D. Squires and attachment from personnel department of employee-owned insurance company in Washington, D.C., (31 October).

McNeely, R.L. and M.R. Kinlow (1987) *Milwaukee Today: A Racial Gap Study.* Milwaukee: The Milwaukee Urban League.

Midwest Center for Labor Research (Ed.) (1985) Labor research review. Special issue, *Workers as Owners, 6*: 1-114.

Mier, Robert, Kari J. Moe, and Irene Sherr (1986) Strategic planning and the pursuit of reform, economic development, and equity, *Journal of the American Planning Association, 52*: 299-309.

Murray, Charles (1984) *Losing Ground: American Social Policy 1950-1980.* New York: Basic.

O'Connor, James (1973) *The Fiscal Crisis of the State.* New York: St. Martin's Press.

Persons, Georgia A. (1987) Blacks in state and local government: Progress and constraints. In Janet Dewart (Ed.), *The State of Black America 1987.* New York: National Urban League.

President's Commission for a National Agenda for the Eighties (1980) *A National Agenda for the Eighties.* Washington, D.C.: U.S. Government Printing Office.

Rehberg, Richard, and Laurence Hotchkiss (1972) Education decisionmakers: The school guidance counselor and social mobility, *Sociology of Education, 45*: 339-61.

Reich, Michael (1981) *Racial Inequality: A Political-Economic Analysis.* Princeton: Princeton University Press.

Reich, Robert B. (1983) *The Next American Frontier.* New York: Times Books.

Reich, Robert B. (1987) *Tales of a New America.* New York: Times Books.

Report of the National Advisory Commission on Civil Disorders (1968) New York: Bantam.

Rist, Ray C. (1970) Student social class and teacher expectations: The self-fulfilling prophecy in ghetto schools, *Harvard Educational Review, 40*: 411-50.

Rosen, Corey, Katherine J. Klein, and Karen M. Young (1986) *Employee Ownership in America: The Equity Solution.* Lexington, Mass: D.C. Heath.

Rosen, Corey, and Michael Quarrey (1985) How well is employee ownership working? *Harvard Business Review, 87*: 126-32.

Rothschild-Witt, Joyce (1985) Who will benefit from ESOPs? *Labor Research Review, 6*: 71-80.

Russell, Raymond (1985) *Sharing Ownership in the Workplace.* Albany: SUNY Press.

Ryan, William (1982) *Equality.* New York: Random House, Vintage Books.

Schuman, Howard, Charlotte Steeh, and Lawrence Bobo (1985) *Racial Attitudes in America: Trends and Interpretations.* Cambridge: Harvard University Press.

Select Committee on Small Business, United States Senate (1979) *The Role of*

the Federal Government and Employee Ownership of Business. Washington, D.C.: U.S. Government Printing Office.
Shaiken, Harley (1984) *Work Transformed: Automation and Labor in the Computer Age*. New York: Holt, Rinehart, and Winston.
Slott, Mike (1985) The case against worker ownership, *Labor Research Review, 6*: 83-97.
Sowell, Thomas (1981) *Markets and Minorities*. New York: Basic Books.
Sowell, Thomas (1984) *Civil Rights: Rhetoric or Reality*? New York: William Morrow.
Squires, Gregory D., Larry Bennett, Kathleen McCourt, and Philip Nyden (1987) *Chicago: Race, Class, and the Response to Urban Decline*. Philadelphia: Temple University Press.
Squires, Gregory D., and Thomas A. Lyson (forthcoming) Employee ownership and equal opportunity: Ameliorating race and gender wage inequalities through democratic work organizations. *Phylon*.
Swinney, Dan (1985) Worker ownership: A tactic for labor, *Labor Research Review, 6*: 99-112.
Thurow, Lester (1981) *The Zero Sum Society: Distribution and the Possibilities for Economic Change*. New York: Penguin Books.
Thurow, Lester (1972) Educational and economic equality, *The Public Interest, 28*: 66-81.
Tidwell, Billy J. (1987) Black wealth: Facts and fiction. In Janet Dewart (Ed.), *The State of Black America 1987*. New York: National Urban League.
Tolbert, Charles M. II., Patrick M. Horan, and E.M. Beck (1980) The structure of economic segmentation: A dual approach, *American Journal of Sociology, 85*: 1095-116.
U.S. Bureau of the Census (1981) *1980 Census of Population, Detailed Characteristics: District of Columbia*. PC 80-1-D10, Table 231. Washington, D.C.: U.S. Government Printing Office.
U.S. Bureau of the Census (1987a) *Current Population Reports* Series P-60, No. 156, "Money Income of Households, Families, and Persons in the United States: 1985." Washington D.C.: U.S. Government Printing Office Table 10.
U.S. Bureau of the Census (1987b) *Current Population Reports* Series P-60, No. 157, "Money Income and Poverty Status of Families and Persons in the United States: 1986" (Advance Data from the March 1987 Current Population Survey). Washington, D.C.: U.S. Government Printing Office, Table 1.
U.S. Bureau of the Census (1969) *Current Population Reports* Series P-60, No.

66, "Income in 1968 of Families and Persons in the United States," Washington, D.C.: U.S. Government Printing Office, Table 11.

U.S. Commission on Civil Rights (1981) *Affirmative Action in the 1980s: Dismantling the Process of Discrimination.* Washington, D.C.: U.S. Government Printing Office.

U.S. Commission on Civil Rights (1985) *Comparable Worth: An Analysis and Recommendations.* Washington, D.C.: U.S. Government Printing Office.

Whittaker, Gerald F. (1977) Capital accumulation through ESOPs: A black perspective, *Business Horizons, 20*: 23-30.

Williams, D.F. (1976) Workers' self-management and social property: A participatory approach to black economic development, *The Review of Black Political Economy, 6*: 438-67.

Williams, Walter (1982) *The State Against Blacks.* New York: McGraw-Hill.

Willie, Charles Vert (1979) *Class and Caste Controversy.* Bayside, NY: General Hall, Inc.

Wilson, William Julius (1987) *The Declining Significance of Race: Blacks and Changing American Institutions.* Chicago: University of Chicago Press.

Wilson, William Julius (1987) *The Truly Disadvantaged: The Inner City, the Underclass, and Public Policy.* Chicago: University of Chicago Press.

Wright, Erik Olin (1979) *Class Structure and Income Determination.* New York: Academic Press.

Zwerdling, Daniel (1978) *Democracy at Work.* Washington, D.C.: Association for Self-Management.

CONTRIBUTORS

Carl Boggs teaches political science at the University of Southern California. He has written extensively on social and political theory, European politics and social movements. He is the author of *Social Movements and Political Power* (Temple), *The Two Revolutions: Gramsci and the Dilemmas of Western Marxism* (South End) and *The Impasse of European Communism* (Westview), among others. He is on the editorial boards of *Theory and Society* and *Socialist Review*.

Diane E. Davis is Assistant Professor of Sociology and of Historical Studies in the graduate faculty of the New School for Social Research. Her research interests focus on urbanization, urban social movements, the sociology of development, state-society relations in Latin America and middle classes and politics. She is currently conducting research on middle-class formation in Mexico with support from the Social Science Research Council. Her book, *Rapid Transit to Ruin: State, Class and Urban Conflict in the Transformation of Mexico, 1910-1988*, is forthcoming.

Susan S. Fainstein is Professor of Urban Planning at Rutgers University. She is co-editor of *Divided Cities*, a book of original essays comparing London and New York. **Norman Fainstein** is Dean of Arts and Sciences at Baruch College and Professor of Sociology in the Graduate School of the City University of New York. The Fainsteins have published extensively on urban political economy, social movements and public policy.

Michael Harloe is Professor of Sociology and Dean of Social Sciences at the University of Essex, U.K. He edits the *International Journal of Urban and Regional Research*. Research interests include housing and urban planning, urban development and economic restructuring and urbanization in Eastern Europe and the U.S.S.R.

Joseph M. Kling teaches in the Government Department at St. Lawrence University in Canton, New York. For many years, he worked in Brooklyn as a youth worker and community organizer. He and Prudence Posner are joint editors of *Dilemmas of Activism: Class, Community and the Politics of Local Mobilization* (Temple University Press), forthcoming.

Su-Hoon Lee is Assistant Professor of Sociology and Director of Planning at the Institute for Far Eastern Studies at Kyungnam University, South Korea. He is author of *State-Building in the Contemporary Third World* (Westview, 1988). His current research interests include global militarization, world inequality and the linkage between local modes of production and the dynamics of the world-economy.

Sidney Plotkin is Associate Professor of Political Science at Vassar College. His research has focused on questions of land use, conflict and power. The author of *Keep Out: The Struggle for Land Use Control*, he is currently working on a study of the political economy of Thorstein Veblen.

Prudence Posner is Director of the Liberty Partnership Program of Associated Colleges in Canton, New York. She has worked at the United Community Centers in Brooklyn as a community organizer, youth worker and director of research and education. She and Joseph Kling are joint editors of *Dilemmas of Activism: Class, Community and the Politics of Local Mobilization* (Temple University Press), forthcoming.

David A. Smith is Assistant Professor of Sociology at the University of California, Irvine. His recent research focuses on comparative urbanization and socio-economic development and network analysis of the structure and dynamics of the world economy. He has had recent articles in *Social Forces, International Journal of Urban and Regional Research, Urban Affairs Quarterly* and *American Sociological Review*, as well as a contribution to *Semiperipheral States in the World-Economy* (Greenwood, forthcoming).

Gregory D. Squires is chair of the Department of Sociology and a member of the urban studies program faculty at the University of Wisconsin, Milwaukee. His research has focused on the process of urban development and its implications for minority communities in major metropolitan areas.

Comparative Urban and Community Research gratefully acknowledges the following people for their reviews of articles submitted to this Review.

Janet Abu-Lughod
Miguel Basañez
Sophie Body-Gendrot
Stephen Brush
Craig Calhoun
Susan Clarke
Pierre Clavell
Philip Cooke
Mike Douglass
Peter Evans
Norman Fainstein
Susan Fainstein
Reynolds Farley
Joe Feagin
Roger Friedland
John Friedmann
John Gilderbloom
M. Gottdiener
Ted Gurr
William Hanna
Chester Hartman
David Harvey
Jeffrey Henderson
Richard Hill
Dennis Judd
Ira Katznelson
Martin Kenney
Francesco Kjellberg
Mickey Lauria
John Logan
Larissa Lomnitz
Jeffrey Lustig
Peter Marcuse
David Meyer
Harvey Molotch
Lisa Peattie
Keith Pezzoli
Chris Pickvance
Adolph Reed
Bryan Roberts
Herbert Rubin
Carol Smith
David Smith
Edward Soja
Clarence Stone
Todd Swanstrom
Ivan Szelenyi
Bernadette Tarallo
Richard Tardanico
Charles Tilly
Christian Topalov
John Walton
Allen Whitt
Howard Winant
Sharon Zukin